T0284880

IMPROVING LEARNING AND MENTAL HEALTH
IN THE COLLEGE CLASSROOM

TEACHING AND LEARNING IN HIGHER EDUCATION
James M. Lang, Series Editor
Michelle D. Miller, Series Editor

A list of titles in this series appears at the end of this volume.

IMPROVING LEARNING AND MENTAL HEALTH IN THE COLLEGE CLASSROOM

....

ROBERT EATON, STEVEN V. HUNSAKER, and BONNIE MOON

West Virginia University Press · Morgantown

Copyright © 2023 by West Virginia University Press
All rights reserved
First edition published 2023 by West Virginia University Press
Printed in the United States of America

ISBN 978-1-952271-80-9 (paperback) / 978-1-952271-81-6 (ebook)

Library of Congress Control Number: 2022049988

Book and cover design by Than Saffel / WVU Press
Cover photograph by Rawpixel.com / Shutterstock

In the quiet heart is hidden
Sorrow that the eye can't see.

—Susan Evans McCloud

CONTENTS

....

PREFACE

....

Friends have often asked us why we wrote this book. For each of us, the answer is different.

Rob

....

For me, part of the impetus was my return to the classroom on a full-time basis in 2016 after an absence of a few years because of leadership assignments. Even though I'd known in the abstract that mental health challenges were a growing problem for many college students, I was taken aback by how many of my students were struggling academically because of them. My heart ached for those students, who desperately wanted to succeed but were overwhelmed, often with anxiety or depression.

I help teach a semester-long course to new faculty members each year, and one semester, a professor suggested spending a day to discuss mental health challenges. We added the subject, and I found I couldn't stop exploring it. I began wondering what things we as teachers do unknowingly that might exacerbate or even precipitate some mental health challenges for our students. Conversely, I began exploring what teachers could do to help eliminate unnecessary stress and discouragement for their students by being a bit more intentional about some of our choices in course design and teaching techniques. Eventually, I proposed a radical idea to Kelly Burgener, the academic vice president and my boss—to take a sabbatical for a semester to work on this project, even though I was serving as the associate academic vice president for learning and teaching at the time. Remarkably, Kelly consented, which made this book possible.

During that semester, I led a faculty learning community in exploring how teachers can affect the mental health of their students. Steve and Bonnie graciously participated. In our group, Steve was by far the most steeped in the scholarship of learning and teaching. Bonnie's personal experience brought a zeal for the subject, her background in math and statistics contributed important perspective, and her organizational skills supplied us with much-needed structure in an ambitious project. Soon, both Steve and Bonnie joined me as coauthors.

From the outset, we want to be clear that the principal expertise we bring to this book is being teachers who are passionate about helping our students. Steve teaches Spanish, Bonnie teaches math, and I teach religion. But none of us have a degree, let alone an advanced degree, in psychology or a related field. Nor are we experts in cognitive psychology or licensed to be counselors. Those facts have given us more than a little trepidation as we wade into the areas of both mental health and cognitive psychology. Of course, we've sought to ground all our analyses and pedagogical recommendations in peer-reviewed scholarship by those who do have the requisite expertise. And we have invited those with such expertise to review our manuscript and set us straight, as necessary. Ultimately, however, the responsibility for any mistakes is ours alone.

We gratefully acknowledge the help of many friends and colleagues. Elizabeth Eaton Warner provided exceptional assistance in editing all the chapters, with the candor and clarity that perhaps only an author's child can freely offer. We could not have asked for a more insightful and supportive editor than Michelle Miller. I particularly appreciate James Lang's early encouragement and support, including connecting us with West Virginia University Press, whose editorial approach aligned perfectly with ours. We appreciate both Derek Krissoff's editorial oversight and Sara Georgi's able assistance in finalizing the manuscript, as well as Dana Johnson's meticulous editing. Our colleagues Mike Abel, Rex Butterfield, David Miller, Rachel Huber, Paul Roberts, and Shane Cole participated in numerous discussions about the topics in this book, sharing their insights and summaries of relevant sources. Shane was particularly helpful in helping us find relevant journal articles. We also appreciate Peter Felten of Elon University, who generously granted us access to an early copy of his and Leo Lambert's *Relationship-Rich Education: How Human Connections Drive Success in College*. As we had suspected, the book was enormously helpful in our own research.

We are grateful to several others who reviewed the manuscript and provided incredibly helpful feedback that has made this book much better: Jon Skalski, John Hilton, Rex Butterfield, Yohan Delton, and Samuel Clay. I am particularly grateful to Sid Palmer, who graciously temped for me in my role as associate academic vice president for learning and teaching while I took leave to work on this project.

Finally, we very much appreciate the support and insights of Brian Schmidt, who provided us with early encouragement and valuable feedback throughout the project. He helped us believe we could pull off something this audacious.

—Rob Eaton, Rexburg, Idaho, January 2021

Steve

....

Recently, my wife, Susan, and I were visiting family members. In an attempt to engage a nephew in conversation, in what seemed to me to be an overly loud voice, I called out, "Daniel, how are you?"

No response.

Again I called out, "Daniel, how are you?"

No response.

I called out four times, each time not more than five feet from Daniel. He didn't ever hear me.

I have Parkinson's, an irreversible, progressive neurodegenerative disease. Since my diagnosis in 2010, I have come to understand the degenerative part of "irreversible, progressive neurodegenerative disease." Depending on my medication levels, I do not have the ability to write by hand in any useful way. Typing is awkward and slow. My right hand and leg shake as if to the irregular beat of some silent song. I have become prone to uncomfortable cramping in my left leg that sometimes makes my walks to and from work an exercise in endurance to the end. And I have today a much softer voice and a much less nimble mind than I had just a few years ago.

All of this represents a powerful temptation to withdraw into silence. If I might be talking nonsense, and if people can't hear me anyway, why not retreat further and further into the silence of the void?

What does my struggle with Parkinson's disease have

to do with a book on helping students who struggle with mental health issues? Perhaps nothing more than a certain measure of empathy for those students whose mental health challenges go by in silence, unnoticed by so many. I am not interested in comparing symptoms and challenges with anyone else. I just want to avoid creating crises for students who struggle with anxieties large and small. For me, it isn't about making the college or university safe or stress free for students; rather, it is about learning to avoid unintentionally increasing the tension that students already experience.

—Steve Hunsaker, Rexburg, Idaho, January 2021

Bonnie

Michael showed up to my class with bloodshot eyes and could not sit still. He was disengaged as his group worked on their project, unable to focus and contribute. The next day he didn't show up at all. I wondered if he would end up dropping the course. Surprisingly, Michael returned the next week. I followed him out the door at the end of class and asked him about the inconsistency of his attendance and if there was anything I could do to help.

He broke down. He mentioned a few of his struggles and explained that he was dealing with depression. Depression? If this had been a few years earlier, I may have thought, "Well, this will pass." I know some people may even say, "Just get over it." Yet those same people would never look at a broken femur bone cutting through their friend's jeans and say, "Just get over it." Some pain is visible, while other pain is hidden and even tragically minimized.

Born in Chile during an era of government unrest and

economic hardship, I have only lately started to understand the political and financial hardships my parents overcame. With my older sister and me in tow, they fled my father's native land two years before President Salvador Allende was assassinated in a military coup. All my life, I have observed my parents' strength and perseverance and have had very little understanding of mental health challenges.

When did my perspective change? Let me start in the darkness. Dark and suffocating. Debilitating and hopeless. These are words I would have never used to describe myself nor my mood before the fall semester of 2015. I'd always been a positive and resilient person. I had disappointments and moved forward. That fall, during the first weeks of the semester, I woke up with a searing pain piercing through my heart and exiting my back. Thinking it would go away, I drove to campus in pain and started teaching classes. I ended my second class early and headed to an urgent care center. A battery of tests determined I had experienced a spontaneous pneumothorax, or a partial lung collapse.

After some consultation, my doctor and the pulmonary specialist decided not to operate to inflate my lung. They were hopeful—as was I—that it would heal with rest and deep breathing. My lung eventually began to improve, but I was not prepared for the emotional turmoil that followed. I had a sudden onset of fear. In addition to the collapsed lung, my focus fixated on past troublesome family events, and this misguided rumination threw me into a pit of discouragement and deep despair. My resolve was failing, and my mind was grasping for understanding.

I was broken. It was more than just being anxious or downhearted. I lost my appetite. I no longer wanted to participate in daily activities. The depression finally engulfed everyday living, and I soon took a medical leave from work.

Sleep escaped me and magnified the intensity of the darkness. I began to worry for my life as I lost thirty pounds in one month. I vanished into dark waters and could not pull myself out—I could not will my way better. After three months of paralyzing anxiety and drowning depression, I miraculously found my way to skills, people, and resources that would eventually save my life and heal me.

When Rob shared his vision of this Helping, Not Hindering project at a college meeting, I was excited and hopeful. He expressed a desire to help teachers better understand some of the mental challenges students face and how faculty can help. I had been a faculty member with little understanding of depression until I went through it myself. Having healed and moved forward, I know there are tools, skills, and resources that can make a difference. My hope is that education, understanding, and some specific ideas will be shared in this book to help teachers understand students like Michael. We don't lower academic expectations, but awareness and understanding can go a long way to help these students grow and progress in our courses.

—*Bonnie Moon, Rexburg, Idaho, January 2021*

INTRODUCTION

....

If a group of malicious social scientists were designing a societal petri dish to create mental health challenges, they would be hard pressed to come up with anything more effective than the US higher education system. For starters, consider the timing: students traditionally embark on their college experience during the very period in life when most mental health challenges initially manifest themselves, with nearly 75 percent of lifelong mental health challenges emerging by the midtwenties.[1]

On top of that, many college students leave home and their established networks of support, often for the first time. Such disruption might unsettle the most emotionally seasoned among us, let alone eighteen-year-olds. "The college years are a period of often intense anxiety about *belonging*: Do I fit in?" observes Paul Tough in *The Years That Matter Most: How College Makes or Breaks Us*. "Can people like me feel at home here?"[2]

For many students, such feelings of self-doubt are most intense during the first year at college. And for first-generation students and students from underrepresented identity groups, such feelings can be exacerbated by doubts about belonging at their university. Michelle Obama describes how she felt when moving from the South Side of Chicago to Princeton University: "It was jarring and uncomfortable, at least at first, like being dropped into a strange new terrarium, a habitat that hadn't been built for me."[3]

Alexis McKee is a first-generation college student who also happens to be our research assistant for this book. We knew she was incredibly capable, meticulous, reliable, and hardworking—and that she was interested in mental health issues and had a goal of becoming a teacher. But until this book was in its final stages, we had no idea about the extent that anxiety had affected her life and transition to college. She gave us permission to share her story, including her name.

Alexis has dealt with anxiety for as long as she can remember. In fact, when her third-grade teacher taught the students about anxiety and then told them it was a "sometimes feeling, not an all-the-time feeling," Alexis remembers laughing and becoming a bit confused. "The feeling we learned about was something that I experienced almost constantly. By the time I was a junior in high school, I had been in therapy for several years, tried almost every [antidepressant drug] available, and missed far more school than I should have. I felt alone."

Neither of her parents attended college, but Alexis dreamed of becoming a teacher and knew she'd need a college degree to fulfill that dream. Visiting potential colleges brought new anxieties for Alexis: "I felt out of place. This was uncharted territory for my family. I honestly did not know if I would be able to survive college. I am shy, horribly shy. I hide in grocery stores from people I know so that I don't have to make small talk. How could I possibly make it in a place where you have to create a second family?"

Alexis's anxiety about embarking on the college experience may have been more intense than most students', but it was far from unique. During this season of emotional vulnerability, students embark on an educational experience that feels to many of them like a high-risk, high-stakes competition—one that in all likelihood will have a profound impact on the rest of their life. In Tough's incisive critique about the power of the college years to make or break entire lives, he notes, "Young adults who didn't have a college degree were almost four times more likely to be living in poverty as those who did. The unemployment rate for Americans with only a high school degree was double the rate for Americans with a bachelor's degree. . . . It sometimes felt as though the country was splitting into two separate and unequal nations, with a college diploma the boundary that divided them."[4]

Not many college students are aware of precisely how dramatic the difference is between the economic futures of the average college graduate and others, but most sense they are engaging in a perilous rite of passage that—justifiably or not—results either in some kind of lifelong societal stamp of approval or an irrevocable status of failure. About 40 percent of students who begin the journey toward a bachelor's degree will fail to earn it within six years. For those who attend open-enrollment institutions (like most community colleges), the odds of finishing the race are even lower: 69 percent fail to earn a bachelor's degree within six years.[5] The odds are worse still for low-income, first-generation college students: 89 percent leave without a degree.[6]

Even those high-achieving students who earned stellar grades in high school often bump up against new kinds of disappointments in college. Some who easily earned good grades in high school are slammed by the need to spend much more time studying outside of class. Others discover that hard work alone had often guaranteed good grades in high school, but that's not always the case in college. These realizations can rock the foundation of even the most apparently healthy, success-bound, new college student. For perfectionists, the changes can be devastating.

"Our students are in one of the most highly uncertain times in their lives, filled with novel experiences that they haven't yet developed the tools to manage and thrown into a new environment with entirely new people and new systems they don't yet understand," observes Sarah Rose Cavanagh in *The Spark of Learning: Energizing the College Classroom with the Science of Emotion.* "Moreover, they are also in a time of life in which they are beginning and ending romantic liaisons with greater frequency than at any other time of life. Our students, in essence, are simmering in a giant vat of emotional soup."[7] In short, if college were proposed as a grand, randomized experiment, few institutional review boards would dare approve it, given the risks to the participants.

Not surprisingly, then, mental health challenges have long been an inevitable aspect of college life, perhaps more so in the information age than ever before. Many of us who teach college students have noticed an alarming trend in recent years: a growing percentage of our students are struggling—often quite seriously—with mental health challenges. The results of a nationwide survey in 2017 of over sixty thousand students at ninety-two schools painted a deeply troubling picture of the mental health of the current generation of college students:

- Nearly 4 in 10 had been so depressed at some point in the past year that they found it difficult to function.
- Nearly 61 percent had experienced overwhelming anxiety

at some point in the year, with over 1 in 4 students experiencing it within the previous two weeks.

- Over 10 percent had seriously considered suicide at some point in the year, and 1.5 percent had attempted it.
- In the two weeks prior to taking the survey, 19.5 percent of the respondents had felt "things were hopeless," and over 51 percent had felt that way at some point in the year.[8]

Worse still, these kinds of indicators are moving in the wrong direction. What has always been a steady flow of mental health challenges in colleges is becoming a flood. According to the authors of one analysis, "The normal, developmental stress that accompanies this life transition has escalated into significant mental health crises for increasing numbers of students."[9] Counseling centers at universities have experienced an increase in the frequency, complexity, and severity of cases of students with mental health challenges.[10] According to the Healthy Minds Study, in 2009, 8 percent of college students had been diagnosed with depression. By 2019, that figure had more than doubled to 18 percent.[11] And such increases in mental health challenges among college students are not limited to the United States. In the United Kingdom, for example, a 2017 report found "that 94 per cent of Universities reported that they had experienced a sharp increase in the numbers of students trying to access support services, sometimes as high as a threefold increase over the period of 2012–17."[12]

To be fair, some of the statistical increases in reported cases of students with mental health challenges and of visits to counseling centers likely stem from a couple of developments. First, we have made real progress societally in destigmatizing mental health challenges, making it likely that students are now more comfortable seeking counseling help or admitting to mental health challenges than in the past. Second, significant improvements in medications have enabled some people to attend college who might not have been able to attend at all in the past.[13] Still, there is a broad consensus among researchers that something has drastically changed. For those of us teaching in today's college classrooms, it's difficult to deny the existence of what the *New York Times* calls a "national epidemic of students dealing with depression, anxiety and suicidal thoughts."[14]

What kind of impact do mental health challenges have on students? One study of over three thousand graduate and undergraduate students at four universities showed that students with mental health challenges were worse off, in statistically significant ways, than students without mental health challenges—in almost every aspect the researchers measured. The magnitude of the gap between how these two sets of students felt about college life is striking:

- One in four of those with mental health challenges was dissatisfied with their academic experience, while only 1 in 10 of the other students were. The researchers conclude that "mental health problems were a significant predictor of academic dissatisfaction and drop out intentions, while positive mental health was a significant predictor of satisfaction and persistence."
- Twice as many students with mental health challenges (30 percent compared to 15 percent) doubted whether higher education was worth the investment of their time and money.
- Students with mental health challenges were significantly less confident they would complete their degrees.

- A whopping 40 percent of students with both anxiety and depression indicated their mental health hurt their academic performance six or more days in the past four weeks.[15]

The bottom line of the study is that "mental health is a significant predictor of both dissatisfaction and confidence in ability to persist." Students with one mental health condition were 1.86 times likelier to be dissatisfied with their academic experience, and those with two mental health conditions were 2.6 times more likely to be dissatisfied.[16]

Not surprisingly, students living with mental health challenges are far less likely to complete their college education and earn a degree. In one study, students with depression were twice as likely to leave school before completion.[17] Another recent study concluded that two-thirds of college students who withdraw do so for mental health reasons.[18] A 2010 study also showed how mental health affects graduation rates, finding that 4.7 percent of students—roughly five million a year—drop out of college in the United States alone due to mental health challenges.[19] In fact, according to one study on the first-year experience, the most common reason students give for seriously considering deferring or withdrawing is their "wellbeing or 'emotional reasons.' "[20]

Failure to earn a college degree deprives these individuals of greater earning power. In 2019, the median income for twenty-five- to thirty-four-year-old college graduates who were working full-time was $55,700. For their peers with a high school degree only, the median income was $35,000.[21] Over the course of a career, some estimates suggest that the difference in the relative earning power of the average high school graduate and college graduate is more than $1 million.[22] Moreover, the average student who ends their college journey before earning a degree leaves with $14,000 in student loans but without the greater earning power to pay them off.[23] But perhaps even more costly is that instead of coming away from college having confirmed their capacity to do intellectually hard things, many who leave without a degree walk away emotionally scarred, concluding they just aren't college material. For too many students with mental health challenges, rather than fanning the flame of hope, college extinguishes it.

Moreover, some of these college students try to end their misery by taking their own lives. Among Americans fifteen to twenty-four years old, suicide is the second-leading cause of death.[24] And in the US, eighteen- to twenty-five-year-olds attempt suicide far more than any other age group.[25] The US suicide rate increased 25.4 percent from 1999 to 2016.[26] But since the 1950s, the suicide rate in this age group has tripled, according to the American College Health Association.[27]

Students with mental health challenges aren't the only ones affected. The escalation in levels "of depression and anxiety, along with increased suicidal ideation, impacts not only the student dealing with depression but also the roommates, floor-mates, teammates and classmates."[28] Concerned roommates often assume the role of caregiver, sometimes helping keep their friends alive, even if it requires occasional around-the-clock vigils. College administrators are becoming increasingly aware of the collateral costs borne by students who struggle to help friends or roommates fighting thoughts of suicide.

We fully recognize that many of our students arrive on our campuses and in our classes with preexisting mental health challenges. Whatever the causes, emerging adults are experiencing mental health challenges at a much higher prevalence than in the past. And whether our students arrive with such preexisting conditions or develop them on our campuses, a significant and growing percentage of our students are coping with substantial emotional challenges. As the US surgeon general concludes in a special advisory issued in 2021, "Mental health challenges in children, adolescents, and young adults are real, and they are widespread." In fact, these problems are so severe that he referred to them as "a mental health pandemic."[29]

Simply encouraging those students to try harder is not enough to help them cope with the challenges overwhelming too many of them. Consider Alexis, whose transition to college was emotionally turbulent. "My first semester was rough. I cried almost every day for three months. The anxiety that I had gotten [under] control during my senior year of high school returned with a vengeance. I struggled to learn what the professors wanted out of their students, and as a result, I spent every day doing homework for about thirteen hours. I rarely slept or ate and struggled socially."

Plausible theories for this escalation in poor emotional health point to everything from rampant smartphone use to helicoptering parents. Others suggest that social media conditions us to constantly compare ourselves to others. Yet other possible causes for the spike in mental health challenges among college students include greater financial stresses and even "widening participation" in higher education.[30] But in this book, we focus on dealing with the reality of our students' symptoms rather than divining the underlying causes of those symptoms.

Given the magnitude of what's at stake, it's not surprising that the impact of mental health on college students has been the subject of a growing body of research.

However, relatively little of this research derives from the social sciences, let alone focuses on the role teachers can play in helping students better cope with mental health challenges.[31] In a fascinating bibliometric analysis of tens of thousands of articles written about mental health and college students, *professor, teaching, classrooms, mentoring*, and *coursework* are not among the terms that appeared twenty-five times or more in this vast body of literature.[32] In other words, teachers—arguably the most important asset an institution has in helping students with mental health challenges—have been largely overlooked.

In the rich literature on student success, it's quite clear that interactions between students and faculty members affect student satisfaction more than any other variable.[33] Teachers have a chance to listen to students, connect with them, and lift them in a way that no other university employees can. Three engineering professors and deans argue in *Inside Higher Ed* that as important as other people on campus are, "the classroom is the one place where every student shows up, and it might well be the place where we can turn the tide of mental health on campus."[34]

Interestingly, students are more focused on the impact of their professors on their mental health than are most scholars researching in this area. Recognizing that little research had been done on "measures that universities could take to reduce environmental stressors," Chi Baik and her colleagues decided to ask students themselves. To be exact, they asked 2,776 students this question: "What can be done to improve student well-being?" More than any other topic, most answers dealt with "academic teachers and teaching practice, indicating that academic teachers can play an important role—perhaps more important than previously recognized—in supporting student wellbeing."

The students' responses made clear that college teachers "have the potential to enhance and support student mental wellbeing (and conversely, to have a negative effect on well-being)."[35] Baik and her colleagues don't call for teachers "to become mental health experts, either in diagnosing mental health difficulties, or in counselling students experiencing psychological distress." Instead, they argue that sound teaching practices "would reduce the stressors that students experience in the learning environment."[36]

To be clear, our aim is neither to help professors become pseudocounselors nor to ask overstretched faculty to invest much more of their limited time. While we will discuss some things faculty can do as noncounselors in the course of our usual mentoring, our focus is primarily on changing the way we do some things we are *already* doing—working smarter, not harder. We recognize that most faculty members—especially adjunct faculty members—are stretched thin already. Our hope is that rather than adding to already full plates, the ideas in this book will make life for teachers, too, a bit more manageable. As we make some minor adjustments in how we interact with students and design our courses, we can help more of them succeed, eliminating a few student-relations headaches in the process. In essence, we believe that wisely practicing some preventive pedagogical care up front can save us some time and energy in dealing with more acute academic cases later in the semester.

Our advice certainly won't help students completely conquer their depression or anxiety—that's not our aim. But by focusing on how we can help rather than hinder students, we hope to support them in moving in a positive direction on the mental wellness continuum. As Cavanagh argues, "Given how common anxiety is in higher education,

and its host of negative effects on achievement and performance, strategizing it out of our classes could have a powerful effect on student learning outcomes."[37] As teachers,
almost all of us do at least some things that unintentionally and unnecessarily create stress or discouragement for
our students. And those practices interfere with learning
more than most of us realize.

On the other hand, among the myriad of teaching practices proven to benefit all students, some are especially
beneficial to students with mental health challenges. We
can and should get better at identifying both kinds of
teaching practices—those that help and those that hinder.
Aspen Institute president and former college president
Dan Porterfield says regarding college and mental health,
we have to figure out "what is enabling great learning and
what is blocking great learning."[38]

As teachers weigh the relative costs and benefits of
each practice with alternatives chosen from among proven
teaching strategies, most of the time we'll discover that
not only can we remove some unnecessary pain from our
students with mental health challenges but we can also
improve learning for all our students. In *Cheating Lessons*,
James Lang writes that "the best practices for reducing
cheating in our courses coincided with the best practices
for increasing learning."[39] Similarly, the best practices for
reducing unnecessary stress and discouragement are usually the best practices for increasing learning. In other
words, we can simultaneously create a much better experience for our students with mental health challenges and
help all our students learn more.

Such a shift requires greater intentionality on the part
of teachers. To us, being intentional means carefully and

consciously considering all the relevant factors and the potential consequences of any course of action we are contemplating. Doing something on purpose is not enough: we need to be complete and robust in our conscious deliberations to be truly intentional. Even many of us who have been quite thoughtful about our pedagogical practices have overlooked what should now be a critical consideration in all our teaching decisions: how they will affect the mental wellness of our students.

Or perhaps we do give passing consideration to the impact an anxiety-inducing assignment or policy might have on students, but we glibly underestimate those impacts if we haven't experienced them ourselves. Knowing that some difficulties are desirable and that some fears and anxieties subside over time, we figure our students will eventually be fine. But sometimes, the fear and the anxiety are more than just a bad case of the butterflies. Indeed, the three of us have come to recognize personally, parentally, and professionally that anxiety, depression, and the many other mental health challenges are every bit as real as cardiovascular disease and diabetes.

How do we balance sensitivity to the negative effects of our teaching practices on students with mental health challenges with the need to be academically rigorous? We recommend engaging in what we call a psychological, pedagogical cost-benefit analysis. With such an analysis, we examine which teaching strategies to adopt, retire, or modify by considering each of the following:

- **Our true outcomes.** What is it we're really hoping to accomplish with this policy, assignment, or classroom technique?

- **The psychological costs and benefits.** What impact does this practice have on my students with mental health challenges? How much does it help or hinder them?
- **The pedagogical costs and benefits.** Just how effective is the practice in helping students learn?
- **Ways to temper any negative effects.** Are there ways we can modify the practice to preserve its pedagogical benefits while reducing its psychological costs?
- **Alternatives.** What techniques could we use instead to accomplish the same outcomes? How do they compare pedagogically and psychologically?

When we engage in this kind of intentional analysis, we won't eliminate all difficulties for our students with mental health challenges, and we wouldn't want to. We're mindful of the argument that if parents and teachers remove all stressors from children's lives, we'll deprive them of the chance to develop resilience. We recognize that the path to lasting learning is replete with what learning psychologist Robert Bjork calls "desirable difficulties." Powerful techniques, such as spaced learning, retrieval practice, and active learning, can all be more difficult for students in the short run but lead to more substantive learning in the long run. But as Bjork himself acknowledges, difficulties in learning are not inherently positive. "The term has become popular, and sometimes people portray it as, 'If I just make things hard on somebody, they'll learn better.' And it's not that, so much. It's that these selective difficulties induce the very processes that create long-term retention and understanding."[40]

The key is intentionality. When our assignments, policies, or practices inflict so much stress that they interfere with learning, we are not creating desirable difficulties.

Instead, we are unintentionally creating needless difficulties. One principal purpose of this book is to help eliminate needless difficulties, not desirable difficulties. Intentionally engaging in the kind of psychological-pedagogical cost-benefit analysis we have outlined can help us discern the difference between the two.

We have encountered a few colleagues who feel as if they face a choice between maintaining academic excellence and lowering expectations. But designing learning experiences with our students' mental wellness in mind does not require us to simply lower the bar or our relevant expectations. We have an obligation to employers, graduate schools, accreditors, and students themselves to ensure that our learners gain desired levels of competency and mastery. We propose a third way: becoming more creative and effective in helping as many students as possible succeed in meeting our learning outcomes.

Here's one concrete example of what we're suggesting. One of our first steps in researching this book was talking to two professionals from our student counseling center. When we asked them what curricular requirements or teaching practices triggered anxiety, both promptly mentioned oral presentations. That stung. We considered ourselves reasonably sensitive, aware teachers. Yet for years, Steve and Rob had taught an interdisciplinary general education class about Pakistan in which they had required students to give oral presentations. There were some obvious benefits to requiring such speeches. Assuming students could just work through a bit of anxiousness, we had never consciously weighed the emotional price that the assignment would extract to produce the benefits. As oblivious as we were of that impact, we certainly had not engaged in an intentional assessment of how the costs and benefits of these traditional in-class presentations stacked up against alternatives.

How central was this assignment to our outcomes? To be honest, we had never articulated an outcome related to this particular assignment. Our unwritten, unspoken outcome was partly to help students hone communications skills and partly to push them to research a subject enough to develop a bit of expertise. And unlike in a public speaking course, neither outcome was particularly central to the course.

What were the psychological effects of our assignment? For many of our students, there were probably no negative effects at all. That would have been the case for us as students, as well—which may be why we didn't consider how giving a live presentation in front of a class affects students with high anxiety or who are introverts. But if we had conducted a survey or focus group or just informally asked for feedback on our assignments, we might have easily learned years earlier what our colleagues in the counseling center had told us. For that matter, if we had read Susan Cain's *Quiet: The Power of Introverts in a World That Can't Stop Talking*, we would have better appreciated the psychological costs of such an assignment for some of our students. Cain is a delightful, brilliant, self-avowed introvert who now speaks quite capably about her best-selling book in front of crowds of hundreds of people.[41] But one of her first experiences with public speaking came in eighth grade, when a teacher cold-called her to the front of the class to improvise a scene. She froze, standing in awkward silence for what seemed like forever. Her teacher undoubtedly thought she was somehow helping Cain develop resilience, but in reality, she set back Cain's progress as a public speaker by years.

Could we have tempered the negative effects of our oral presentation assignment? Cain doesn't advocate sparing introverts the stress of learning how to speak publicly, but she does argue for being deliberate and wise about providing the scaffolding that helps budding speakers incrementally improve. "You don't start by giving a TED talk," she explained to a group of over eight hundred participants at the 2019 Educator Summit. "We can prevent our students from acquiring these fears in the first place by making sure that when we ask them to do something potentially scary like speaking in public," we don't stretch them unduly. On a discomfort scale of 1–10, Cain argues, it's better to start students in the 4–6 range rather than in the 8–10 range.[42]

Years after the initial design of our Pakistan course, a new cohort of instructors modified the oral presentation in a way that inadvertently did just what Cain recommends. They changed the assignment to adapt the course to a hybrid format, with the three-credit class meeting only twice a week. Instead of having students give oral presentations live in class, our successors assigned students to record and share narrated slideshows. This allowed students to choose when to spend an hour each week watching and learning from their classmates' oral presentations. Interestingly enough, the quality of the presentations improved markedly, as students were able to record a presentation multiple times and then submit the best take. Unwittingly, the new group of teachers had found a way to reduce stress for many of the students *while improving the course quality for all students.*

What about other alternatives? Years later, in a completely different setting, Brigham Young University–Hawaii linguistics professor Mark Wolfersberger told us about a tactic he regularly uses in language classes to give students a chance to practice presenting without having one student speak to the entire class. He divides students into groups of four, where each student presents to the three other students. Then he mixes up the groups and repeats the process three times. This simple technique significantly reduces stress while tripling the amount of practice students get.

There's simply no way around some practices that will cause acute stress in certain students. Indeed, college teachers would be negligent if we didn't prepare some of our students for high-stress and high-stakes certification exams in their fields after graduation. But we always make wiser decisions when we (1) focus on our actual outcomes, (2) consider the psychological costs of our teaching and design practices, (3) weigh the benefits of the technique, (4) explore ways to temper the practice's negative effects on students with mental health challenges, and (5) consider alternatives that still achieve our outcomes.

We don't pretend that striking the right balance is easy. In some ways, we're like football coaches who have to decide how much hitting with pads to allow during the preseason and practices. If coaches don't allow enough contact, their players are soft and unprepared for the fray of battle during games. But if they allow or encourage too much hitting, they're likely to lose some key players to injury before the season has even begun. The best coaches are intentional as they try to strike the right balance. And they can't be very intentional if they are ignorant of or underestimate just how much damage daily preseason contact can cause.

Frankly, we don't know exactly where to draw the line when it comes to removing stressors from the lives of college students. But taking a hard look at the potential consequences of our practices and policies on students with mental health challenges can only help us make better-informed decisions as we decide which practices to keep, which to jettison, and which to modify. If nothing else, as we comb through the constantly growing pile of effective, evidence-based pedagogical practices, being sensitive to students with mental health challenges gives us a useful filter in our search for the next good practice to adopt.

In the chapters that follow, we first examine how stress, anxiety, and depression can interfere with our ability to learn. In each subsequent chapter, we tackle some of the research that supports adopting a particular strategy, such as doing more to build a sense of community among students in a course. We then put theory into practice, suggesting several tactical ways to implement the strategy, drawing from the scholarship of teaching and learning, our colleagues' best practices, and our own.

Our aim is to provide a series of practical and strategic teaching tips grounded in sound psychological and pedagogical research that helps college professors teach in a way that not only helps more students with depression and anxiety succeed but enables all our students to engage more, and even thrive. In terms of teaching modalities, some of our suggestions may be a better fit for face-to-face settings, while others might better lend themselves to online teaching. We hope these principles will be useful in any teaching medium, even if they require some adaptation.

Our approach is also more modular than many all-or-nothing teaching philosophies that, while very powerful, can also be daunting because they require a wholesale overhaul of teaching techniques. Ours is more of a buffet of ideas in the spirit of James Lang's *Small Teaching: Everyday Lessons from the Science of Learning*, offering suggestions that readers can choose from without having to commit to an entire pedagogical scheme. We invite readers to consider our suggestions individually, acting on those that seem most promising and doable, rejecting those they judge to be counterproductive, and putting off for now those that feel overwhelming. Finally, we hope this book will be a catalyst for further research and rigorous examination of how teaching practices and course designs affect our students with mental health challenges.

....

CHAPTER I

WHY ANXIETY AND DEPRESSION MATTER FOR LEARNING

....

Anxiety and depression inhibit learning. In many ways, cognition is a zero-sum game. That is, whatever effort we expend coping with anxiety or depression saps us of valuable neurological resources we need for learning. Actually, it's a bit more complicated than that. A jolt of short-term stress at the right time produces a shot of adrenaline and cortisol that actually boosts cognition and can even save lives. But too much cortisol for too long can seriously interfere with some critical aspects of our thinking.

A recent experience of one of our friends demonstrates this dramatically. Bruce Yerman lived in Paradise, California, and on the morning of November 8, 2018, he got word that he needed to evacuate his home within an hour because of a raging wildfire. His wife told him by phone to grab their daughters' art, so he scrambled from room to room gathering paintings done by his five daughters, as well as his bicycle. He managed to hook up a small trailer to his car. Fortunately, his wife arrived from work after driving against traffic, just in time to grab some important papers and a few pieces of clothing for each family member. But as the smoke from the fire increased, so did the fog in Bruce's brain: "The smoke thickened. I could hear the fire's roar in the nearby canyon as ash and burning embers fell like snowflakes. My brother-in-law phoned to see if we had evacuated. 'Get out now, my mother is caught on Pentz Road, surrounded by fire,' he said. . . . We checked on neighbors and headed out of town."

After Bruce and his wife escaped, their house burned to the ground. All that survived of their physical possessions was what they managed to grab in that small window of time before evacuating. With hindsight, Bruce was not impressed with his own choices in one of life's high-stakes tests. "My journals, girls' memory boxes, and some special memory-gifts remained at home. . . . We could have collected those items as well." An educator with a master's from Stanford University and a doctorate from the University of Minnesota, Bruce is a very bright guy who normally thinks quite clearly—but not when he experienced the unimaginable stress that comes with knowing he had to evacuate his home in a matter of minutes, perhaps never to see it and its contents again. "My brain was shutting down as the urgency increased," he explains.

Bruce's conclusion? His experience changed him, not just as an educator but as a person: "I have great empathy for those who are working through challenges related to illness, employment, health, or family and the effects of stress. I'm slower to judge. I seek to understand others—I have greater patience."

In this chapter, we explore some of the research explaining why Bruce's brain shut down under intense stress and why chronic anxiety makes learning much more challenging. In addition, we examine the negative impacts of depression on learning. In each chapter that follows, we then explore strategies for preventing and combating some of these effects.

Stress Diverts Limited Cognitive Resources

Bruce's personal experience is consistent with the findings of multiple studies. Kerry Ressler, chief scientific officer at McLean Hospital in Belmont, Massachusetts, and professor of psychiatry at Harvard Medical School, explains that "when one part of your brain is engaged, the other parts of your brain may not have as much energy to handle their own vital tasks." [1] As the authors of one study conclude, "When faced with stressful situations, normal thought processes can be impaired including the ability to focus attention or make decisions requiring deep thought." [2] In the case of math anxiety specifically, Cavanagh colorfully notes that it "appears to disrupt performance by hijacking part of one's working memory capacity via worrying thoughts, leaving fewer cognitive resources to direct to the problem at hand." [3] One student we interviewed (we'll call her "Sheila") explained how her anxiety affects her ability to focus in class: "I have noticed that coping with my anxiety is often distracting while I am in class. It's hard to give my full attention to the teacher when I have so much commotion and loudness happening within me!"

One possible explanation for why anxiety interferes with our working memory is the attentional control theory. According to a team of European professors, this theory posits that anxiety undermines cognitive performance because it increases "bottom-up, stimulus-driven, processing of threatening information." That processing leads us to fixate more on our negative thoughts—like whether we'll be able to pass a test or finish an assignment on time. Anyone who has needlessly stewed about negative possibilities that never come to pass is not surprised to learn that "anxious people automatically scan their environment for threat cues, which then capture their attention, making it more difficult to disengage from this information." As we expend mental energy focusing on such distractions, "insufficient resources remain for the task at hand."[4]

John Medina, a developmental molecular biologist and the director of Seattle Pacific University's Brain Center for Applied Learning Research, summarizes the research on stress and learning in these broad terms: "Stressed people don't do math very well. They don't process language very efficiently. They have poorer memories, both short and long forms. Stressed individuals do not generalize or adapt old pieces of information to new scenarios as well as nonstressed individuals. They can't concentrate. In almost every way it can be tested, chronic stress hurts our ability to learn."[5]

While a few cognitive processes actually seem to benefit from certain forms of stress, high or chronic stress clearly interferes with "higher-order cognitive functions supported by the prefrontal cortex."[6] J.R.R. Tolkien puts it more simply when describing Bilbo's riddle competition with Gollum: "He began to get frightened, and that is bad for thinking."[7]

Dual expert Judy Willis practiced neurology for fifteen years before returning to a university to obtain her teaching credential and a master's degree in education. She then taught elementary and middle school students for ten years, giving her a unique perspective on pedagogy and the brain. She notes that while anxiety inhibits learning, if "teachers use strategies to reduce stress and build a positive emotional environment, students gain emotional resilience and learn more efficiently and at higher levels of cognition."[8]

High Anxiety Undermines Learning

Generally, studies show that high levels of anxiety under-mine college students' performance both cognitively and affectively. One study of over two hundred engineering students not surprisingly found that students "who have high anxiety levels achieve low academic performance."[9] Another showed that college "students with high anxiety had poorer study skills and achieved lower first-semester GPAs than students with low anxiety."[10]

Our physiological responses to stress are complex yet concrete, and they vary throughout the learning process. Consequently, the way and extent to which stress affects our ability to learn hinges both on when it occurs and how intense it is. With the right timing and dosage, stress can arouse our senses, make us alert, and focus our attention—all of which come in handy for protecting ourselves and dealing with crises.[11] Even in academic settings, modest amounts of stress can be helpful: "While a high level of anxiety in students has been shown to inhibit student academic performance, in some instances a moderate amount of anxiety has been shown to improve student motivation and performance."[12] Contrast the pleasant buzz created by a no-stakes gamified quiz with the intense stress created by a final exam worth half the total course grade.

One fascinating set of experiments showed that rats learning how to find a hidden platform in a water maze actually remembered what they learned better as the temperature of the water cooled and their corticosteroid levels increased—but only up to a point. When the water became too cold, it then impaired rather than enhanced their performance. So, while a certain level of extra cortisol from stress may sharpen our cognitive abilities, stress overload seems to impair them.[13]

As Medina concludes in *Brain Rules*, "When moderate amounts of hormone build up to large amounts, or when moderate amounts of hormone hang around too long, they become quite harmful. . . . Stress hormones can do some truly nasty things to your brain if boatloads of the stuff are given free access to your central nervous system. That's what's going on when you experience chronic stress. Stress hormones seem to have a particular liking for cells in the hippocampus, which is a problem because the hippocampus is deeply involved in many aspects of human learning."[14]

Over the long haul, sustained stress not only impairs our memory but dampens our creativity as well. "Long-term stress is literally killing the cells in your hippocampus that contribute to the deterioration of your memory," notes one brain researcher. "But it's also zapping your creativity."[15]

Stress Can Lead to Depression

Another problem with chronic stress—and it's hard to imagine many seasons of life more chronically stressful than the college years—is that it opens the door to other more serious problems, including depression. "Chronic exposure to stress can lead you to depression's doorstep, then push you through," notes Medina. And the effects of depression can be even more devastating than those of anxiety: "Depression is a deregulation of thought processes, including memory, language, quantitative reasoning, fluid intelligence, and spatial perception."[16]

Unlike stress and anxiety, there really isn't a point along the depression spectrum where a dose of discouragement can be a catalyst for learning. With depression, the news is all bad: it undermines cognition, academic performance, and persistence toward a degree. One clinical psychologist who also teaches at Harvard Medical School cautions that "depression can actually change your ability to think. It can impair your attention and memory, as well as your information processing and decision-making skills. It can also lower your cognitive flexibility (the ability to adapt your goals and strategies to changing situations) and executive functioning (the ability to take all the steps to get something done)."[17] One study showed strong evidence of a significant, negative relationship between depression and academic performance among college students. Even students experiencing "moderate levels of depressive symptoms" performed worse academically than students with little or no depression.[18]

In light of such research, it's not surprising that even when controlling for prior academic performance and other variables, "depression is a significant predictor of lower GPA and higher probability of dropping out." The correlation is even stronger when students have both depression and generalized anxiety disorder.[19]

Studies show that psychological distress powerfully affects students physically, cognitively, and emotionally. When psychological distress is chronic, it's especially detrimental to students' ability to perform academically. A survey of college students reveals a correlation between mental health challenges and lower motivation, academic satisfaction, and self-efficacy.[20] Unfortunately, even when students take antidepressants, which can be helpful in many ways, these cognitive challenges remain. Although there is some evidence regarding the effectiveness of antidepressants in conjunction with psychotherapy, a recent large study casts serious doubt on whether such medications help with cognition. Researchers asked one thousand people taking antidepressants for depression to undergo a barrage of cognitive tests. Ninety-five percent of the participants showed no cognitive improvement.[21] In other words, even our students who are taking medication to help with their depression are likely to be cognitively hamstrung.

In discussing research about the effects of depression on cognition, an important disclaimer is in order. Numerous studies about stress involve interventions temporarily subjecting participants to stress, making it possible to examine the effect of stress on cognition in randomized settings that can reveal causality. But to our knowledge, virtually no such studies exist involving depression—quite understandably. Consequently, most of the studies we discuss are correlational rather than experimental, making it impossible to confidently infer causality. Is it depression that causes poorer academic performance or poorer academic performance that causes depression? Or could they have a symbiotic relationship in which each has some influence on the other?

The good news is that for our analysis, our prescribed approaches work with any of these answers. As we strive to help all our students learn more effectively and to do so in ways that are less likely to lead to or exacerbate depression, we can positively influence both factors. The tactics we suggest in this book are beneficial, regardless of whether depression or academic performance is the independent variable.

There's Cause for Pause in Judging

We mention in our introduction that divining the origin of mental health challenges is beyond the scope of this book.

But one strand of research we found bolstered our commitment to not judge students with mental health challenges as having brought their struggles upon themselves. Researchers Vincent Felitti and Robert Anda and their team surveyed over seventeen thousand participants in a seminal study about eight different categories of potential traumatic events in childhood, including various types of recurring abuse and factors, such as living with someone who engaged in unhealthy or hazardous use of alcohol or drugs. Participants received an adverse childhood experiences (ACE) score from 0 to 8, depending on how many of these types of sustained traumatic experiences they had endured as a child.

Felitti and Anda then monitored this group for five years, tracking everything from hospitalizations to suicide attempts to deaths. What they discovered was "a powerful relation between our emotional experiences as children and our adult emotional health, physical health, and major causes of mortality in the United States. Moreover, the time factors in the study make it clear that time does *not* heal some of the adverse experiences we found so common in the childhoods of a large population of middle-aged, middle-class Americans. One doesn't 'just get over' some things." [22]

The breadth of factors correlated with childhood traumas is sweeping. Among other conditions and features, "hepatitis, heart disease, fractures, diabetes, obesity, alcoholism, occupational health, and job performance" all have "a strong, graded relation to what happened in childhood." For example, a man who has endured four forms of childhood trauma is 390 percent more likely to contract chronic obstructive pulmonary disease (COPD) than a man who has suffered none. Of course, people who smoke are much more likely to contract COPD than nonsmokers. And it turns out that the "higher the ACE score, the greater the likelihood of current smoking."[23]

On the mental health front, participants who had an ACE score of 4 or higher—meaning they had been exposed to four different forms of abuse and other traumas as a child—were *460 percent* more likely to experience depression as adults than those who had experienced no such traumas in their childhood. Comparing those same two groups for attempted suicide, the research team found that participants with a score of 4 or higher had attempted suicide at a rate of *1220 percent* more than those with no childhood traumas.[24] In fact, having experienced childhood trauma in any one of the categories "increased the risk of attempted suicide 2- to 5-fold." And someone who had an ACE score of 7 or 8 was more than thirty-one times as likely to have attempted suicide.[25] Finally, these researchers were struck by the fact that "adverse childhood experiences are vastly more common than recognized or acknowledged." Indeed, one in four participants had been exposed to two categories of trauma, and one in sixteen had been exposed to four.[26]

If we can't change our students' childhoods, why does knowing all this matter? For those of us privileged to have experienced little or no childhood trauma, it should give us pause when we are tempted to wonder why some of our students struggle so much with mental health challenges. Neither we nor Felitti and Anda are suggesting that childhood traumas explain all adult mental health conditions. Nor are we implying that students with higher ACE scores are doomed, only that they may need some professional help in processing some of these traumas. For us, the bottom line is that when we are tempted to assume our students' mental health challenges stem solely from coddling, a lack of willpower, or use of smartphones, we might want to generously allow for the possibility that different childhood experiences may be substantially contributing to their current emotional challenges. Such recognition can help us withhold judgment and cultivate the compassion we need to become more intentional about how we can help rather than hinder our students with mental health challenges.

Mental Health Isn't Binary

College students deal with a wide variety of mental health challenges and conditions. According to the fall 2019 National College Health Assessment (the most recent prepandemic survey available to us at this writing), over 29 percent of students had been treated or diagnosed for anxiety in the last twelve months. Depression ranked next, with 23 percent of those surveyed having been diagnosed or treated for it in the last year. Other mental health conditions were less common but no less challenging: 8.6 percent of students had been diagnosed at some point with attention deficit disorder or attention deficit hyperactivity disorder, 4.7 percent with posttraumatic stress disorder, 4.1 percent with obsessive-compulsive disorder, 3.7 percent with eating disorders, 2.1 percent with bipolar disorder and related conditions, 1.3 percent with autism spectrum disorder, and 0.4 percent with schizophrenia.[27] While we focus primarily on students with depression and anxiety in this book, our hope is that students with any mental health condition will benefit from the changes we recommend.

We should also differentiate between mental health challenges and mental health conditions. Many people struggle with stress and anxiety without qualifying for a diagnosis of generalized anxiety disorder. Similarly, students may experience significant amounts of discouragement and what we would colloquially call "depression" without it being severe enough to constitute depression as defined by the *Diagnostic and Statistical Manual of Mental Disorders* (DSM). But even mental health challenges that don't constitute diagnosable mental health conditions can affect students' ability to learn. Thus, in this book, we are less concerned about what label a clinician would apply to a student's symptoms than we are about the degree to which any of our practices create enough stress or despair to undermine learning. A brain researcher at the Center for Healthy Minds at the University of Wisconsin–Madison puts it this way: "I'm kind of a believer that there aren't any clear-cut points between subclinical and diagnosed anxiety. It's a continuous spectrum where uncertainty plays an increasing role, increasing the suckiness of unpredictability." [28]

We acknowledge the multiple approaches to viewing mental health, including the categorical approach, which "represents mental health and illness as a dichotomy"—someone either is or isn't clinically diagnosed with depression. By contrast, with the continuum approach, mental health and mental illness are treated as "the two opposite poles of a continuum. Thus, there are various degrees of health and illness between these poles, with most of us falling somewhere in between." [29]

For us, thinking of mental health in terms of a continuum rather than as discrete binary categories of diagnoses is more fruitful as we consider the impact of our teaching practices on students' mental health and well-being. It seems naïve to think that stress and discouragement can significantly affect student performance only once they become severe enough to be clinically diagnosed as having generalized anxiety disorder or depression. One fascinating study categorized students into four groups based not only on their level of clinical symptoms but also on their levels of subjective well-being. The researchers found that students in the high well-being, low-symptom category had the highest GPAs. Even among those students who were not experiencing any clinical symptoms, students who rated their own well-being at higher levels were more engaged than students who rated their well-being as low. Even when students were experiencing clinical symptoms of mental health challenges, if their subjective well-being was high, they "had better study habits, were more engaged with faculty and peers, had higher intrinsic motivation, and felt a greater sense of belonging in the university community than the individuals with low subjective well-being. Accordingly, positive well-being seems to be an important component of an optimal college experience." [30] Again, it's difficult to know which way the causal arrow points in this correlation, but our suggestions in this book can help improve both academic performance and wellness.

In short, our aim should not be just to help students better cope with their clinically diagnosed mental health conditions. Instead, our goal should be to help students—wherever they are—edge toward the positive end of the well-being continuum.[31] The World Health Organization (WHO) describes mental health as "a state of well-being in which every individual realizes his or her own potential, can cope with the normal stresses of life, can work productively and fruitfully, and is able to make a contribution to her or his community." [32] We succeed whether we help students with clinical diagnoses in finding more joy and purpose in college, prevent students with signs of

depression and anxiety from developing full-fledged diagnosed conditions, or even help students with no symptoms
of depression or anxiety at all become happier. In every
case, students will be better off academically as they move
in the right direction on the mental health continuum.[33]

As we explore in greater depth in chapter 8, conceiving
of wellness and mental health challenges in this way has
given rise in recent decades to the field of positive psychology. While psychology has focused traditionally on mental
illness and other deficits, positive psychology focuses on
mental health and human flourishing broadly, promoting
optimal levels of functioning. The teaching strategies we
advocate in this book thus benefit not only students with
clinically diagnosed mental health conditions but all students, wherever they are on the wellness spectrum.

Stress and Other Triggers Affect Each of Us Differently

Of course, different learning activities and policies affect
each student differently. One research team examining the
impact of stress in learning noted a "considerable individual variation due to genetic background and life history."[34]
Not only do the timing and amount of stress affect how we
respond, but so does our preexisting stress level. For example, in one important study, groups of volunteers at different levels of anxiety tried to discern any emerging patterns
while being shown a series of images that included either
angry or happy faces. High-anxiety participants struggled
to adjust their learning rate as quickly when viewing angry
faces compared to when viewing happy ones.[35]

That's worth remembering when teachers are tempted
to judge how much consternation our assignments and

policies create based on our own experiences alone, especially when our college experience may be decades old and
involve a very different set of circumstances. What may
have created little stress for us might result in much higher
levels of stress or discouragement in some of our students.
In fact, given the academic success almost all professors
experienced that qualified them for their current positions, it's quite possible that a disproportionate percentage
of us thrive academically under stress. That may make it
hard for us as teachers to imagine a completely different
response from some of our students. Simply remembering
that we are all wired a bit differently from one another in
how we respond to certain stressors can help us be more
sensitive to the fact that some assignments we might
enjoy, such as oral presentations, could trigger significant
anxiety for some of our students.

Conclusion

Ultimately, no college professor is imposing as much stress
on students as Bruce and his wife experienced in the face of
a fire that was about to engulf their home. Yet, after reading
the previous sentence, Elizabeth Eaton Warner, Rob's daugh-
ter and a relatively recent college graduate, commented, "It
can feel that way though! . . . College is an extremely high-
risk and high-stakes endeavor. So while you're not worrying
about physically dying from a fire, failing [or] passing a class
can seem just as important for a student's future in a lot of
ways."

Many of our students experience our courses against
an intense emotional and psychological backdrop. While
few, if any, of us are intentionally creating stress-inducing experiences, some of our assignments and policies

unwittingly exacerbate the anxiety and depression many of our students experience—undermining their ability to learn and function optimally. Researching and writing this book has certainly helped the three of us recognize just how much stress some of our own assignments and policies have unnecessarily created for some of our students. On the other hand, many professors are already doing some important things that help reduce unnecessary stress and discouragement.

As we mention in the introductory chapter, our goal certainly is not to remove every cause of stress from students' lives. First of all, we don't want the authors of *The Coddling of the American Mind* coming after us. Second, the *Coddling* authors have a point: perhaps one cause of our current societal challenge with young people's mental health is parents and others trying to remove every source of stress in their children's lives rather than helping them develop resilience. If teachers eliminated all stress-inducing academic tasks, we would hardly be preparing our students for employment and life.

Our aim is not to remove every learning activity any student might find stressful. Instead, it is to be more intentional about designing everything from syllabi to assessments to late policies. This process requires consciously weighing the negative mental health benefits of practices against their cognitive and curricular benefits. As we have implemented this approach ourselves, we have almost always found solutions—which we share in the chapters that follow—that simultaneously make life better for students with mental health challenges *and* improve learning for all our students.

CHAPTER 2

. . . .

BECOME NATURAL MENTORS

. . . .

To augment our research for this book, in the fall of 2020, we conducted a few "focus groups" with students who were experiencing mental health challenges. The term is in quotes because the focus groups might more accurately be called interviews or group interviews, since our numbers were quite small. Still, what we learned poignantly illustrates students' concerns. And perhaps the clearest theme that emerged from these interviews is that students care a lot about how much their professors care about them.

For example, Trisha (we use a pseudonym for all but one of the students we quote) wrestles with both anxiety and depression. She told us about a Spanish teacher she had in high school who began the first day of class by saying, "I want you all to succeed, and I know that everybody's lives are different. And I know that you guys are gonna have problems. And if you guys ever need anything . . . , even if it's not Spanish, please, please, please come to me. I would love to help!" Beginning the semester with that offer and expression of concern made a huge difference to Trisha, and she ended up talking with him about the challenges brought on by her anxiety and depression. Generalizing from that and other experiences, Trisha concluded that "just knowing that a teacher actually cares about you and they want you to succeed just takes away a lot of anxiety with the class because you know that at least somebody is rooting for you."

We also conducted a survey of 279 students, asking them about their mental health status and about how they felt about a variety of the practices we examine in this book. The most important variable to the students we surveyed was having professors who they felt cared about them personally, with a mean response of 5.51 on a scale of 1 to 7. Students who feel connected to their teachers have an entirely different college experience than those who don't. A 2018 survey of college graduates found that graduates who had seven to ten "significant" relationships with their professors or staff were "more than three times as likely to report their college experience as 'very rewarding' as compared to graduates with no such relationships." [1]

The consequences of students' relationships—or lack of relationships—with professors carry far beyond graduation. A groundbreaking study of more than thirty thousand US college graduates, *Great Jobs, Great Lives: The 2014 Gallup-Purdue Index Report*, revealed that teachers play a critical role in shaping the college experience of students who thrive after graduation. Among other things, the degree to which alumni thrived significantly correlated with whether students had a teacher or mentor who cared about them. According to the researchers, "Feeling supported and having deep learning experiences means everything when it comes to long-term outcomes for college graduates." [2]

Just how great was the impact? Graduates fortunate enough to have "felt 'supported' during college (that professors cared, professors made them excited about learning, and had a mentor) were nearly three times as likely to be thriving than those who didn't feel supported." [3] Even students who simply felt their professors cared about them were 1.7 times more likely to be thriving in all areas.[4] But perhaps the most revealing and most troubling finding was that only 27 percent of students strongly agreed that their professors cared about them. And only 22 percent had someone who acted as a mentor.[5]

Mentoring matters for all students, but it is especially important for students with mental health issues. In this chapter, we explore both why teachers' level of genuine support for their students has such an influence academically and emotionally and how we can become more effective, natural mentors. The strategies we examine include combining high expectations for students with high levels of support, shrinking the psychological gap between us and our students, getting more students into our offices, and making the most of whatever mentoring opportunities we get. Finally, we discuss the line between the kinds of help professors can appropriately provide to students with mental health challenges and the kinds of situations that require professional assistance.

Theoretical Framework

Mentors Matter

Joe Cuseo, an influential scholar on student success and mentoring, notes that research demonstrates how the "frequency of student-faculty interaction correlated significantly with every academic achievement outcome examined, including: college GPA, degree attainment, graduation with honors, and enrollment in graduate or professional school."[6] Cuseo speculates that out-of-class interactions between professors and students have a strong effect because of the less formal context and more casual nature of such conversations, the lack of evaluation, and the individual attention faculty can give students in such settings. The collective impact of teachers talking to students outside of class, states Cuseo, is that "it makes students feel significant and that the college cares about them."[7]

Data from a 2019 Gallup survey of college graduates suggest that students do indeed equate the level of concern they feel from faculty members with the university's overall concern for their mental health. In fact, if participating alumni strongly agree their teachers cared about them "as a person," they are three times more likely to also strongly agree that their school is "passionate about students' mental health." Similarly, graduates "who strongly agree that they had a mentor who encouraged them to pursue their goals and dreams are more than twice as likely to also strongly agree that their school handles mental health issues with vigor."[8]

Conversely, other research confirms the troubling corollary: when students "perceive faculty to be remote, discouraging, or biased, they are likely to avoid interactions and to disengage from college."[9] The gist of the research is that the relationship students have with their professors is a two-edged sword. While positive relationships lead to multiple benefits for students, "a negative relationship can have an immensely negative impact upon the motivation of a student."[10] This is especially true for students with disabilities.[11]

Natural Mentors Can Help Students Better Manage Mental Health Challenges

Natural mentors do much more than just help graduates have more pleasant memories about college. Having a trusted natural mentor strongly correlates with positive mental health for students. In one fascinating nonexperimental study, researchers examined the influence of natural mentors on over six hundred African American "emerging adults" during the five years following high school. They defined *natural mentors* as someone other than a parent who youth feel they can turn to for guidance in making important decisions or who inspire them to do their best. In other words, such mentors need not have been assigned and might include anyone from a teacher to a custodian. Among other benefits, young people with natural mentors were less likely to experience depressive symptoms, suggesting that having a natural mentor may serve as a "protective function." Emerging adults "who had a natural mentor presented greater decreases in depressive symptoms over time." [12]

Obviously, having a natural mentor didn't totally shield these emerging adults from stress, but it did moderate its impact, resulting in less depression. This impact was especially important at a critical juncture of the participants' lives: "The insulating effects of natural mentoring relationships on emerging adults' psychological health are more pronounced when adolescents graduate from high school and begin to experience increased levels of transitional stress." [13] Thus, college teachers have a unique opportunity to play the role of natural mentors for students—simply by being someone students can turn to for advice and a bit of encouragement during an emotionally critical juncture in their lives.

The effect of having natural mentors extends beyond students coping better with stress and discouragement. In some cases, the effect is nothing short of lifesaving. In one study, over ten thousand high school students from thirty-eight different schools were asked to list up to seven of their closest school friends and up to seven "adults in your school who you trust and feel you can talk to about personal things." They were also asked about whether they had considered or attempted suicide. The researchers then contrasted the average number of adults listed by students at each school with the average number of suicide attempts. Among other things of note, there was a significant inverse relationship between the number of natural mentors and the rate of attempted suicides. The more natural mentors were listed at a school, the lower the average number of students self-reporting suicidal thoughts and behavior.

In fact, a decrease of just 10 percent in the number of students who did not list any adults as natural mentors correlated with a 20 percent reduction in the average number of students who attempted suicide in a high school.[14] Simply having more adults in their school they trusted to talk to about personal things corresponded with significantly fewer attempted suicides. Research shows that the more social support youth have, "especially during times of stress," the less likely they are to be overcome by depression.[15]

Not only can concern from faculty members help students better manage their mental health challenges, but it can also boost their happiness, moving them toward the positive end of the mental health continuum. Harvard economist Ronald Ferguson and several colleagues conducted a massive study of sixteen thousand classrooms of grades 6–9. With the objectivity and analytical rigor you would expect from economists, they examined which teaching behaviors boosted and which dampened students' agency—or students' ability to take actions that pragmatically solve problems and shape future outcomes. Ferguson and his colleagues were struck by the impact that teachers' level of concern for students has on their students' happiness, concluding that when teachers are caring, "students are happier, more inclined to seek help, more future oriented (i.e., interest in college and what happens after high school), more conscientious, and more inclined to believe in the possibility of getting smarter (i.e., they develop more growth mindset)." [16] We recognize there are important differences between the junior-high classrooms Ferguson's team studied and those in which we teach, but enough similarities compel us to give serious consideration to their findings.

Young Adults Are Often Reluctant to Seek Professional Help for Their Mental Health

Recognizing three facts can inspire us to be more careful about the verbal and nonverbal cues we give our students: (1) many of our students struggle with mental health challenges, (2) most students are reluctant to seek the help they need, and (3) students look for signals to gauge our attitudes about mental health challenges.

In fact, among students who are experiencing suicidal thoughts or have had a mental disorder for twelve months, only one in four gets help.[17] In the World Health Organization's massive 2019 survey we discussed in the last chapter, over thirteen thousand students were asked, "If during this coming school year, you developed an emotional problem that caused you a lot of distress and interfered with your school work, how likely would you be to go to the student Counseling Center for help?" and "How likely would you be to go somewhere else for help, like to your doctor, a mental health professional, or religious advisor?" Only 24.6 percent of the college students who responded indicated they would definitely get help. Of the remaining 75.4 percent of students, 8.8 percent indicated that they had a 12-month suicidal ideation, including 7.8 percent who reported having had a 12-month suicide plan.[18] That is, nearly six out of one hundred college students have a plan for taking their lives and have admitted they would not seek help.[19]

In other surveys, the leading reasons students have offered for not being willing to seek help include feeling like they need to handle the problem alone, preferring to talk only with family and friends, and being embarrassed.[20] One survey respondent articulated the concern about stigmatization this way: "There is a negative stigma attached to any mental illness, as soon as you say that you've got one, people judge you and start thinking of you differently." Another added, "I was afraid of what people might have thought of me." One respondent tellingly noted a reluctance to impose on others who are busy: "I feel that others didn't have the time to help me." Another young adult was skeptical of how someone would respond who didn't really understand the significance of mental health challenges: "Not many people are fully aware and educated on mental illnesses. This causes them to say insensitive things such as: 'get over it,' 'can't you feel happy?' "[21]

The students we interviewed recognized that some of their professors take mental health challenges more seriously than others. When students perceived that their teachers minimized the seriousness of mental health challenges, they were reluctant to approach them when these challenges affected their ability to complete assignments in a timely fashion. For example, Jonathan, a student who has attention deficit hyperactivity disorder (ADHD), acknowledged, "I have a lot of problems reaching out for help because I always seem to fall behind on assignments, and then I'm too embarrassed to ask for help because I feel like I should be able to get everything done on time."

The students we interviewed seemed particularly sensitive to the signals their professors send about how they feel about mental health challenges. Abigail explained that when she gets overwhelmed, freezes up, and fails to turn in an assignment, "I'm way too scared to email my professor." She worried the professor would "hate me and think that I'm a slacker."

Others in the focus group shared her concern, in part because most of them had encountered a professor or two who was dismissive of mental health issues. "It sucks when the first day of class, . . . a professor talks about mental health like it's a joke, and he doesn't believe it because he's old school," admitted Theresa in one of our focus groups. "You just don't want to go to them, you know. You're just like, 'Great, I'm screwed in this class.' " Randy echoed the comments of Theresa and Abigail, explaining that a few teachers "think that we're just using mental health as an excuse, or they don't believe it's real."

By contrast, when professors make it clear that they are mindful of just how much poor mental health can interfere with academic performance, Trisha, who deals with both anxiety and depression, genuinely appreciates it. "I don't want to say that they should baby their students that have mental health issues, but if they're trying to at least help them or be understanding, then I think that makes a world of difference." Rob includes a provision in his syllabi to preemptively address such issues, something we discuss more in the next chapter. Recently, one of his students wrote an email thanking Rob: "I would once more like to show my appreciation to you for being so understanding and accommodating to students who have struggles with their mental health. I don't believe that I had any problems that interfered with the class but having had some of these problems in the past, knowing that you are understanding of such situations helped me to feel safer in your class, which was a great feeling." Just as some golfers play better when they know they have a mulligan to use—even if they never do—simply knowing their professors take mental health challenges seriously provides an emotional safety net for some students.

The bottom line is that in addition to the typical fears created by the imbalance of power between professors and students, those learners with mental health concerns face an extra layer of fear that their issues will be dismissed or they themselves will be seen as entitled. Those fears are often rooted in experience with a small but memorable minority of professors. Incidentally, to a person, the students in our focus groups did not expect professors to excuse them from completing assignments. Instead, what they were hoping for was some flexibility based on an understanding that their challenges were real. Explained Sheila, whose primary mental health challenge is anxiety, "I hate when people lower the bar, like if you have anxiety." She has had teachers offer to excuse her from assignments altogether, but that's not what she wants. Instead, she's just hoping for some flexibility with deadlines if her anxiety interferes too much.

In sum, faculty members have the potential to become natural mentors at a critical stage of emotional development in their students' lives. They don't have to be mental health experts or even have lots of time-consuming pseudocounseling conversations with students to make a difference. Simply being someone students feel they can turn to when they need help has the potential to improve academic performance, boost happiness, reduce loneliness and depression, and even decrease suicide attempts.

Putting Theory into Practice

Too many of our students are graduating without feeling that level of support. Despite our good intentions, time limitations make it difficult for us to have the kind of personal relationships with all our students we wish we could have. Becoming more effective natural mentors—without treading inappropriately into territory that is the exclusive purview of counselors, psychologists, and psychiatrists—can be a bit challenging. But if we can be more intentional about connecting with students personally and making the most of those relationships—especially with those who need such support the most—we can help more students thrive in college and beyond.

Be Mindful of Your Vibe

Even for those already philosophically focused on our students, the daily grind of answering email, grading papers, and preparing to teach sometimes leads us to rush through our interactions with students, eager to move on to some tasks we can finish and cross off the list. Yet, according to our survey, the vibe professors give off makes a big difference to students: those who perceived their professors cared about them as a person were nearly twice as likely (a mean of 5.51 on a scale of 1 to 7) to approach them than when the professor "seems really busy" (2.83). Sheila, who experiences anxiety, noted that whether professors came across as very busy was "a make-or-break thing." When her teachers seem busy, she said, "I'm just too self-conscious to actually go, because I feel like they have more important work." She has even noticed professors multitasking while talking with her, and other students in the focus group mentioned similar experiences. Such experiences were very much the exception for these students, yet they were also clearly seared in their psyches.

Students sometimes gauge how busy their professors are by how quickly they respond to emails. One participant in our focus groups, Allison, juggles both ADHD and depression. When it takes professors several days to get back to her—or when they don't respond at all—she said, "I feel like my professor doesn't have time to answer a valid question that I would have," so she doesn't ask them any more questions.

Of course, one significant challenge for most teachers, caring or not, is that we *are* busy. Still, realizing the impact of the vibe we give—caring or busy—can inspire us to be more intentional about what messages we give our students. One simple way for teachers to move our interactions in the caring direction is to assume that during every office hour, some students could really benefit from some help with an issue they don't initially raise with us. Rob remembers a day when he nearly missed such an opportunity. He saw a former student in the hallway, and the student mentioned he was planning to transfer to another school. As on most days, Rob's plate as an academic leader and professor was overflowing, so he was about to wish the student well and get back to his office to get some things done. But something prompted Rob to ask this student why he was considering transferring.

That question opened the door to a conversation in Rob's

office, where this student shared some deeper frustrations he was experiencing at a predominantly white school as a Black student. Rob listened intently and ultimately shared a few thoughts. The young man left with a determination to stay and, hopefully, with a greater feeling of belonging. But the daily grind almost prevented Rob from discovering and helping this student with needs hidden beneath the surface. Simply looking for an opportunity to help one student in life each day or even each week can help us rise above the pressing demands of our profession to recognize the important opportunities it provides.

Shrink the Psychological Distance

It's easy to forget how daunting a professor's persona can be to many of our students. While our credentials and capacity can be a source of respect, they can also be a source of intimidation—something that creates a psychological gap between professors and students. In the first chapter, we mention the survey conducted by Chi Baik and her colleagues asking students what could be done to improve their well-being. The students' most common suggestion was that "their wellbeing would be improved if academic teachers—both lecturers and tutors—were more approachable and understanding of diverse student circumstances." [22] This jibes with multiple studies showing that "student anxiety decreases as instructor immediacy increases." [23]

Given the psychological distance inherent between professors with advanced degrees and young college students, our task is to find ways to shrink that gap. This is especially important, given the reluctance of students with mental health challenges to seek the professional help they need. Teachers who manage to connect with students are in a position to help convince them to get that help, or even just introduce them to other valuable resources. In their report on how to create caring cultures, the Association of College and University Educators offers some simple suggestions for how faculty members can make clear to their students that they are approachable:

- Share with your class at the beginning of the semester that they can talk to you if they are struggling for any reason.
- Include mental health resources on your syllabi along with the more typical academic and tutoring resources available to students.
- Ask advisees about how much sleep they are getting, if they are feeling stressed, and urge them to practice self-care.
- Check-in with individual students you are concerned about and ask directly how their semester is going. If they defer to a default or vague response (i.e. "I'm fine" or "I'm good"), gently push for a little more detail. . . .
- Share a story about when you needed help while in school, if you feel comfortable. Doing so is a powerful way to show students that seeking help is a sign of strength.[24]

Another way to reduce the psychological gap between us and our students is to humanize ourselves, acknowledging some of our mistakes and growth. In fact, doing so might help dispel some students' fixed mindset about their teachers' expertise and capacity. We explore the concepts of fixed and growth mindsets at length in chapter 5, but the basic notion is that if teachers believe people (including our students and ourselves) are either naturally good or naturally bad at things, with little potential for improvement, we suffer from a fixed mindset. But if we believe that we all have the potential to significantly improve, given the right resources and opportunities, then we have more of a growth mindset. When we let students see that we have also struggled and grown along the way, we paint a more accurate picture of who we really are: imperfect beings with the capacity to grow. It may also create an environment where students are more willing to appropriately disclose some of their challenges in private, out-of-class conversations.

Jason Hunt, a biology professor at BYU-Idaho, almost always has multiple students in his office during his office hours and beyond. Students flock to him. He explains his approach this way: "Developing my classroom culture is the most important thing that I do as a teacher." Highlighting the importance of belonging, openness, and authenticity in his relationships with his students, he adds, "My classroom culture is one of vulnerability and trust. I work to establish this by sharing my own vulnerabilities each day in class. I'm very open with my weaknesses, the mistakes I've made and how I remedied those mistakes. I also encourage students to adopt a value system of growth mindset, self-control, gratitude, and respect for others. Each thought that I share revolves around these values. For example, I often share a thought of how I was kicked out of my first class in graduate school for not coming prepared. I explain the anger and embarrassment I felt, the fight to not just quit, and then how I found the strength to return to class and change my approach to education."

According to Jason, "one crucial step" must follow the creation of a classroom community built on vulnerability and authenticity. Once the culture has been established, "I must stay true to my word," he explains. For example, when a student finally dares to challenge something Jason says in class, his response makes or breaks the tone for the entire semester. "If I receive it well, being careful to correct with kindness, or, more importantly, to accept correction when I'm mistaken, my students gain trust in me."

Steve has found that a form of Jason's purposeful vulnerability can bring a powerful authenticity to a class. He was in the habit of taking a few minutes near the end of the first day of each semester to make his students aware of his struggle with Parkinson's disease. In a classroom setting, where his tremor, soft voice, and ongoing battles with the computer mouse were "on display" for all to see, that conversation seemed more practical than self-indulgent. Since those challenges were less evident in a videoconferencing environment, he stopped sharing that information with his students when he was no longer in a classroom with them. However, on a day in class when the tremors and muscle rigidity were particularly vexing, Steve, in frustration, apologized for the delay and blamed the problem on the Parkinson's—something he hadn't mentioned previously. One student's response changed his view on sharing his vulnerability. That student simply said, "It's all right. You can tell us."

We can also help to shrink the psychological distance between our students and us by not overreacting when they fall short. Jim Kanan, a professor of sociology at Western Kentucky University, recalls a student who was struggling so much that she was even finding it hard to get to class. One day, she arrived very late. Jim describes what followed this way: "She said she feared some scolding comment from me, but was instead greatly relieved and put at ease when my only comment (she included it in quotes with this story in the written portion of the evaluation) was 'Ms. X, I am just very pleased that you are here, and I will always be glad when you make it here.' " [25] This welcoming gesture was a small thing to Kanan, but to any student in this situation, such a generous reaction can go a long way to establishing a personal connection with their professor.

We recognize that most of these behaviors take place *in* the classroom, but great connections with students outside of class usually begin with good rapport in class. As Cuseo notes, when "students feel comfortable engaging with instructors in class, they are more likely to seek out opportunities to connect with faculty in out-of-class contexts." He cites a vast body of research showing that "instructors who have frequent out-of-class contact with students often give signals about their accessibility and approachability by behavior they exhibit in class." [26]

Of all the behaviors listed for building rapport and establishing immediacy, perhaps none is more critical than one simple gesture. Cuseo cites earlier work by Charles Bonwell and James Eison concluding that "perhaps the single most important act faculty can do to improve the climate in the classroom is to learn students' names." [27] In one study about the importance of learning students' names, many students indicated that when professors learn their names, they "feel valued in the course," they feel like the instructor cares about them, and they feel more invested in the course. Some said that they "would feel more comfortable talking to the instructor about topics unrelated to the content, such as scheduling conflicts or personal struggles." And almost 12 percent felt they performed better in courses where their teachers knew their names. [28]

Stephen Courtright, a professor of management and the director of executive education at the University of Iowa, believes that "belonging must be created on the very first day of class, because first impressions make for lasting impressions." He uses a variety of memory techniques to learn students' names on day one. As students file into class on the first day, he greets them individually and asks their names. Then he begins class by betting them he can name all of them. When he manages to pull it off—to the dismay of his students—the class often erupts into applause. And over the years, according to Courtright, many students have said in their evaluations that "this single act of memorizing student names immediately created a culture of belonging and safety in the classroom." He acknowledges this is easier to do in smaller classes; he's never done it in a class with more than forty students. But when he can, it helps "students feel they belong by creating a direct connection with me as their professor."[29]

One of the students in our mental health focus groups, Allison, feels validated when her professors know her name: "It makes me feel important, it makes me feel valid. It's like, 'OK, they care that I'm here. They care about my opinion.' " Explained Sheila, another student in the focus group: "I feel like when they know my name, I know that they see me." Echoing the thinking of Courtright, she explained that for her, the simple fact that teachers learn her name creates "an emotional connection. . . . There's just a human connection that's important psychologically to me."

When students sense the concern that comes from learning their names, it also creates a greater willingness to reach out to their professors. Jed explained, "It's like, wow, these guys actually care. Now, I know I can go to them if I got issues with something." Jed, who described himself as having twice survived attempts at suicide in the last three years, found it especially powerful when faculty members knew his name on the first day of class. To him, that effort somehow sent the message that they were willing to accept him as he was.

Trisha is a student who describes herself as a "very stubborn person" who is typically reluctant to get help. She also describes herself as "somebody who has a lot going on in their head," including both depression and anxiety. But "if a professor knows my name and tries to talk to me . . . , I will be so much more comfortable with approaching them. . . . If I need help or anything, it's like it makes me feel like they want to help me, . . . that they would want my success, in a way." She contrasted a biology professor and a chemistry professor she had during the same semester. Even though the biology class had at least three times as many students, her biology professor made the effort to learn every student's name. "He would always get my name right," she said with a smile, and that made her much more comfortable asking questions in class, something that normally causes her stress.

Finally, when asked what professors could do to be more approachable, Sheila, whose anxiety and depression cause her some issues, mentioned that the first impression of the semester was the first class, and it was "super essential" how professors acted toward students. Similarly, she said it mattered what teachers did before class, whether they were engaging with students and asking about them. She really appreciated it "when they try to actually make a personal connection to you. Then it really helps. Then I actually want to go to them for [help] because I know that they actually care." Whether it's learning students' names, showing vulnerability, or chatting with them before class, when we take steps to build immediacy and shrink the psychological gap between us and our students, we open opportunities for more meaningful personal interactions out of class as well.

Make the Most of Office Hours

Office hours are the perfect time to proactively establish personal connections with students, yet there's quite a gap between how professors and college students view office hours. In one survey of over six hundred students, the researchers asked whether students used office hours and what would make them more likely to use them. Two-thirds of the participants reported never having used office hours. When asked what would make them more likely to use office hours, the students' most frequent response was some variation on not understanding why they would ever use them. One student answered candidly, "Office hours are kind of weird"—a quote the researchers loved so much that they used it in the title of their article.[30] Several other students illuminated some reasons for not taking advantage of office hours:

- "I have no idea what I would go to office hours for."
- "If I was doing very, very, very bad in the class and there was no way for me to improve. Or if I needed to get grade changes on any previous exams. Most likely, though, never really going to use office hours."
- "Office hours are dependent solely on the approachability of the professor. Some professors make you feel like a burden for coming to office hours and interrupting their work. Or they make you feel stupid for asking some questions or being concerned with your grade."[31]

Most students in the survey thought of office hours in

fairly narrow terms: you use them only if you have a question you can't get answered in some other way. They saw office hours as "the last resort they can turn to when an academic crisis" occurs rather than an opportunity to connect with or learn from faculty members.[32]

Conversely, colleges tend to envision office hours as a time when teachers and students bond while exploring ideas more deeply together. According to these researchers, then, one of the main reasons office hours are so underutilized is that there's a "mismatch between students' perceptions and institutional design of office hours."[33]

In some ways, technological tools such as email are definitely a blessing, making it easier for students to communicate with their professors. But the flip side is that some of the kinds of questions that once got students to come to our offices—literally opening the door to conversations and relationships—now get handled quickly with fairly impersonal emails. That may be good on the efficiency front, but it doesn't do much to build personal relationships. The authors of the study on office hours recognize that the historical approach to office hours may be falling out of favor, but they suggest updating our tactics rather than abandoning the effort to connect with students.[34]

One way to do this is by permitting students to take advantage of office hours via videoconferencing tools—a technology that virtually all our students became acquainted with during the COVID-19 pandemic. For some students, meeting virtually with professors lowers the psychological barriers to entry, allowing them to remain in the security of their residence hall or apartment, if they choose. The University of Washington's Center for Teaching and Learning points out another reason for offering students the option of meeting with us remotely. As important as in-person office hours are, they "risk serving only students who live close to campus and have flexible schedules. Many students work, have family responsibilities, and long commutes to class." It recommends holding office hours online to "provide all your students with greater access."[35] Stefan Stoll, an associate professor of chemistry at UW, has been doing this for years. Stoll says he reaches far more students than when he offered only face-to-face office hours. "There's a higher barrier when you have to make a decision to get to campus."[36]

Another way to eliminate logistical hurdles is to update our calendars and give students access to them using a calendaring tool. That way, their access to us isn't limited by the few hours we designate at the outset of the semester as appropriate times for meeting with us. Especially as more students become comfortable with such scheduling tools, we suspect that increased flexibility in meeting times will result in greater student use of office hours.

Our colleague Jason Hunt does something else to lower the barriers to entry to his office: he works with his door open. "My office door is always open; when a student peaks around the corner, I immediately invite them in. My colleagues often ask how I get any work done. My reply is two-fold. First, maybe the work I'm doing with students is the work I'm really supposed to be doing. Second, most students are not morning people, so early morning is a great time to do the 'other' work—writing, grading, planning, etc." There may not be a more effective way to show students that they belong than to make it clear that we organize our time to be available for them.

Another simple idea is to take office hours to the students. Shaun Vecera, a professor at the University of Iowa, decided to do for office hours what bookmobiles do for libraries: he moved them out of his office and into a conference room in the residence halls where students live. "I actually get really very good foot traffic because of that," he explains.[37] Similarly, we can hold office hours immediately following class on benches or chairs outside the classroom. Bonnie recently started letting students know in one class that she would stick around for fifteen minutes after class. Since then, she has met with more students than she had all semester. Often students' questions were quick and simple, maybe not something they felt warranted a trip to Bonnie's office. And one student she talked with after class then mustered the courage to come to her office hours. Whether it's letting students meet with us via videoconferencing or taking office hours to where they live, the key is to find ways to lower the psychological barriers to entry that prevent far too many of our students—especially those who most need the help—from showing up at our official office hours.

As obvious as this may seem, a simple way to get more students to use office hours is to do more than just mention them in the syllabus. We can periodically remind students about when and where our office hours are, help them understand their broader potential ("I'm happy to talk with you about any aspect of challenges you're facing in college, even if they don't relate directly to this class"), and assure them that we *actually* want them to come. "By taking time and effort in class to announce that they welcome office visits from students," argues Cuseo, "faculty send students a stronger, more sincere message than simply listing office hours on the syllabus, which students may interpret merely as perfunctory fulfillment of an institutional requirement." [38] And even if students don't take advantage of our office hours, Cuseo cites studies showing that "student retention may be enhanced even if students simply *perceive* faculty to be available and interested in them." [39]

Consider Requiring Students to Meet with You Once

In their wonderfully enlightening book *Relationship-Rich Education: How Human Connections Drive Success in College* Elon University's Peter Felten and Leo Lambert share the experience of Holly Graff, chair of the humanities department at Oakton Community College, who implemented a requirement in her curriculum that students meet with her in her office. She was surprised at how much of a difference these meetings have made: "I've been teaching here a long time, and I still am in contact with some of my students from twenty years ago, but when I added the one-on-one conferences, it transformed me and my teaching. My departmental colleagues have said the same thing. I am not just getting to know the students with whom I might have the greatest affinities; instead, I am getting to know all my students, and there's a big difference between those two things." [40]

But how would you find the time to work in interviews with all your students from even one class? Phil Allred and Rex Butterfield, then chair and vice-chair of BYU-Idaho's department of religious education, came up with an intriguing way to do just this. The impetus for their innovation was an inspiring conversation with the president of the college, Henry Eyring, who charged them to find ways to help more students succeed. From his doctoral research on student success, Butterfield remembered the potential power of having faculty members meet individually with each student. But he and Allred also worried it would be too much to mandate for every course on top of all that teachers were already doing.

That led them to focus their efforts on one required course that was unusual in that students from all the sections of the course gathered for a giant lecture six times during the semester. Together with colleagues who taught that course, they decided to move the content for those large lecture sessions into podcasts students could watch or listen to online—thus freeing up six hours of class time for faculty members. They then added the requirement that all students in the course meet with their professor for five to ten minutes over the course of the semester, with priority given to first-year students. Participating professors were given a script with a few simple questions that helped them get to know students better, questions inspired by what research showed were common reasons for dropping out of college. The professors were encouraged to use the interview as a kind of triage, identifying students who might be academically at risk for leaving without a degree and could benefit from further contact.

They measured the percentage of students in these sections who remained at college the next semester, comparing the figure to the university's average. Although it wasn't quite statistically significant, 14 percent more students in the course with the interview remained enrolled. And there was a statistically significant difference for international and male students. In talking with individual students about the required interviews, Butterfield and Allred also discovered that a number of students with mental health challenges felt they particularly benefited from the personal contact with their professor.

In some cases, students met numerous times with their professor beyond the requirement. "I felt more comfortable meeting a few other times to get extra help," explained one young woman who struggled with anxiety and depression. In fact, the follow-up conversations with her professor led to his helping her find a job. That act helped her "feel a little more secure and anchored," she explained. "I felt cared about. . . . I knew someone cared, at least, and was rooting for my success, even if I didn't at the time feel super capable or very successful."

Oakton Community College has created a similar requirement for all classes taught by teachers who volunteer to be part of the Faculty Persistence Project. According to Felten and Lambert, professors who participate commit to meet with each student in their classes for ten to fifteen minutes. They also commit to learn students' names, return an assignment with useful formative feedback, and set high standards with high support—all within the first three weeks of the semester. The results have been astonishing: "Students in Persistence Project course sections are more than 24 percent more likely than their peers to return to Oakton the next semester, and the positive effect is even greater for students who identify as African American." [41]

A colleague at BYU, John Hilton, teaches larger classes, where meeting with each student individually is less feasible. Instead, he schedules lunch with eight students at a time, with the students bringing their own lunch. These lunch sessions create a more relaxed setting for him to get to know his students and for them to get to know him. Each semester, about twenty of two hundred students take him up on the invitation. At the outset of the semester, he also has students complete a questionnaire about themselves. Using the help of a teaching assistant and some boilerplate language, he responds with a personalized comment to every student. In two or three hours, they send messages to two hundred students, showing them from the outset of the semester that they are important to him.

Mentor in the Moment

As valuable as office hours can be, if we limit our thinking of mentoring opportunities to office hours, we may be over-looking some of our most valuable moments with students. Even if students steadily stream to our offices seeking advice with open hearts and minds, using office hours as the sole method for establishing personal connections severely limits the number of students we personally reach. Felten and Lambert acknowledge the impracticality of expecting every student to have the kind of time-consuming, life-changing "sustained relationship between a scholar and a protégé" that often comes to mind when we think of mentors. "One-on-one mentoring is an academic ideal but nearly impossible to scale at the undergraduate level because the sheer quantity of protégés overwhelms the number of available mentors," they concede. "The math just does not work at most institutions." Fortunately, much shorter interactions can still have a significant influence on students' lives.

Consequently, Felten and Lambert urge teachers to look for what Brad Johnson of the United States Naval Academy calls opportunities to be a "mentor of the moment" or what Sean James of California State University– Dominguez Hills calls "mentoring on the run"—"those times when you are passing a student and just ask them a simple, pointed question" or say something to help students "gain understanding and belonging." [42] Such opportunities often arise unexpectedly, and the mentoring takes place informally.

Despite their relative brevity, argue Felten and Lambert,

"mentoring conversations have the potential to be conse-
quential moments in the lives of students."[43] With a bit of
intentionality, we can even transform digital communication from what Felten and Lambert call "transactional
practices toward relational ones."[44] For example, a student
might email us asking when an assignment is due. In addition to answering her question, we might ask how long
she has been at college, what she likes best about it so
far, and what is most challenging. A kind question or two
might open the door to an important conversation, even
via email.

Another simple but remarkably effective tool is to make
a point of arriving early enough to class to be able to sit
down next to a student or two for a short conversation.
Many teachers have long believed in doing this but still
struggle to arrive at class early enough to log in, pull up our
slides, and get everything in place in time to comfortably
chat with individual students before class starts. Far too
often, we are busy dealing with some technological glitch
right up until class starts. Even if a student wanted to approach us, our body language lets students know we are
preoccupied and cranky—anything but approachable. Yet,
as Lisa Nunn points out in her wonderfully practical book
*33 Simple Strategies for Faculty: A Week-By-Week Resource
for Teaching First-Year and First-Generation Students*, "first-
year students told me that they use the minutes before and
after a class as a kind of testing ground for building up the
courage to come to our office hours."[45] Making sure we are
available to students before and after classes is a simple
but important way to be more approachable and to cultivate immediacy.

Perhaps most crucial for mentoring in the moment is
to develop the discipline to slow down enough to listen,

observe, and engage in personal conversations rather than simply cutting to the chase. For example, we might get an email from a student letting us know they will be missing class to attend a funeral and asking if they can make up the absence. If we jump right to answering the administrative question, we miss a critical opportunity to develop and demonstrate concern. We can build a surprising amount of rapport with students just by taking a few extra seconds in every email exchange—no matter how mundane the original question or comment—to try to connect with them in some personal way.

Be Strategic in Prioritizing the Students You Help

We might not have the time to interview the students in all our courses, but what if we focused strategically on reaching out to a few more students who might most benefit from our help? Simply narrowing the field of those we are trying to reach opens up possibilities that are impractical if we try to do something with or for all our students. One of our colleagues who used to invite students in a particular class to his home for breakfast once a semester had bemoaned the fact that he'd had to abandon the tradition because his class had grown too large. But then it occurred to him that if he invited only the class's first-year students, the size of the group would still be manageable.

Another area to focus our limited time is on students who have fallen behind in class. Especially if you have assignments throughout the semester rather than only at midterms and finals, tracking their performance alerts you when students are at risk of not succeeding academically. Getting a failing grade is a pretty sure sign that a student is struggling and in need of help, motivation, or both.

Given that both anxiety and depression undermine students' capacity to cope and learn, we are not surprised that a disproportionate number of the students who are having a difficult time academically are also having a difficult time with their mental health, often undiagnosed and untreated. (Of course, at the other end of the grading spectrum we also encounter anxiety-ridden students who suffer from perfectionism.) And even for those students whose performance has not been affected at all by their mental health issues, these students are still in particular need of our help.

Another fruitful area to focus our efforts is on any students who may lack a natural sense of belonging at their college. Felten and Lambert argue that "relationships are especially powerful for students who for any reason might feel they are on the margins of higher education, including first-generation students, people of color, and LGBTQIA people." [46] We explore this issue in greater detail in chapter 6 when discussing the importance of building community, but it's worth noting here that, paradoxically, some of these students may be the least likely to have mentors. In a 2018 poll of college graduates, first-generation college students—arguably those who may benefit most from meaningful mentoring relationships—were almost three times more likely than children of college-educated parents to lack any influential relationships. Fifteen percent of such students reported they have no such relationships, while only 6 percent of students with college-educated parents experienced such lack of support. [47] Just as Allred and Butterfield found that their efforts had a greater influence on international students—many of them at BYU-Idaho are from Africa—Felten and Lambert argue that "student-faculty interactions are the single most significant factor in positive educational outcomes for students of color and are also especially significant for first-generation students." [48]

One reason positive, personal relationships with teachers can have such a powerful effect on some students is that they can address a need for confirmation of their potential and worth. "When faculty know who their students are and know something about them, it provides students with a strong sense of personal validation—they feel valued, recognized as unique human beings, and sense that faculty care about them as individuals," explains Cuseo. "Personal validation is important to all college students, but it is particularly important to underrepresented college students from families without a college-going tradition who may experience the 'imposter syndrome'—a feeling that they do not belong in college or are there under false pretenses." [49] (We also explore imposter syndrome in greater depth in the chapter on building community.)

Just how can we reach students who could most benefit from some personal contact with faculty members? It's more challenging to address this need with first-generation students and students of color than it is with students who are failing a course and do not share either of these identities. With students who are struggling academically, we can be forthright about why we are seeking them out. However, if we are clumsy in the way we try to help students who might feel they are on the margins of college life, our efforts to help them feel supported may come across as condescending and do more harm than good. Our suggestion, then, is to reach out to a variety of students with different backgrounds and identities, so that there is no discernible pattern among the students you chat with before class or invite to your office.

Perhaps the most important way to avoid appearing patronizing is to avoid *being* patronizing. And that requires both scrutinizing our own hearts for bias and adopting a growth mindset for all our students. Some disadvantaged students might initially underperform, leading fixed-mindset faculty to assume such students lack academic potential. Conversely, professors who have the greatest impact on their students never seem to give up on them. In fact, as Sarah Ketchen Lipson and Daniel Eisenberg point out, there is "a robust literature documenting the importance of teacher expectations for student achievement—students, particularly those from disadvantaged backgrounds, are more likely to succeed when teachers expect students to do so." [50]

In a seminal study, a Harvard psychology professor and a California elementary school principal examined the phenomenon of observer-expectancy, also known as the Pygmalion effect, with teachers and grade school students. They learned that when teachers were told that some students were about to blossom based on preliminary gifted testing (even though the researchers had selected the students randomly), the teachers treated the students labeled as "bloomers" differently, and those students ended up blossoming after all: "The results of the experiment . . . provide further evidence that one person's expectations of another's behavior may come to serve as a self-fulfilling prophecy. When teachers expected that certain children would show greater intellectual development, those children did show greater intellectual development." [51]

Similarly, studies show that students invest more time studying when they perceive we believe they can succeed. [52] In the Healthy Minds Study we discussed earlier, almost half of the students who were flourishing indicated their professors believed they could succeed. Conversely, among those with at least one mental health challenge, only 25 percent felt their professors believed in them.[53]

Reach Out to Students Proactively

Being strategic in our efforts to establish personal connections with students requires us to be intentional not only about who we reach out to, but when. An obvious example is learning students' names: making that investment during the first week of the semester reaps far more dividends than learning them the last week of the semester. Similarly, when we receive notifications from the disabilities office about students who need accommodations, a bit of preemptive kindness in the form of a quick phone call asking how we can best support them can go a long way to easing some students' anticipatory anxiety.

Another key opportunity for helping students comes within the first two or three weeks of the semester—right when the wheels start to come off academically for many students. Rob used to reach out much later in the semester, only to realize students had often dug a hole so deep it was difficult or impossible for them to recover at that point, even with plenty of faculty support. He then moved up his intervention to midterms. He finally realized that he'd have the greatest impact by reaching out to most of the same students by the end of the second or third week. At that point, he scans the students' grades to identify which students are earning a D or worse, writes individual emails to the students, and lets them know that he noticed they are falling behind and that he wants to help them get back on track before it's too late.

In earlier years, Rob extended a blanket invitation to

come to his office for help. Now he sends an electronic calendaring link and invites them to schedule an appointment at the time that works best for them that week. Since making these simple changes, Rob has seen a much higher percentage of these struggling students come to his office to meet with him. Interestingly, a significant percentage of those students are also dealing with mental health challenges. Helping students in those situations has proven to be one of the most rewarding parts of Rob's job each semester.

Rob's experience confirms what scholars like Cuseo already knew: it's important for faculty members to "initiate outreach to low-achieving students" because research shows that "students who most need learning assistance are typically the students least likely to seek it out on their own."[54] By reaching out to them individually, inviting them to meet (rather than merely announcing our availability), and sending them an electronic calendaring link (rather than asking them to look up our office hours and limiting students to those time slots), we lower psychological barriers to entry for students who most need help.

Midterms and the end of the semester are also a good time to remind students that your office door is open and you're eager to help, especially if they are feeling overwhelmed. Another important time to intervene is when a student's performance or attendance suddenly drops. Too often we are surprised at the end of the semester when a student who was actively engaged during the first half of the semester has stopped turning in assignments or attending class without our realizing it. Staying on top of sharp drops in performance is important, since such a sudden change can be a red flag for mental health challenges. Learning management systems make it especially manageable for professors to stay up-to-date with their students.

Finally, while many of our programs are structured so that we're most likely to develop personal relationships with students when they are seniors, it's when they are in their first year that many could most benefit from a kind comment, a reassuring conversation, some academic encouragement, or a pitch for using the counseling center on campus. As we seek to have the greatest effect on individual students with our limited time, one guiding principle is that helping sooner is better—earlier in the semester and earlier in a student's college experience.

Counsel Widely but Wisely

We have found these two things to be true for the vast majority of the academically struggling students we invite to meet with us: (1) they are doing poorly not just in our class, but in most of their classes, and (2) no other professor has reached out to them yet. This means that teachers who are willing to offer help proactively to such students are uniquely positioned to improve not only students' performance in their class but also students' overall college experience.

Taking full advantage of that singular opportunity requires us to take a somewhat holistic approach. We certainly don't want to become students' psychiatrist or counselor, but a bit of generous listening and wise counsel from caring faculty can do wonders in identifying and addressing some of their root problems. Students might come to our office because they are wrestling with a concept or falling behind in class, but their root problems are often poor study habits, lack of discipline, doubting the value of college altogether, working too many hours at a part-time job—or mental health challenges. When we care about our students, ask questions, and actively listen for clues in their answers, we often discover root problems that explain the academic symptoms we are seeing. And whether our expertise is in math or Spanish, we don't need to be trained counselors to offer some helpful advice to help them succeed academically.

We can start by taking a few minutes to get to know the students and see how they're doing. As tempting as it is to jump in and help them with their math problem, asking a few simple questions to get to know students better can create the foundation for important personal connections. Rob's father was a journalism professor who liked to say that everyone was a walking feature story, if you just asked the right questions. Similarly, every one of our students has an interesting—and often illuminating—backstory. The better we get to know students, the more we tend to care about them. Moreover, like learning their names, taking the time to ask a few personal questions is validating—evidence that they matter to us.

We might begin with simple, open-ended questions, such as, "What's been the best part of your experience here? What's most challenging?" When we follow up their answer to the latter questions with a simple, "Tell me more about that," we often begin to discover some of the deeper concerns and challenges students have. We also love the idea of asking students, "What's your story?" We have been surprised by how much students will share in response to this simple question, if we ask with genuine interest. Rob recently asked a student this question and learned that he had been abandoned on the roadside as a baby by his mother in his birth country because he had a cleft palate.

He lived in an orphanage until he was adopted by parents from the United States. Needless to say, that backstory helped Rob see this student in a different light.

As we talk with students and ask them questions, listening carefully is essential. Reflecting on lessons he has learned through conversations with his students, Jason emphasizes the need to avoid going into lecturer mode as soon as a student enters his office. "As a teacher I want to do just that—teach! However, when a student shows up at my office, they usually aren't there to listen to me. Tutors can teach, the book can teach, I teach in the classroom, but I have discovered that my office is a place for me to listen. Once I figured out that students who make the effort to come to my office often need more than just teaching, I began to listen, and that changed everything." Jason's generous listening sends a powerful message: You don't have to have everything figured out to belong in our class or at this university.

In interviewing hundreds of students on multiple campuses, Felten and Lambert "heard over and over from students how much simple interactions matter. When the person asking this question took a minute to practice the art of generous listening, students felt that they mattered."[55] Part of listening generously includes being alert for clues that might point us toward those deeper, unmet needs—subtle hints in conversation that can lead to important questions. Just the day before writing this, one of us asked a student how she was doing. "I'm doing a lot better today, thanks," she replied. Following up on that hint, we learned that the prior day had been one of the worst in this student's life and that she'd come closer than ever before to taking her life. We were able to contact the campus counseling center and get her the help she needed.

(In the next section, we talk more about how to respond to such information.)

In the report *Creating a Culture of Caring*, the Association of College and University Educators (ACUE) suggests a simple approach of validating, appreciating, and referring. They encourage teachers to acknowledge the difficulty of the mental health problems a student is facing with phrases like "that makes sense" or "that sounds difficult." That also means it's important not to judge students' conduct or minimize their feelings. "In many cases, struggling students can be helped through a show of compassion, with active listening and appropriate responses." [56] Appreciation involves thanking students for trusting you enough to divulge their challenges. Finally, when students have more severe problems, as we will discuss later in this chapter, the key for any nonclinician is to refer students to expert help. [57]

As we listen, in particular to students who are falling behind academically, we often learn that they aren't studying very much or very well. According to a 2019 survey of first-year college students, more than half of them spent an hour or less studying per day in high school. And this was apparently enough for almost all of them to earn As and Bs, since just over 97 percent of these students reported earning those grades in high school. [58] Many students fail to grasp—let alone transition to—the higher expectations at the college level. When an hour a day isn't enough for them to succeed in college, they are often puzzled. In our experience, simply encouraging such students to treat college like a full-time job often sparks a perspective-shifting epiphany. And for students who have been trying to get by with an inadequate investment of time, spending more time studying often reduces the stress and discouragement that comes from being perpetually behind and underperforming in their classes.

Discovering and pointing out that students aren't studying nearly enough to succeed academically is relatively easy; helping them choose to study more is a much bigger hurdle. One intriguing approach for helping others make important life changes is motivational interviewing, a counseling technique that originated in the context of addiction recovery. At its core, motivational interviewing relies heavily on gently using questions to help others explore their feelings about how things are going and what changes they might want to make. The basic premise is that rather than lecturing others about how they ought to change, we ask questions that help them discover changes they might want to make and explore why they want to make them. Then we provide support in helping them accomplish goals they have chosen for themselves.

In our context, we might ask students, "What's going well so far, and what is challenging? If you could make just one change that you think would help you learn more in all your classes, what would it be?" Students often already know why they are struggling academically. With a bit of gentle nudging and support, they will often choose to set a goal to improve in some way—a goal that they then own. We can then follow up with encouragement as they strive to achieve that goal. As we discuss in chapter 4, when students exercise agency and choose their own path, they tend to be much more motivated than when they are assigned or asked to do something.

Some of our students know just what's expected, but they have a hard time mustering the discipline to put in the study time. For these students, we've found it can be helpful to ask what their biggest distractions are. We then brainstorm some realistic adjustments they could make. Using principles of motivational inquiry, we can ask students which of several possible changes they think could realistically improve their academic life the most. One student who was spending lots of time watching videos decided to study two hours for every one hour of video she watched—hardly an ideal distribution of time for a dedicated college student but a manageable yet significant step forward for her. A week later, she returned to Rob's office, energized by what a difference that simple change had made in her college experience. A simple willingness on the part of concerned faculty members to help students succeed in college rather than just on the next assignment can transform a student's entire college experience.

Finally, we should note that some students with mental health challenges—especially anxiety—face an entirely different kind of problem. Driven by perfectionism, these students are sometimes unable to be at peace emotionally, despite their best efforts, with anything other than perfect grades. You might recall that in her first semester of college, Alexis (currently our research assistant) was studying thirteen hours a day, fearing she might get something wrong. "My roommates went out with friends while I stayed in to do homework," she recalls. "Once, my roommate actually picked me up and carried me out of our apartment, yelling that it was time for me to take a break."

The pivotal point in her college experience came when two of her teachers helped her see things differently:

> It was the words of two professors that changed my life. One professor told us about how important it is to find balance. Sometimes, we have to do our best and then move on

and make time for the things we enjoy. As another professor put it, "Life is about learning the art of good enough." That quote has stuck with me. I share it with everyone. Having professors that openly address matters such as anxiety and perfectionism in class is life changing. Hearing a professor say that it was okay to just be okay, to not place all of your self-worth in your GPA, changed my life. That is not to say that I am cured, I still get upset when I get a B on a test, but I have learned when it is time to put the books down and talk to my friends.

Know Your Limits, and Connect Students to Expert Resources

What happens if you're getting to know a student with academic challenges and looking for the root causes, and you learn that the student is depressed and struggling to get out of bed most days? To answer that question, consider an analogous situation: You're playing soccer with some friends, and one of them crumples into a heap after colliding with another player. Your friend says she's fine and tries to walk it off, but you see a bone protruding. No one argues that you should try to fix the broken bone yourself. But you'd certainly let your friend know that having a bone poking through the skin is a pretty good reason to go to the hospital or urgent care. You'd probably even give her a ride. In this case, you're not inappropriately providing a medical service to your friend for which you are neither licensed nor qualified. You're just wisely connecting a friend in need with someone who is qualified to meet that need.

Similarly, it doesn't take a professional counselor to know that if students haven't been able to function because of anxiety or depression, they would be prudent to see a mental health professional. We can lower the barriers to entry for students by letting them know about the counseling services available on our campus. Perhaps more importantly, we can help persuade them that rather than trying to push through alone and in pain, getting help is both the brave and wise thing to do. Being willing to get help is an important part of being gritty. Just like when we break a leg or have an aching cavity or get stumped by a math problem, growth-minded people get help when they're having panic attacks or can't get out of bed because they're so depressed.

Indeed, of everything we suggest, perhaps nothing professors can do to help students with mental health challenges is more important than persuading those in acute need of professional help to seek it out. Recall that three-fourths of college students indicate they would not seek help, even if a serious mental health challenge arose in their lives. If we do the kinds of things described in this chapter and that so many teachers already do, we build social capital with our students. We may be one of the few adults in their lives in a position to persuade them to get the help they need. We are absolutely not suggesting that we invite our students to lie down on a couch in our offices while we extensively probe their mental health history or condition. What we are suggesting is that college professors are uniquely positioned to recognize red flags and persuade students to seek the help of professional mental health-care providers. We can aid students in overcoming their fears and inhibitions and perhaps inspire them to get help—help that could change not only their college experience but also their lives.

Even if students are not suicidal and are still fairly functional, we can point them to online resources and wellness practices short of professional help. We appreciate the insights of Jeremy Hsu and Gregory Goldsmith of the Schmid College of Science and Technology at Chapman University, who offer instructor strategies to address student stress and anxiety: "Although instructors cannot (and should not) serve as health professionals, instructors can learn about common mental health challenges relating to stress and anxiety. Instructors who familiarize themselves with and are aware of mental health challenges can better direct students to the proper resources and likewise will have greater insight into how to approach these conversations with students if and when they arise."[59] That said, when in doubt, we should always err on the side of referring students with mental health challenges to professionals who can determine what level of help a student needs.

For helping students with problems that seem to be more significant, the first step is to be informed about the resources available in our university and community. On some occasions when we have had students with pressing mental health challenges, we have walked with them directly to the counseling center. It ensures they make it there without changing their minds and removes psychological and logistical barriers to entry, such as being too embarrassed or not knowing where it is. Where such resources aren't available, even giving students the phone number of a local or national suicide hotline such as the National Suicide Prevention Lifeline (800–273–8255) may help save a life. (The student who nearly took her life two days before we wrote this section chose not to go through with it because she made a call to such a hotline.) Some may feel more comfortable texting, in which case they can use the crisis text line 741741 for free crisis counseling twenty-four hours a day. If what you believe is a life-threatening situation arises, and there are no other alternatives, in the United States you can always call 911 and inform emergency services.

When teachers identify a potential mental health crisis and help connect students with appropriate resources, we are playing a gatekeeper role. One government report on suicide prevention identifies gatekeepers as "individuals in a community who have face-to-face contact with large numbers of community members as part of their usual routine." Such individuals might be trained to "identify persons at risk of suicide and refer them to treatment or supporting services as appropriate." [60] Like the friend who gets the injured soccer player to urgent care for what looks like a broken leg, a gatekeeper spots a potential mental health problem in students and then helps get them to professionals for care. In a thorough examination of mental health challenges among college students by the *Chronicle of Higher Education*, Sarah Brown advocates "training faculty and staff members as gatekeepers who can spot students in distress and ask them the right questions." [61]

The Jed Foundation, a nationwide group dedicated to reducing the rate of suicide among college students, also recommends training "frontline faculty and staff members, as well as peers, to recognize and refer anyone in distress." [62] In *Creating a Culture of Caring*, the ACUE notes that although "faculty cannot (and should not) be expected to replace the role of mental health professionals, they can take actions as helpers, not clinicians, to support struggling students." [63]

A 2021 report on the role of faculty in student mental health provides important insights into this role that a growing number of professors are playing. Primary author Lipson and her colleagues asked thousands of faculty members questions about being a gatekeeper. The researchers learned that "faculty are in need of mental health gatekeeper training, defined as programs designed to enhance an individual's skills to recognize signs of emotional distress in other people and refer them to appropriate resources. Over half of faculty (55.8%) report that they do not know if gatekeeper trainings exist at their institution. Only 28.8% report that they have participated in a training program. Among those who report that they have undergone such training, 71.5% found it 'helpful' or 'very helpful.' " [64]

One gatekeeper training program is QPR, which stands for *question, persuade, refer*. It's built on the assumption that just as nonmedical professionals can play an important role in the event of an emergency that calls for performing CPR or the Heimlich maneuver to save a life, with a bit of training and practice, most of us could do more to help prevent suicide among those within our influence. The aim is not to replace mental health professionals but to persuade people in need to turn to them for expert assistance. [65]

Studies make it clear that short training such as QPR can significantly improve the capacity of gatekeepers to act effectively in a crisis. In one study testing the effectiveness of QPR, the participants were employees in a variety of roles, such as faculty members and resident assistants, at five different universities. The researchers first recorded video of the participants' interactions with an actor role-playing a suicidal student—in essence, a pretest. The participants then participated in a one-hour QPR training session. Following the training, they tried role-playing again. Researchers rated only 10 percent of the participants as adequate in the pretest role-playing, but that figure jumped to 54 percent in the posttraining role-playing. Wendi Cross and her colleagues concluded that gatekeeper "training enhances suicide-specific skills for the majority of participants." [66]

In sum, whether or not we have been formally trained, professors are potential gatekeepers. Consequently, spending a bit of time in training like the kind the QPR program provides can be a wise investment of time for any professor who wants to better know how to deal with situations where students may be suicidal. At a minimum, when professors believe students are in danger of taking their own lives, we should connect them with professional help as quickly and effectively as possible.

While we might use gatekeeper techniques such as those outlined in the QPR program, Felten and Lambert caution against exceeding the limits of our expertise and authority as teachers. "Mentors also need to recognize the limits of their own capacities and the professional boundaries that guide their relationships with students." Because most campuses are rich with support resources, often our role will be to provide what they refer to as "a warm handoff" as we connect students with others who can help them in more specialized ways.[67] QPR provides great training in how to do just that.

In addition to recognizing the limitations of our competence, it's important to remember the limitations of our capacity. When students do open up to professors, sometimes their problems can overwhelm *us*, especially if we feel like we have to solve all their problems ourselves. That's why Nunn believes that a "key element in self-care is the willingness to set boundaries. I am a firm believer that caring about my students' well-being does not require me to overextend my emotions, my in-box, or my work-life balance." [68] Felten and Lambert also remind us that we "do not need to solve every problem or provide every answer to matter in the lives of students. Sometimes students just need to be heard." [69]

Conclusion

Given the rising levels of mental health challenges among college students—including a growing number of suicides and suicide attempts—there has never been a greater need for professors to proactively and strategically establish personal connections with their students. We can't do everything, but if we are intentional and creative, we can become natural mentors who personally influence more students than we thought possible. The source of a natural mentor's power to influence students must be genuine concern—something that we cannot fake but that we can foster. As our concern grows, we look for ways to shrink the psychological distance between us while still maintaining an appropriately professional relationship. Whether it's chatting with students individually before class or offering office hours through videoconferencing, we can look for innovative ways to lower the physical and psychological barriers to their conferring with us. Recognizing that the risks and hurdles are higher for some students than others, effective natural mentors intentionally make an effort to give some attention to the students who could most benefit from validating personal contact. And effective natural mentors don't wait until the semester is nearly over to reach out to students in need.

As they provide support to students, natural mentors invest a bit of time to get to know their students as people. They then listen carefully, looking for clues that lead to students' deeper concerns or needs—needs that often transcend the question the student initially asked about an assignment. Expecting to help students with broader issues such as poor study habits, imposter syndrome, or doubts about college making sense for them, natural mentors do what they can to help students thoughtfully address root challenges. In doing so, they often facilitate students' own discovery of solutions to such problems, rather than simply lecturing them on how to change.

Might faculty members who confide to their students that they have grappled with mental health challenges themselves—or even professors who develop a reputation as being compassionate and reasonable about such challenges—become magnets for such students? That is definitely a possibility. Indeed, we know that faculty members who are female or belong to underrepresented ethnic or racial groups often find themselves doing a larger share of mentoring students. As Shampa Biswas, a professor of politics at Whitman College, writes, "I realized early on that I was going to be a magnet for students of color, international students, and women who took my classes and frequented my office. But I didn't know then what I know now: that faculty members who are female, nonwhite, or both perform a disproportionate share of the care work at institutions like mine." [70]

To preserve our own health and well-being and keep our jobs manageable, even as we strive to be more intentional in connecting with students with mental health challenges, we have to establish the kinds of limits Nunn sets for herself. Then, without feeling guilty that we can't do everything for everyone, we can happily help as many students as possible. Given how many students have serious, untreated mental health challenges, we can even be grateful that we are in a position of trust—a position to make a difference. As natural mentors, we have the potential to persuade students to get the professional help that could not only let them finish college but change their lives. And recognizing our own limitations, we do what we can to provide a warm handoff to the professional experts best positioned to help them.

....

CHAPTER 3

DESIGN COURSES KEEPING STUDENTS WITH MENTAL HEALTH CHALLENGES IN MIND

....

Once when Rob was revising a course in preparation for the next semester, he asked his seasoned teaching assistant for her input on how it could be better. "Too many moving parts," she commented, without hesitation. "Students hate it when there are so many balls to juggle, so many different assignments to keep track of." Rob felt like each assignment was necessary and useful. And, collectively, the amount of work the course required of students was within the university's recommended parameters. But the TA's objection wasn't that there was too much work; her concern was how the work was organized.

With a few tweaks, Rob consolidated what felt like a collection of unrelated assignments with haphazard deadlines into a single recurring assignment: a weekly hands-on project. Even though the specific assignment varied from week to week, students knew that some kind of experiential learning assignment would be due every Saturday night. They still had the same amount of coursework to complete, but keeping track of what was due and when involved far less work. Just as it's easier to memorize more words when they are organized in a meaningful way, simplification and predictability lightened students' overall cognitive load without reducing their learning. In interviewing students with mental health challenges, we were surprised at just how big of an issue course design was for them. The wisdom of a TA and a bit of intentionality improved Rob's course for all his students, but especially for his students with mental health challenges.

For these students, course structure and policies may be an even more important variable in their experience than our teaching techniques. Courses that have too many assignments that don't follow clearly established patterns can overwhelm them, while courses with too few assignments create the stress-inducing high stakes that undermine learning. And some policies can sap students of incentive and hope rather than fostering a growth mindset.

In this chapter, we first discuss research highlighting several issues to consider when creating course assignments and policies and organizing the course in a learning management system (LMS). We then articulate seven principles that harness the insights of this research: being clear, proactively addressing mental health challenges, avoiding unnecessarily high-stakes assignments and draconian late policies, breaking up larger assignments into smaller chunks, guarding against extraneous load, providing students with the incentive and opportunity to master material not initially understood, and fostering a mastery mentality.

Theoretical Framework

Research from a variety of sources and disciplines reveals some important considerations in crafting assignments, organizing courses, and establishing policies. These principles may seem unrelated, but each can help us be more mindful of how our course structure and policies affect our students with mental health challenges.

Anxiety Sets in When Students Feel like a Class Is Moving on without Them

In a survey we conducted of BYU-Idaho students, we asked how much stress a variety of practices caused. To our surprise, the highest-rated item by half a point on a scale of 1 to 7 was "not understanding course material and the class is moving on anyway." And of practices that helped reduce anxiety, the second-highest-rated item was being given the opportunity to continue practicing outcomes until they are mastered.

Anxiety is what neuroscientists call "a future-oriented emotion," where individuals' anticipation of "the future induces anxiety largely because the future is intrinsically uncertain."[1] Against that cognitive psychological backdrop, then, consider the snowballing effects of compounding ignorance as knowledge cracks become knowledge gaps. As the complexity of what we expect our students to master increases, holes in their learning invariably increase anxiety. Without being given adequate opportunity and resources to first master the foundational content, some students may well feel like they are moving on to a lesson about unicycle riding when they haven't really mastered riding a bike yet.[2] For many, that's when panic sets in.

Uncertainty Fosters Anxiety

With a few notable exceptions—like being surprised with gifts or by a book's ending—most of us aren't big fans of uncertainty. "Uncertainty itself can lead to a lot of distress for humans in particular," observes Dan Grupe, a scientist at the Center for Healthy Minds.[3] Our aversion to uncertainty is so great that in one study, when given a choice between experiencing a shock now or a potentially milder shock in the future, the vast majority of participants opted "to experience the same pain sooner rather than later and were willing to accept more pain in order to hasten its occurrence."[4] Of course, how each of us reacts to uncertainty is different, just as we have varying degrees of allergic reactions to different foods. Grupe compares intolerance of uncertainty to "a psychological allergy."[5]

Researchers have even devised a scale for measuring just how allergic we are to uncertainty: the Intolerance of Uncertainty Scale. Uncertainty is a problem particularly for those with generalized anxiety disorder and obsessive compulsive disorder,[6] but as noted in the previous chapter, Grupe sees us all as being somewhere on a continuum of anxiety. The further along we are on the spectrum, the more problematic uncertainty becomes for us.[7] As we'll discuss in the section on practical application, syllabi and rubrics offer a great opportunity to provide the kind of clarity to our students about our expectations that can reduce unnecessary anxiety.

High-Stakes Assessments Can Hinder Cognition

As we discuss in the previous chapter, research has consistently shown that a moderate shot of stress at the right time can boost cognition, but too much stress can be cognitively debilitating. The Yerkes-Dodson law suggests that moderate levels of "arousal" actually boost performance, while too much arousal causes people to perform worse on difficult tasks.[8] Studies have borne out this phenomenon in a variety of settings: when the incentives—and thus the stakes—get too high, performance decreases significantly.[9] For example, in one study, over 70 percent of the participants performed worse in a cognitive game when the financial stakes were higher. According to Angelos Angelidis and his colleagues, the key takeaway with such research is that moderate "levels of stress, including [cognitive performance anxiety], enhance cognitive performance, but higher levels have detrimental effects."[10]

There's also quite a bit of variation from individual to individual with respect to how well we learn under acute pressure. But one consistent finding seems to be that acute stress has a more negative impact on the cognitive performance of individuals with higher levels of anxiety than those with more typical levels of anxiety. In one study where subjects in the experimental group underwent a stressful intervention while doing math, their cognitive performance suffered. And for those individuals who started out with higher levels of anxiety, the effects were even stronger: the stressful intervention led to a lower-performing working memory, "especially in vulnerable individuals." Participants with higher preexisting anxiety scores were "slower under stress."[11]

The Law School Admission Test (LSAT) is a classic example of a high-stakes exam: it plays a huge role in determining where applicants get accepted to law school, which in turn influences employment opportunities throughout their legal career. In his podcast, *Revisionist History*, Malcolm Gladwell takes on the LSAT, arguing that rather than measuring reasoning capacity, the exam is really testing the ability to solve problems quickly. In fact, as Indiana University law professor William Henderson notes in the article that inspired Gladwell's incisive rant, "Within the field of psychometrics, it is widely acknowledged that test-taking speed and reasoning ability are separate abilities with little or no correlation to each other." [12]

In his podcast, Gladwell compares taking tests to playing chess. He talks with a chess player ranked number 11 in the world. But in blitz chess, in which only three minutes or so are allowed per move, the same player's ranking shoots up to number 2. Conversely, other players who don't do as well at blitz chess excel under the traditional rules, where they have much more time to consider a variety of moves. Similarly, Henderson found that the LSAT predicts well how students will fare on timed exams, because both kinds of tests are the exam version of blitz chess—breathless cognitive sprints rather than more measured marathons. But if you change the rules and give law students a take-home test or a paper to write, the LSAT proves to be a relatively weak predictor of success with such exams. The actual practice of law is much more like completing take-home exams and writing papers than taking timed exams that put a premium on quickness, such as the LSAT and most law school finals. As Henderson concludes, "The current emphasis on time-pressured exams, therefore, may skew measures of merit in ways that have little theoretical relationship to the actual practice of law." Gladwell muses, "When we decide who is smart enough to be a lawyer, we use a stopwatch." [13]

Henderson also notes the unfortunate impact these assessment choices have on students of color: "Because the performance gap between white and minority students tends to be larger on the LSAT than [undergraduate grade point average] (the other important numerical admissions criteria), heavy reliance on time-pressured law school exams is likely to have the indirect effect of making it more difficult for minority students to be admitted through the regular admissions process." [14] Understanding the impact of the stress created by make-or-break exams—especially for certain students—allows us to be more intentional as we craft our assignments and assessments for our courses.

Hopelessness Is Not Helpful

According to one article, "Decades of research show hope is a robust predictor of mental health. Not only does it make life more enjoyable, experts say, but hope also provides resilience against things like post-traumatic stress disorder, anxiety, depression and suicidal ideation." [15] Recognizing the importance of hope can help us better appreciate just how debilitating hopelessness is. In fact, as our colleague Jon Skalski, a BYU-Idaho psychology professor, points out, it is "more precise to describe hopelessness, rather than depression, as a major precipitating factor for suicide; individuals who are not clinically depressed, yet are hopeless, will sometimes take their own lives." [16]

Feelings of hopelessness are exacerbated when the structure of a course doesn't allow students to turn in late work for any kind of credit, retake tests, or resubmit assignments. In such traditional scenarios, the lack of incentive for students to fill in their own knowledge gaps and cracks saps them of both hope and motivation to recover from a poor start.

Extraneous Load Can Hamper Learning

Unwittingly, professors sometimes add to our students' cognitive burden with tasks or concepts that aren't essential to learning the material in question. Cognitive psychologists call such complicating factors *extraneous load*. "Research has shown that removing extraneous load—that is, aspects of a task that make it difficult to complete but that are unrelated to what students need to learn—is helpful," note Susan Ambrose and her colleagues.[17]

Imagine learning about new concepts in a second language you mostly—but not fluently—understand. Having to learn in a language in which you're not fully proficient would create extraneous load, often increasing the time it takes to complete reading by a factor of two or three. (For our students who speak English as a second language, this is not hypothetical.) In this case, the extraneous load may be unavoidable, but in some cases, we unwittingly create extraneous load by having students tackle two or three new things at once. For example, in one study, researchers asked students to demonstrate a mathematical concept in a spreadsheet. Some students received sequential instruction, focusing first on how to use the spreadsheet and then proceeding to the mathematical application. Others concurrently learned how to use the spreadsheets and do the math. The researchers found that for students who didn't already know how to use spreadsheets well, having to simultaneously develop that skill and the math skill was just too much. They performed better when they could learn the skills separately.[18]

Our hunch is that such a fusion of tasks is even more challenging for students with higher levels of anxiety. Indeed, many of the comments from students in our focus groups invoked this concept without knowing its name. We found focus-group student Allison's description of how last-minute changes affected her especially interesting: "It increases my anxiety; it increases my mental energy that I have to put into planning what I'm going to do, [so] that I can't put as much energy into what I'm actually supposed to be doing." That's extraneous load.

Another student told her sociology professor that she loved his class and theory was her "jam." Unfortunately, because of her emotional well-being, she said, "I need to take it down to just one course this semester." She then elaborated further, identifying one of our favorite academic technology tools as the source of some of her anxiety: "In all honesty, it was the pressure of the reading Perusall grade thing that was too much for right now. Pressured reading . . . I don't know. I'm a paper pencil person and that was kinda too much stressful expectation, as odd as that may sound." (Incidentally, our own experience with this marvelous tool has led us to believe that using the default algorithm for grading leads to quite a bit of uncertainty and thus a fair amount of associated anxiety. We try to minimize that by significantly tweaking the parameters for grading to remove as much guesswork as possible for students.) For this student, learning to use a new collaborative tool while simultaneously completing a substantive assignment created extraneous load.

Putting Theory into Practice

How can we take advantage of these insights from the research to create more compelling, more positive, and less stressful course structures and policies? And how can we do that without lowering the bar for our students academically? We suggest seven principles.

Be Clear

Done well, syllabi and course materials reduce uncertainty—and thus reduce stress. Done poorly, they exacerbate stress. The students we interviewed especially valued simplicity, consistency, and clarity in the layout and design of a course. "Consistency is the key," observed Trisha. Allison shared Trisha's perspective: "I thrive on structure." Sheila, whose principal mental health challenge is anxiety, added, "The stress of an assignment that doesn't have clear instructions or a reasonable timeframe can bring me into big panic attacks."

Clarity is important not only in instructions for assignments and announcements of deadlines but also in how student work will be graded. When teachers are clear about expectations and consistent in grading, we create an atmosphere of fairness and predictability. That's why it's important, as Sarah Rose Cavanagh argues, to "aim for clarity and complete transparency in the reasoning behind your assignments, your activities, and which criteria students will be graded on."[19] Knowing what is required to earn a particular grade can decrease unnecessary anxiety for students. And, as with virtually all our recommendations, it can lead to greater student effort and learning. Just as studies have shown that "workers' perceptions of fairness and trust are also key drivers of their work effort,"[20] surely students are more willing to invest effort in a course they perceive as fair than in one that feels arbitrary. Lisa Nunn argues that this is especially important for first-generation and first-year students: "First-year students in general, and first-generation students especially, sincerely do not know what our expectations are. We can alleviate a lot of unnecessary stress by simply being explicit about how we are going to assess their learning and how they might best prepare for it." [21]

Similarly, students may understand some of our policies better and resent them less if we explain the rationale behind them. Instead of bluntly stating administrative rules with all the sensitivity of a lawyer drafting an insurance contract, we can kindly share the thinking behind them in accessible prose. And instead of merely setting forth assignments and deadlines, syllabus writers could weave in a bit of explanation for why they have included those assignments in the course, planting seeds of enthusiasm in the process.

Nunn also notes how some unwritten policies, such as requiring responses in complete sentences even in a math class, make perfect sense to professors but catch some unsuspecting students off guard. The result is we unintentionally irk students and leave some wondering if they are cut out for this game of college, whose unwritten rules may feel like traps. A simple solution, suggests Nunn, is to "be explicit with our students about why we require the things that we do, why we dock points when we do, and what our goals are for each of our particular rules and assignments. . . . We can mitigate some of the hard feelings and resentment"—and, we might add, unnecessary anxiety—"by simply explaining why we do what we do." [22] As the philosopher Friedrich Nietzsche said, "He [or she] who has a why to live can bear almost any how." [23] The syllabus is the perfect place for being explicit about the whys behind our hows.

Even if we state policies clearly, providing a simple explanation for their rationale can transform our language from cold to warm. James Lang admits that after a "few years of yelling at my students on my syllabus" about their use of electronic devices, he finally "learned to explain my (evolving) policy more clearly." [24] Here's an explanation one of us provides in our syllabi for our late policy:

> Why can't you submit assignments for credit when they're more than a week late? The deadlines actually help you. First, enforcing deadlines helps you stay on track and not get behind, which is what can happen if there are no firm deadlines. (That's definitely what happens for me without deadlines.) Second, enforcing deadlines ensures your memory is accurate for things like how many days you have read. Third, enforcing deadlines helps you develop the kind of responsibility that will be a blessing to you in employment and many other things.

When setting the tone for your class, perhaps even more important than the syllabus itself is the presentation of your course in an LMS, which has become a digital extension of the classroom. Our LMSs are powerful tools, but they are also fraught with opportunities for creating uncertainty and confusion through software errors. For instance, when we copy a course from a previous semester, if we're not careful, we may end up with some links that no longer work, some dates that no longer make sense, and some instructions that are outdated. Despite our best efforts, we invariably end up with some glitches. Those glitches can annoy any student, but they may disproportionately vex certain students, like those who score high on the Intolerance of Uncertainty Scale. Thus, one of the simplest yet most important things we can do to create a positive overall setting for students is to ensure that our links work and our instructions make sense, both in the syllabus and in the LMS.

Beyond making sure our instructions are clear and links are functional, how we organize our materials for students in our LMS can go a long way to increasing or decreasing confusion and the stress that comes with it. When professors had not kept assignments, links, and deadlines updated in the LMS, the students we interviewed found it very frustrating.

Sheila is a student who struggled so much with anxiety and depression in high school that she dropped out of all her extracurricular activities. She commented, "For me, it is so much more helpful if [professors] are really specific, because then it takes all the guessing and worrying out of it for me." When students experienced unclear instructions, ambiguity about deadlines, and confusing layouts in the LMS, the collective impact was unsettling uncertainty. Adam has been diagnosed with attention deficit disorder, anxiety, and depression, and he has dropped a course because of frustrations stemming from confusing course layout. "It wasn't very clear . . . where you were supposed to go and what the assignment was and when it was due," he explained. Conversely, referring to when courses are well organized with a consistent pattern of deadlines, Jed said, "It just takes that much pressure off your shoulders."

Until 2018, BYU-Idaho's campus-based faculty members had each organized their courses in an LMS independently, guaranteeing that students taking multiple classes would encounter multiple organizational schemes (and, in many cases, multiple LMSs). But when we chose to move to a new LMS in 2018, the instructional design experts urged us to take advantage of the clean slate. For starters, we required all faculty members to move to a single LMS, now that we had one with broad faculty support. (Ninety-two percent of our faculty members supported the change.) That meant students—especially new students—would no longer have to master several LMSs.

Recognizing how fiercely independent faculty members (including the three of us) are, our learning and teaching team chose not to mandate a single organizational scheme for courses in the new LMS. But with the help of our online colleagues (who do use a single, consistent course template), we offered each faculty member the choice of a limited number of templates that were organizationally similar. Faculty members were free to reject the templates altogether and create their own approach, but those who adopted one of the suggested templates received more support transitioning their courses to the new system. Over 80 percent of the faculty chose one of the templates, resulting in more consistency across courses and, we believe, cleaner and more intuitive designs.

Adam, in his fifth year of college at the time of this writing, was already attending before our conversion to a single LMS. Juggling classes in multiple LMSs sometimes caused him to miss deadlines. He has vastly preferred the simplicity of having all his courses in a single LMS. In addition, since our college's conversion to Canvas, he appreciates that all his professors now use a similar layout with weekly modules. "I know exactly what to check on what class. I can go in, and it's the same route through every class. And so it's simple finding what to do with that date, because it's the same path, every time." Another student in our focus groups, Trisha, added, "I freaking love modules. I love when teachers just have a module for every day, and each module . . . tells you exactly what you need to know so you're not scrambling around trying to figure out what was due." With well-organized modules, Trisha doesn't get stressed out because she can't find things. "If everything's organized, it's one less thing for me to worry about, because I'm already so stressed out about assignments—I'm stressed out about life in general."

Converting to a new LMS provides a unique opportunity for improvement. Still, even without a college-wide conversion, faculty members individually and colleges collectively can approach the design of their courses more intentionally, choosing to create a more intuitive and thus less stressful digital learning environment for their students.

Guard against Creating Extraneous Load

The notion of breaking large tasks into their components is useful not only for huge assessments—like law school's single-assessment final—but also for individual assignments that may seem small but have some embedded complexity. One way to eliminate extraneous load and the anxiety that often accompanies it, especially when introducing tools that may be new to some students, is to first give them an assignment that orients them to the tool before using it in a more substantive way. For example, we may make the first assignment an ungraded freebie so that students can first learn how to use the new tool without undue pressure. This is an example of *scaffolding*, a process originally suggested by psychologist Lev Vygotsky, in which "instructors temporarily relieve some of the cognitive load so that students can focus on particular dimensions of learning."[25] Providing scaffolding helps students learn in a more manageable way that leads to fewer knowledge gaps and cracks.

Ambrose and her colleagues point out that such support is often necessary because, as experts, professors simply don't "experience the same cognitive load as novices." Consequently, we often have "performance expectations for students that are unrealistically high." By allowing "students to focus on one skill at a time," we are "temporarily reducing their cognitive load and giving them the opportunity to develop fluency before they are required to integrate multiple skills."[26]

We inadvertently create extraneous load when we assume students understand foundational concepts that they haven't yet grasped, forcing them to try to master two concepts concurrently when we thought we were assigning them only one to learn. "Because of the phenomenon of expert blind spot, instructors may have little conscious awareness of all the component skills and knowledge required for complex tasks."[27] The key to avoiding such mistakes on our end, according to Ambrose and her colleagues, is to step back and break down everything required to master something—"decomposing the task." "Decomposing complex tasks helps instructors pinpoint skills that students need to develop through targeted practice."[28] Ultimately, decomposing tasks can reduce unnecessary stress and enhance learning by allowing students to tackle new concepts in more manageable ways than when we ask them to do or learn multiple new things at once. Sequenced approaches simplify the learning process, allowing students to first master discrete concepts before having to complete tasks that require them to integrate their knowledge of multiple concepts.

Address Mental Health Challenges Proactively

Today, boilerplate syllabus language addressing sexual harassment and disabilities is part of any university's prudent efforts to comply with federal law and create an atmosphere of equity. Given how often mental health challenges create difficulties for students and challenging grading issues for faculty members, why not address this in the syllabus pro-actively? Alternatively, enlightened faculty members might share some thoughts on the subject with students in class or by email early in the semester. The ideal language would lower students' stress level, invite important dialogue be-tween affected students and the teacher, and establish a fair framework. It might read something like this:

> A growing number of students are experiencing mental health challenges to varying degrees. Doing what you can to stay ahead and on top of depression or anxiety by wisely taking care of yourself will be a key to succeeding academi-cally. But even then, sometimes these challenges can affect your ability to complete the required work. Or a particular assignment might trigger anxiety for you in ways I have not anticipated. Or maybe you reach a point where you just can't get yourself to class at all.
>
> In any of those cases, please come and talk with me, or at least send me an email. I'll listen and do what I can to help. But the sooner you share your challenges with me, the bet-ter I can help. To pass the course or earn an A, you'll still need to do every bit as much work as other students, but we may be able to find some creative ways to help you do that—especially if you approach me when your problems arise, instead of at the end of the semester.[29]

Randy, one of the students we interviewed, felt that having language like this in a syllabus would make it clear that the teacher understands the reality of mental health challenges some students experience. "To me, it just makes us still feel like a person." One first-semester student in our mental health focus groups happened to be in one of Rob's classes. When she read his section in the syllabus about mental health, she said, it "was the most reassuring thing. Oh my goodness, it was crazy good." The language resonated with her, even though she never needed to take advantage of this provision. Just a bit of recognition, on our part as teachers, of the reality of these students' problems can destigmatize mental health challenges, open the door to the professor's office, increase the odds of a student getting the necessary help early in the semester, and guard against an increasingly common scenario where a student shows up the last week of the semester, desperately trying to make up for a semester of not attending class or completing assignments.

Some might fear that preemptively announcing the possibility of flexibility could lead some students to slacken their effort. But Barbara, another student in one of our focus groups, said, "When a teacher is up front about their flexibility to work with mental health challenges, I feel like I work harder in their class, because I already feel closer to them." And in several semesters of including this provision in his syllabus, Rob has yet to encounter a student trying to take undue advantage of it.

Avoid Creating Unnecessarily High-Stakes Deadlines and Assignments

When professors look at course structures through the lens of mental health, an important question to ask is whether we are unnecessarily creating acute stress or discouragement by making the stakes higher than they need to be for any single deadline or assignment. In particular, we might examine the severity and flexibility of our late policy and the number of major assignments. When we combine a course structure featuring only a few assignments with severe late policies administered without any exceptions for extenuating circumstances, that trifecta can create emotional problems on both the front end and back end of major assignments. Before high-stakes assignments are due, stress is the main response. After one is missed, discouragement and despondency come into play.

The students we surveyed were significantly more likely to experience anxiety in courses with only a few major assignments (rated a mean of 5.03 on a scale of 1 to 7) than in courses with many small assignments (3.18). Such data support the argument Josh Eyler makes in *How Humans Learn: The Science and Stories behind Effective College Teaching*: "The higher the stakes, the higher the potential anxiety. If we create more low stakes assignments (or even, dare I say, ungraded assignments where students get feedback on their progress), we are creating an atmosphere that is friendly to curiosity. We cannot blame students for being uncurious if we have created courses that privilege high-stakes performance." [30]

None of us has assignments with stakes as high as the LSAT, but any time we put a tight timeline on an assessment, we are probably measuring, at least in part, something other than what we intend to be measuring. Under the pressure of time limits, even students who know the subject matter perfectly well may choke. Taking tests with time limits was also one of the more stressful situations students encounter, with a mean response of 4.88 on a 1–7 scale in terms of their anxiety level. Even timed low-stakes quizzes given in class create anxiety for some students. "Students identified that their anxiety in science classrooms increased when they felt they did not have enough time to think through a clicker question," conclude the authors of a study on active learning that we will explore in depth in chapter 7.[31]

Even without imposing time limits on tests, we can unnecessarily create acute stress through the choices we make in designing a course's deadline policy and assignments. Consider what is at stake for students taking two different courses. The first course has only three assignments—a midterm, a paper, and a final, each worth a third of the total grade. And the late policy is entirely old school: nothing is accepted after the midnight deadline, no matter what. In the second course, there are ten assignments, each worth a tenth of the grade (not because that is ideal but because that simplifies the math for this illustration). Students can submit each assignment up to a week late, losing three percentage points of the assignment's total value for each day beyond the set deadline.

In both cases, a student has put off the assignment until the last day. Granted, the procrastination is purely the student's doing, yet it's a reality for so many college students. In the first course with the midnight deadline, one third of the overall grade is at stake. If the student misses the deadline, he is virtually doomed to fail the course. In the second course, if the student doesn't complete the assignment until the next day, she risks losing only 3 percent of 10 percent of the total grade—or 0.3 percent. In other words, the stakes for the assignment deadline in the traditional course are literally more than 100 times higher than in the course with more assignments and a more nuanced late policy. Because the risk of not completing an assignment on time is so fundamentally different between the two courses, so are the stress levels of the students taking them.

The fewer the number of assignments and the more draconian the late policy, the greater the pressure each deadline creates. When asked what kinds of things make them less willing to approach professors, one young woman who has anxiety said, "Some of the professors I struggle talking with the most are ones who, at the very beginning [of the semester] say, 'This is my syllabus. It's very strict; if you have any conflict unless someone is literally dying, don't talk to me about it.' " Another student who grapples with anxiety explained that just the thought of such deadlines was very stressful. On the other hand, if she knew she could turn in an assignment late with a modest penalty, that approach was "so much more motivating and relaxing," even if she never ended up needing to use that option. Another student in our focus groups, Trisha, said that when teachers "have super strict late policies, then I'm gonna be so much less likely [to talk with them]. I'm just gonna take the C." She admits that most of the time she simply lumps it. But if "a teacher makes it clear . . . that they care about their students and that there are certain circumstances where late work could be accepted, then I'm definitely going to be much more likely to reach out to them."

Sadly, then, the old three-assignment model of a class with a midterm, a paper, and a final—all of which students tended to cram for or write up in the hours before they were due—created a scenario in which students undertook a good chunk of their most important learning each semester under highly stressful circumstances that were also least conducive to learning. And when every professor takes a harsh approach to late policies with a limited number of major assignments, the aggregate experience for college students is four to six years of intense bouts of anxiety triggered by deadlines.

Moreover, when students miss those deadlines—as some invariably will—the lack of opportunity to complete and submit the assignment for some portion of credit creates an even bigger emotional problem for many. With no possibility of turning in an assignment belatedly for even partial credit, they may lose hope, potentially leading to a downward spiral of discouragement. Many late policies make it mathematically impossible at some point in the semester for students to pass the class, even if they were to make up every assignment they have missed. Students who realize this often do the understandable thing: they lose hope and stop engaging in the class altogether.

This is especially true where there is a combination of a small number of assessments or assignments in the course and rigid late policies. "I freak out," said Trisha, when asked how she felt about such scenarios. "I'm kind of like, 'Okay, great. I'm going to fail this class, and there's nothing that I can do about it.' And then at that point I just give up."

Perhaps most significantly, unyielding late policies limit learning in an even more fundamental way: once students miss a deadline for any reason, they have no incentive to belatedly complete the assignment. If the purpose of the assignment was merely to assess learning, then such a policy might be a decent approach. (Even then, it deprives the student and teacher of feedback on how well the student is learning.) But if the teacher was hoping students would actually learn something by completing the assignment, the late policy ensures that students who miss the deadline won't learn that content or develop that skill. One young woman in our focus groups who has struggled with social anxiety her entire life said that such policies puzzled her because she thought the "whole point of doing assignments is to learn." When professors don't accept late work, even with penalties, she explained, "The student has no motivation to actually do it anymore, because they can't turn it in at all."

What Lang writes in *Cheating Lessons* about severe consequences for cheating applies with equal force to all-or-nothing late policies: "A student who automatically fails an assignment on which he has cheated [or not turned in time], and which he has no chance to redo, also fails to learn anything from that assignment. So harsh and uniform punishments will put an automatic stop to the learning that the course was designed to instill in the students."[32]

Consider a physics class full of interrelated concepts that students need to learn sequentially. What if there are only five deadlines and the professor has a policy of not accepting any late work? If any students miss that first deadline and don't learn what they would have by completing the assignment, they almost certainly create a critical gap in their knowledge. As we discuss at length in chapter 4, that knowledge gap has serious downstream consequences, as the students' lack of understanding of the foundational concepts compounds with each new concept that is layered on the faulty foundation. As knowledge cracks become full-blown knowledge gaps, students' anxiety snowballs.

Finally, it's worth noting that more nuanced late policies combined with having assignments throughout the semester also aligns more closely with most real-world jobs. That matters, since many professors justify rigid late policies by arguing that we are preparing our students for employment. While a few tasks in some professions have inflexible deadlines with dire consequences for noncompliance, few of our graduates will work in jobs where their bosses give them no credit at all for completing a task a day later than originally requested or promised. Nor will their annual evaluation be based solely on their performance of three or four discrete tasks.

Over time, we've applied the first prong of our proposed cost-benefit analysis to our own late policies, considering what outcome we were really trying to achieve. We realized that our late policies were causing us to fail some students simply because they didn't turn in the assignments within our specified window, even though they attended class faithfully and could have eventually completed all the required work at an acceptable level. We decided that as important as helping them learn responsibility was, it shouldn't account for such a large part of the overall grade. So we built in some leniency that allowed students to make up past work—for example, making it possible for them to pass the class, albeit while capping their grade at a C–, a much lower grade than if they had turned in the assignments punctually. Such an approach offers both consequences for tardiness and the possibility for redemption for students who might otherwise throw in the towel. We have personally seen many students through the years take advantage of such modest mercy, mastering concepts they would not otherwise have mastered, and passing courses they would not otherwise have passed—thus avoiding the disappointment and depression that often come with failing a course.

We should also emphasize one important exception to our recommendations for modifying the combination of deadlines and assignments that create acute stress: disciplines where students eventually need to take a high-stakes exam in order to work in the field, such as nursing. In such fields, we would be doing students a disservice if the first high-stakes exam they encountered was the real thing after graduation. Yet even in these fields, we can phase in the amount of stress over the course of an entire program, rather than bombarding students with intense stress from the first semester through the last.

There's no ideal late policy we believe all teachers should adopt. But when we design late policies intentionally—deliberately weighing the costs and benefits of various options, especially on students with mental health challenges—we believe most of us will move in the direction of nuanced and principled flexibility. The result would be not only less stress for most students but also more learning, with more students completing more assignments.

Promote Mastery

What happens when some students don't master all the critical concepts from a unit? Even if we break up bigger tests into multiple tests, if we assess students' mastery of concepts and material only once, we give them no structural incentive or opportunity to go back and learn what they missed. At least from the standpoint of grades—which we argue can play an appropriate utilitarian role in motivating students—there is no reason for students to figure out what they didn't know and learn it better. And without any other feedback than the overall score, they have no idea where they came up short and need to learn more. Our traditional approaches to assignments and assessments, then, tend to lock knowledge gaps and cracks into place.

Lang suggests that to promote a mastery mindset—a corollary to a growth mindset—we can "begin by designing an assessment system that rewards intellectual growth in your students. The very simplest way to do this is to allow students the opportunity to practice and take risks, fail and get feedback, and then try again without having their grades suffer for it." Such a simple practice could do much to alleviate the anxiety our surveyed students experienced when a class moved on before they had mastered the material. Similarly, we can cultivate a mastery mindset and reduce discouragement from poor performance on initial assignments when we "weigh later assignments in the same sequence more heavily than earlier ones." [33]

Why don't we build in more opportunities, incentives, and resources to master the concepts that students may have difficulty with at first? One impediment may be the notion of accountability—the sense that allowing second chances may undermine the seriousness with which students approach their learning. That concern is understandable, and we'll address it shortly. But another premise can shape our thinking, sometimes even unknowingly—the notion that students who perform poorly on assessments do so because they lack the intellectual potential of their higher-performing peers.

In that view, students don't perform poorly because they have knowledge gaps or any other remedial barriers to their success. Instead, failure and success are merely a function of students' natural levels of intelligence and perhaps discipline. Subconsciously, we might find ourselves believing that no amount of extra help or opportunity is likely to change those facts. When we see a distribution of students across the grading spectrum at the end of the semester, we may even call it a "healthy spread"—as if we managed to create the perfect system for identifying and elevating only those students with enough innate intelligence or even grit to succeed. In this rather cynical fixed-mindset worldview, our courses are less an attempt to help all students realize their academic potential than they are some kind of intellectual Darwinian sifting exercise. In that old-school view, our principal task as professors is more a matter of sifting than lifting.

One mechanical engineering student we interviewed who has severe depression experienced this mentality firsthand. He had studied math only through algebra, so calculus was a real challenge for him. When he approached the professor designated as his mentor about his discomfort with calculus, the professor suggested, "Maybe you should just go find a job."

Contrast such thinking—of which many of us have been guilty to varying degrees—with something called mastery learning. As Khan Academy founder Sal Khan points out, mastery learning was based on the premise that "all students could learn, if provided with conditions appropriate to their needs." First implemented in 1922 by educator Carleton W. Washburne, this approach briefly flourished and then fizzled out because of logistical challenges. Khan argues that we can now easily overcome some of those logistical challenges with technological tools not available in Washburne's day. He sums up the mastery learning approach this way: "Students should adequately comprehend a given concept before being expected to understand a more advanced one."

Khan points out multiple benefits studies have documented for mastery learning, including longer knowledge retention, students taking more responsibility for their learning, and reduction in the spread between slower and faster students.[34] We're not advocating wholesale implementation of a mastery-learning approach, which still raises some formidable logistical challenges. But we are arguing that teachers can and should do more within existing structures to help all students attain mastery of as many concepts as possible.

For example, when we include quiz or test questions about concepts covered on an earlier assessment, we provide incentive both for students who didn't master those concepts initially to do so and for students who did to review and retain them. Lang argues for setting aside a couple of questions in every ten-question quiz to cover older material. He also lobbies for some kind of comprehensive exam or project at the conclusion of the semester: "If you don't give a cumulative final exam, you are essentially conveying to students that what they learned in the first weeks of the semester doesn't matter anymore."[35]

Allowing and even encouraging resubmissions or retakes fosters a mastery mentality. Lang suggests creating or finding "as large of a question bank as possible" to facilitate this for quizzes and tests.[36] For those of us who might chafe—as we did initially—at the potential such mercy has to undermine accountability, there are some simple ways to address such concerns. If nothing else, teachers can set the maximum grade on each resubmission or retake at several percentage points lower than the previous time, so that students aiming for the highest grades still have the incentive to get things right the first time.

Philosophically, we might consider the converse question. When we don't allow students to restudy concepts and earn additional credit for mastering them, what kind of message are we sending? If a student earns a 60 percent on a test about conjugating Spanish verbs, which scenario do we really prefer: one where she can't get any additional credit for going back and mastering the content—but hopefully learns an important life lesson about preparing better for future tests—or one where she could still earn up to a 95 percent by going back and actually learning everything you hoped she would have learned in time for the first test? As Lang notes, "Nothing says mastery—seriously, nothing at all—like telling a learner that they get to keep practicing and trying until they get it right."[37]

Allowing resubmissions and retakes not only fosters mastery, it foments hope. Perhaps that is why being given the opportunity to continue to practice outcomes until mastered was the second-highest-rated practice among our students. And as one psychologist argues in *Psychology Today*, "Hope is not just a feel-good emotion, but a *dynamic cognitive motivational system*." In fact, studies show that students with more hope perform better academically.[38] Students who earn a 60 percent on the Spanish test still have a formidable challenge ahead, even if they are allowed to retake the test for additional credit. But at least that door is open. Whether or not students choose to walk through the open door, the very fact that it *is* open may be less discouraging and create less panic for students than when they are staring at a door that is emphatically closed and locked.

Third, it's naive to blithely assume that 100 percent of our students will comprehend 100 percent of the material on our first pass. Yet most of our daily lesson plans and semester-long plans are based on this wildly unrealistic assumption, which Doug Lemov, who trains educators, finds incredibly unrealistic. Accordingly, he recommends that teachers "plan for error." Taking that approach leads both to building in reviews and resources to help students grasp material and to creating an environment where students feel emotionally comfortable seeking help with concepts they don't yet understand. Lemov notes that when you create "an environment where your students feel safe making and discussing errors," you can then "spend less time hunting for errors and more time fixing them." [39]

We can fruitfully plan for error—or at least something short of complete mastery—by connecting students with resources they can turn to in reviewing or clarifying concepts they still find challenging. Those resources certainly include academic support centers and relevant portions of textbooks, and in this extraordinary age they almost always include video tutorials posted free online by entities such as the Khan Academy. Many teachers find it helpful to make video tutorials of their own, in some cases. Incidentally, the students we surveyed were much more likely to watch a video a professor had made (a mean response of 5.74 on a scale of 1 to 7) than they were to go to the tutoring center (3.27). Bonnie builds in just-in-time reviews each week. Teachers who are intentional can also foster a sense of community in their classrooms, encouraging students to seek help from and share knowledge with each other to master the material.

Finally, Rob has noticed a psychological benefit for both his teaching assistants and himself since he has begun allowing resubmissions: it's easier for them to hold students to higher standards on the initial submission. For example, in the past, if a well-intentioned student who faithfully attended class throughout the semester fundamentally misunderstood the prompt for the final paper and wrote about the wrong thing, Rob and his teaching assistants had sometimes balked at giving as low a score as the student actually deserved. Today, knowing that they can give him clear feedback with course corrections and that he can resubmit the assignment has made it emotionally easier for Rob and his TAs to grade more accurately. Ironically, allowing resubmissions has resulted in more academic rigor in their grading.

Cultivate a Mastery Mindset

All the structural tweaks and formative feedback we suggest here will do little to fill in students' knowledge gaps and cracks if they simply don't care about mastering the material. Here, we're not talking so much about that small portion of students who might be truly apathetic; that's a different challenge. Instead, our concern is with those who are satisfied with mediocre mastery—those who earn a C– on a paper but don't bother to revise and resubmit it. Our university is virtually open enrollment, which allows us to educate a wide variety of students, including some academic late bloomers. But, at least initially, too many of them are quite content with a B or a C, without realizing that this means they are also comfortable with not fully understanding key concepts or mastering essential skills. An intriguing finding from Ronald Ferguson's comprehensive analysis of junior high classrooms underscores the benefits of cultivating a different mindset in students. Of all the factors Ferguson and his colleagues analyzed in the classrooms, requiring persistence "is the most consistently positive predictor" of the positive outcomes they examined.[40]

Helping students cultivate a mastery mindset isn't easy, because our students have been raised in a very different kind of educational system that fosters a very different kind of mindset. So how can we help our students make the shift? We can start by making the kinds of structural changes we've discussed in this chapter. When we give students the incentive, the opportunity, and the resources to continue studying concepts until they fully understand them, we send the message that helping them master the content is more important to us than the shape of our class's bell curve.

Beyond such structural changes, we can also be mindful of our rhetoric. Do we talk as if the goal of our course or an assignment is to earn a certain grade? Or do we make it clear that our greatest concern is about students learning certain things? Our language reveals what we really care about, and it can rub off on our students. When students do well on an assignment in her online class, Rob's wife Dianne congratulates them not on their grade but on mastering the material. And when they score poorly, she invites them to revise and resubmit their work, not just to improve their grade but to master the concepts. We strongly suspect that students who focus more on mastery than on grades are more resistant to anxiety and depression.

Another way to cultivate a mastery mindset in our students is to help them more fully grasp the consequences of having the kinds of gaps and cracks in their knowledge base that mediocre and subpar grades represent. Too often, students don't recognize that not quite understanding everything you should have learned in Spanish 1 or Algebra 1 will make it much more difficult to succeed in Spanish 2 or Algebra 2. We owe it to students to kindly and fully illustrate the benefits of mastery and the negative consequences of partial or incomplete mastery. Helping them see the real-world relevance of what they are learning also fosters a mastery mindset. For example, it's one thing to get a B or a C in Spanish class. It's quite another to give a doctor inaccurate information when translating for a Spanish-speaking patient because you never quite mastered some false cognates.

Incidentally, developing a mastery mindset fits together

beautifully with developing emotional resilience, as we explore in chapter 5. Students with resilience may be disappointed by low grades, but they understand the truth of what Khan has observed: "If you got 20 percent wrong on something, it doesn't mean that you have a C branded onto your DNA somehow. It means that you should just keep working on it." [41]

Break Down Big Assessments into Smaller Pieces

One great way to avoid creating unnecessarily high-stakes assignments and to promote mastery is to break up large assessments into chunks. We'll illustrate with the extreme example of courses that rely on a single assessment—a final. (Almost all of Rob's courses in law school operated this way.) If we were redesigning such a curriculum, we'd start by breaking that single end-of-semester test into much smaller chunks. Then, even if students were to take tests on one-fourth of the semester's material at a time, at least they could discover whether their study methods were working relatively early in the semester rather than at the end. For that matter, professors would learn long before the end of the semester if a significant number of students had failed to grasp key concepts, giving them a chance to do something about it. And if the final were comprehensive, students would have incentive to master the concepts on which they were weak.

That's why Nunn gives students what she calls "a mini-midterm" just a few weeks into the semester. She argues that "first-year students genuinely do not know if their high school study habits are adequate for college until they get their first midterms back." When they don't get back a graded midterm until several weeks into the semester, that can be "stressful and anxiety producing" for some students. The mini-midterm can "give students a clear sense of how well their high school study habits are serving them early enough to avoid devastating consequences on their GPA and on their emotional health." [42] Lang echoes this sentiment: "Whatever you ultimately expect of them on your major assessments, you should first allow them to practice on lower-stakes, more frequent assessments." [43] Lang quotes cognitive psychologist Stephen Chew as warning: "The actual exam should never be the first time the faculty or the students get feedback about the actual level of student understanding." [44]

Some simple ways to provide such opportunities are to break larger assignments, such as research papers, into smaller chunks; require the submission of a draft on which students receive formative feedback; make exams comprehensive and more heavily weighted later in the semester; and precede major tests with many smaller, low or even no-stakes quizzes. Similarly, the more opportunities we provide for students to practice skills we eventually measure, the more chances they get to learn from their mistakes before being assessed. Moreover, by dividing major assessments into smaller parts, we avoid the intense stress that accompanies high-stakes assessments.

Asking students the same questions on multiple quizzes or exams throughout the semester instead of only on a final exam is an example of retrieval practice. According to retrievalpractice.org, retrieval practice is "a strategy in which bringing information to mind enhances and boosts learning. Deliberately recalling information forces us to pull our knowledge 'out' and examine what we know." [45] One study of retrieval practice among middle school students supports the notion that having more low-stakes quizzes improves student performance, with 64 percent of the participants indicating that "the quizzing reduced anxiety over unit exams." [46] Whether students experienced less anxiety about tests preceded by frequent quizzes because they had learned more and were better prepared or because the quizzes had given them the confidence and self-efficacy that can eliminate unnecessary anxiety, the result was the same: less stress rather than more when assessments were carved up into smaller chunks.

Modularizing tests and other assignments also gives students more granular feedback, enabling them to identify where they have knowledge gaps and cracks. By contrast, the only feedback most law students receive the entire semester is a single number capturing their performance on the final. They have no idea whether they aced certain components of the exam and bombed others and, if so, which elements were which. Similarly, if we assign students a term paper and then simply give them a single number for feedback, they don't know whether they had a great thesis and supporting ideas but terrible mechanics or whether it was a combination of poor organization but great research. Using a rubric with scores for individual components is a simple but huge step forward for grading.

Conclusion

Until Rob began working closely with a colleague who used a wheelchair, he was completely unaware of where most elevators on campus were, which classrooms were difficult to navigate in a wheelchair, and which off-campus retreat sites were wheelchair accessible. Going places with this friend opened Rob's eyes to just how great an impact physical structure could have for someone differently situated than him.

Similarly, many of us who teach in higher education may have excelled in taking timed tests, understanding material on the first pass, juggling a plethora of assignments, and managing deadlines when we were students. Interviewing a number of bright, earnest students with mental health challenges helped open our eyes to just how much the structure of our courses and nature of our policies can affect such students.

As with every other chapter, our recommendations here lead to better learning for all our students, not just those with mental health challenges. We can begin by reducing the kind of confusion and uncertainty that interferes with working memory by being clear in our directions, expectations, and course layout. It also helps to be consistent with our deadlines and to ensure that the course is up to date in the LMS. Simplicity and predictability in course design also help to eliminate extraneous load.

We can significantly reduce anticipatory anxiety for many of our students by expressing some willingness in the syllabus to be flexible in working with students who experience mental health challenges during the course. We can give students more feedback, more practice, more lower-stakes assessments—all helping to lessen acute stress, which undermines learning.

Creating more nuanced and flexible late policies can help more of our students learn more and cause fewer of our students to lose hope. Recognizing that many of our students don't master critical concepts and skills initially, we can build in opportunities and incentives for them to persist with their learning until they master the content. Such a mastery-oriented approach also helps eliminate the panic too many of them feel when a class moves ahead before they understand the foundational material. Finally, breaking up larger assignments into smaller chunks can reduce unnecessary stress and discouragement. And giving students useful, detailed feedback along the way can help them create a much better final project or paper.

Of course, none of this helps unless we can get students to genuinely care about earning more than just a passing grade. But if we make it our aim, we might be able to help more students develop a mastery mindset, leading them to take responsibility for identifying and filling their own knowledge gaps. Helping them cultivate such a mindset will benefit them not only in our class but also throughout their lives.

. . . .

CHAPTER 4

AWAKEN STUDENTS' INNATE DRIVE TO LEARN

. . . .

What kind of motivation drives them matters for all our students, but it's especially significant for students with mental health challenges. When students are fueled by innate desires, such as curiosity, they are much happier, less anxious, and less depressed than when they are driven by extrinsic factors alone.

Imagine establishing a curriculum in your university whose outcomes for students in a single year include accomplishments like these:

- Students will make dramatic increases in their functional independence.
- Students will make significant gains in their ability to think logically.
- Students will become so curious that they ask as many as two hundred to three hundred questions per day.[1]
- Students will advance from a rudimentary mastery of a language to the point where they can tell stories fluently.[2]

What kind of grading structure could compel students to actually achieve such ambitious outcomes? Might a grant be necessary to fund some financial incentives to get students' attention and engagement? Could the lure of promising jobs in a high-paying field do the trick? Or perhaps just some old-fashioned sticks instead of carrots, such as getting dropped from the program if they don't progress enough?

Unbelievable as it sounds, millions of people across the globe master these outcomes each year. A substantial percentage do so with the help of only volunteer instructors. And all of them do it with few or no extrinsic rewards or punishments—they do it just because they want to.

And all of them are four years old.

That's right. The average four-year-old child grows cognitively in remarkable ways, because that's just what they do.[3] We doubt many parents are encouraging their four-year-olds to ask even more questions. But according to at least one survey, if we consider the number of questions asked per day as a measure of curiosity, humans are literally at the apex of our curiosity when we are four.[4] According to another survey, four-year-old girls top the charts with 390 questions asked every day.[5]

And it's not just four-year-old children who accomplish such impressive things without being rewarded by grades or paid for doing so. As of August 2019, 300 million people globally had downloaded Duolingo, the language-learning app. According to *Forbes*, "Digital language-learning generates $6 billion in revenue."[6] That's a lot of money spent by people, not because they have to learn a new language for a grade or for money but because they want to learn it.

If we expand our category of achievers to include people who were paid but not assigned to do specific tasks, we can add a bevy of other remarkable accomplishments to the list—the creation of Post-it Notes, Gmail, Google Translate, Google Sky, and Google News.[7] All these innovations came from employees whose employers gave them a certain percentage of their work week to spend as they saw fit on creative projects they believed would benefit the company. No one told these employees exactly what they were to accomplish, much less gave them a rubric for what would constitute success. They were simply given permission to pursue good ideas, and their innate drive took it from there.

The point is that people—including our students—are naturally curious and eager to learn. Or at least they once were. Psychologists Richard Ryan and Edward Deci, who developed a key motivational theory we discuss later in this chapter, believe such innate drive is at the core of our being: "Perhaps no single phenomenon reflects the positive potential of human nature as much as intrinsic motivation, the inherent tendency to seek out novelty and challenges, to extend and exercise one's capacities, to explore, and to learn." [8] Carol Dweck, whose *Mindset* we discuss in the next chapter, explains that we are all "born with an intense drive to learn." [9]

Don't worry. We definitely don't advocate doing away with structured assignments altogether or letting each class period be an open lab of self-directed experimentation. Nor have we gotten on the bandwagon for eliminating grades entirely, even though we're intrigued by the vibrant discourse on that topic. We still think that some extrinsic motivators provide important instructional scaffolding in the learning process, especially for higher-anxiety students. Like James Lang in *Distracted*, we find that in "contrast to the single-minded view that grades always damage student motivation, other research suggests that the ideal approach to motivating students is a mix of intrinsic motivators (like deep goals) and extrinsic ones (like grades)." [10] Thus, our argument in this chapter is not for the

immediate and complete elimination of extrinsic motivation such as grades. Instead, we make the case for doing all
we can to draw out students' inner drive to learn so that
they move from what Daniel Pink, the author of *Drive: The
Surprising Truth about What Motivates Us*, calls "compliance
to engagement."[11]

We begin by examining why motivation matters so
much, particularly for students with mental health challenges, and exploring a couple of theories that explain the
role and nature of motivation in learning. Then we discuss
how professors can affect what cognitive psychologists
call "motivational climate." Finally, we show how we can
create a motivational climate that draws out our students'
innate drive to learn as we increase their autonomy (or
student choice), enhance the relevance of material (or the
perceived value of what students learn), boost students'
confidence or self-efficacy, and foster a meaningful sense
of purpose.

Theoretical Framework

How Motivation Affects Mental Health

It's well established that when it comes to learning, motivation matters. In *How Learning Works*, Susan Ambrose
and her colleagues argue that "motivation influences the
direction, intensity, persistence, and quality of the learning
behaviors in which students engage."[12] Ryan and Deci cite
studies showing that when our motivation is authentic—
something that comes from within—rather than thrust on
us by external factors, we "have more interest, excitement,
and confidence, which in turn is manifest both as enhanced
performance, persistence, and creativity."[13] In other words,

if we want to transform students' learning experience, there may be no better place to focus our efforts than on helping students become more intrinsically motivated.

Rekindling natural curiosity and the drive to learn is important for all our students, but it's especially important for those with mental health challenges, because extrinsic motivation comes with some real emotional baggage. Ryan and Deci cite one study concluding that "placing strong relative importance on intrinsic aspirations was positively associated with well-being indicators such as self-esteem, self-actualization, and the inverse of depression and anxiety, whereas placing strong relative importance on extrinsic aspirations was negatively related to these well-being indicators." [14]

Thus, anything we can do to awaken students' inner drive to learn may also contribute to their psychological well-being. Among other things, intrinsic motivation improves mood and mitigates anxiety. Studies have shown that when we prioritize extrinsic motivation, such as financial success, over nobler intrinsic motivators, such as family, it leads to more depression and anxiety. [15] Conversely, there's ample evidence that intrinsic motivation "contributes to psychological well-being either by enhancing positive mood states or diminishing negative mood states." [16]

In one longitudinal study in China, Yu Ling and his colleagues asked 462 undergraduate students to complete surveys regarding their motivation, depressive symptoms, and social and academic hassles. Students answered the same questions every three months for a year. The researchers found that when students hit frustrating bumps in the road, those who are less intrinsically motivated experience more depressive symptoms. The researchers conclude that if we can help foster "the development of intrinsic goals" in students, we may ultimately "help to prevent the onset and maintenance of depressive disorders."[17]

In terms of anxiety, studies show that students driven more by an innate desire to learn than by extrinsic motivation—aims like getting the approval of others, avoiding punishment, or getting into a prestigious graduate program—are less vulnerable to anxiety. Just consider how differently students react to a poor grade on an assignment if one student's primary goal is to get a 4.0 and another student is fueled by a desire to understand how the human body works. The disappointing score might send the first student into an emotional tailspin and the second back to the books to see what she didn't fully understand.

An Indonesian study of 365 economics and business students compared students' types of motivation and their levels of anxiety. It found a significant positive correlation between students who were extrinsically motivated and those experiencing anxiety, while there was no such correlation between intrinsic motivation and anxiety. Perhaps intrinsic motivation serves as an antidote for anxiety. As the author of the Indonesian study concludes, "Students who are only motivated extrinsically by grade point or simply want to show their abilities . . . will have high anxiety. Conversely, students who are intrinsically motivated by interest and challenge will have low anxiety."[18]

What Shapes Motivation

Drawing on two theories, the self-determination theory and the control-value theory of achievement emotions, we see the following elements as essential ingredients in the recipe for the type of motivation that lifts students' moods, enhances their perseverance, and elevates their learning:

- Students have plenty of say and choice in what they do and how they go about doing it.
- Students see value in what they are learning and how they are learning it.
- Students feel like they have the ability—perhaps with some stretching and some help—to actually learn or do what they are being asked to learn or do.[19]
- Students feel supported by their teachers, classmates, assignment structure, and other resources.[20]

As Ambrose and her colleagues explain, when "students find positive value in a learning goal or activity, expect to successfully achieve a desired learning outcome, and perceive support from their environment, they are likely to be strongly motivated to learn."[21]

Practical Application

Just as coaches are among "the most important architects of the motivational climate" for their teams,[22] teachers are the principal architects of the motivational climates of their classrooms. Ambrose and her colleagues viewed such environments as existing along a spectrum of supportiveness. They argue, "Without question, the complex dynamics of the classroom, its tone, the interpersonal forces at play, and the nature and structure of communication patterns all combine to either support or inhibit the students' motivation to pursue a goal."[23] Instructor approachability, affect, and attitude also contribute in important ways to the motivational climate.

Sarah Cavanagh contends that "managing the emotional climate of your classroom is the most powerful step you can take to maximizing your students' attention and motivation, which we know are the critical first steps to learning." [24] There are countless ways teachers can shape the motivational and emotional climate to help draw out students' innate drive to learn. Here, we explore just five: fostering a meaningful sense of purpose, increasing student choice, making the curriculum relevant, building students' confidence through providing optimally challenging assignments, and designing opportunities for small wins early in a semester. We also argue that regardless of which particular techniques we use, the overall quality of a course and how it is taught greatly influence the type of motivation students develop.

Help Students Discover an Ennobling Purpose

One of the most potent tools for awakening students' inner drive to learn is to help them develop a meaningful purpose for learning. If students are fueled in their effort to learn by a sense of purpose—especially by a desire to help other people in some way with the knowledge they are gaining—they will have the inner drive to do some very challenging things. Moreover, having a meaningful purpose enhances our capacity to cope with mental health challenges, even though it does not exempt us from them.

Psychologist William Damon, a professor of education at Stanford, is one of the world's leading scholars on purpose. He argues that having a meaningful purpose "endows a person with joy in good times and resilience in hard times, and this holds true all throughout life." [25] Moreover, the research is clear, according to Damon, that purpose "brings a deep sense of satisfaction, well-being, and exhilaration."[26] The benefits of having a sense of purpose and meaning in life also include experiencing, on the whole, "fewer symptoms of depression and anxiety."[27]

To be sure, having an ennobling purpose in life does not magically eliminate anxiety or depression. But as the title of one study indicates, "Purpose in life predicts better emotional recovery from negative stimuli." The study's authors explain that having "purpose in life may motivate reframing stressful situations to deal with them more productively, thereby facilitating recovery from stress and trauma." Thus, even though some people with a meaningful life purpose may also struggle with mental health challenges, such as anxiety or depression, they are likely to cope better with these challenges because of their sense of purpose.[28]

Helping students discover purpose flows naturally from leading them to see how what they are learning is relevant, although the two tasks are not identical. We might begin by guiding students to recognize a variety of real-world ways that they can apply the knowledge they are gaining. Once they begin visualizing those possibilities, we can nudge them toward identifying at least one of those possibilities that looks outward, something that helps make the world a better place.

When students develop such outwardly focused purposes, they develop grit. For psychologist Angela Duckworth, half the grit formula is becoming passionate about some "ultimate goal in an abiding, loyal, steady way."[29] While almost any goal can generate some drive, Duckworth argues that what really "ripens passion is the conviction that your work matters."[30] Indeed, the nature of one's ultimate purpose is so important in the development of grit than in her "grit lexicon," Duckworth defines purpose as "the intention to contribute to the well-being of others."[31] In her study of "grit paragons," Duckworth found that "most gritty people see their ultimate aims as deeply connected to the world beyond themselves."[32] Damon reached the same conclusion: "Only a positive, pro-social purpose can provide the lasting inspiration, motivation, and resilience that is characteristic of a truly purposeful life."[33]

In a study led by cognitive psychologist David Yeager and coauthored by Duckworth and five others, the researchers asked over thirteen hundred high school seniors their motives for attending college. These students were in their last semester of high school, and 99 percent indicated they had applied to college and were planning to attend. The researchers contacted these same students the next fall. What they learned was that the more self-transcendent students' purposes for attending college were, the more likely they were to persist.

Of those whose purposes were rated at the bottom of the purpose scale, only 30 percent of students were still enrolled in college. For those whose purposes were rated in the midrange, 57 percent persisted. And for those whose purposes were rated most self-transcendent, 64 percent were still enrolled. Basically, students whose purpose for attending college focused more on helping others than on getting ahead in life were more than twice as likely to persist.[34] While this was a correlational rather than an experimental study, its findings strongly suggest that if we can help students foster more meaningful purposes for learning, they are more likely to persist.

The bad news and good news is that few of our students arrive at college and in our classes hardwired with a purpose that gets them out of bed each morning, let alone one focused on making the world a better place. Instead, many are simply looking to get ahead. In her extensive study of the iGen (people born between 1995 and 2012), psychology professor Jean Twenge concludes, "In brief: money is in, and meaning is out. Entering college students are more likely to say it's important to become very well off financially (an extrinsic value), and less likely to say it's important to develop a meaningful philosophy of life (an intrinsic value)." [35]

Twenge has the numbers to back up her claim. According to the American Freshman Survey, in 1967, twice as many entering college students said it was important to develop a philosophy of life than it was to become very well off financially. By 2016, those numbers had virtually flipped, with 82 percent of first-year students focused on becoming very well off financially, while only 47 percent showed up to college thinking it's important to figure out their purpose in life. [36]

"Even more than the Millennials just before them," observes Twenge, "iGen'ers think that making a lot of money—winning the economic race—is important." And while some may be fixated on money, others lack focus altogether. As one twenty-two-year-old young woman quoted by Twenge put it, "We distract ourselves online with unimportant things and we are always being 'entertained.' We have stopped looking at life and its deeper meaning and have instead immersed ourselves in a world where the big stuff people think about is how many likes they got on an Instagram post." [37] An undergraduate student, participating on a panel that was asked about when and where they explored life's big questions, replied simply, "We are numb to those issues." [38]

At first blush, these data are depressing. But when we adopt a growth mindset ourselves, they actually paint a picture of opportunity. The very fact that few of our students arrive with the kind of purpose that will most help them succeed in college and in life means we may have a long lever that has not yet been pulled in the fight against mental health challenges. What if we helped our students develop a more ennobling sense of purpose for college and life than just becoming set financially? How would that affect their ability to cope with the kinds of challenges that often have negative effects on mental health? When students want to get an education so they can provide well for themselves or make a living doing something that interests them, they are in a much better position to succeed than if they don't have even such modest aims. But when we help them elevate their vision so that they are driven to succeed academically to somehow help others, the research suggests that they will accomplish more and be happier in the process.

Unfortunately, according to Damon, fostering life purpose "is not even on the radar of the agents of culture that influence young people," including schools.[39] That's why "when it comes to guiding students toward paths that they will find personally rewarding and meaningful, so many of today's schools and colleges fall short."[40] But is it really the place of colleges to raise questions about students' real purposes in life or their hopes to make the world better? Georgetown University's vice provost for education Randy Bass thinks so. "Institutions should be places that ask all students, 'Who are you becoming for other people, not just for yourself?'"[41] Creators of liberal arts education might be bemused—if they weren't troubled—if college educators today balked at the notion of nudging students to grapple with questions of how they can make a positive difference in the world. According to William Sullivan, historically, such questions "have been central concerns of the tradition of liberal education." [42]

In Felten and Lambert's myriad interviews for *Relationship-Rich Education*, the subject of purpose came up so often that they made it one of the four relationship-rich principles that serve as the cornerstones of their book: "Every student must explore questions of meaning and purpose." Moreover, they note that "for many students asking big questions is best done in conversation with people who care enough to take the time to listen generously and to encourage critical reflection." In fact, unless "meaningful questions and relationships are at the heart of the college experience, students are likely to drift aimlessly." [43]

How can we appropriately nudge students toward purposes that are ennobling rather than merely self-serving? One simple way is to help students recognize how what they are studying—whether it's accounting, anthropology, or art—can be used to benefit other people. When we help students make such connections, we not only foster purpose and passion but also help them see the relevance of what they are studying—one of the keys to cultivating intrinsic motivation. Imagine asking students in a personal conversation or in class as part of a reflection exercise these two questions: Why are you in your particular major, and how could you use it to make the world a better place? We might even share how our own purposes have evolved over time and how much more rewarding our work became as we adopted more self-transcendent purposes.

This approach may sound simplistic, but it parallels an elegantly effective intervention used by Yeager and his colleague Dave Paunesku. They asked high school students how the world could be a better place and then "asked them to draw connections to what they were learning in school." The entire exercise took less than an hour, yet compared to students who received a control treatment, "reflecting on purpose led students to double the amount of time they spent studying for an upcoming exam, work harder on tedious math problems when given the option, and, in math and science classes, bring home better report card grades." [44]

Another way to foster ennobling purposes in our students is to highlight how they can use what they are learning to make the world a better place. We might feature people practicing in our field who have used their disciplinary expertise to improve life for others. We could also ask graduates from our programs how they have used their knowledge to bring about positive change, then share some of their responses with our students. For example, imagine how learning about some graduates' most meaningful pro bono experiences could motivate law students and help them focus on more than just snagging the highest-paying job possible. Similarly, reading a letter from a grateful patient who was provided medical translation by one of our graduates could inspire students to master the vocabulary of a new language.

Organizational psychologist Amy Wrzesniewski of Yale has examined how helping employees reframe their jobs in this way affects how they perform in the workplace. After studying how happy and effective employees are in a variety of contexts, Wrzesniewski and her colleagues learned that "people who see their work as a calling are significantly more satisfied with their jobs. They're significantly more satisfied with their lives. They're more engaged in what it is that they're doing and tend to be better performers, regardless of what the work is." [45]

The key is not somehow being lucky enough to find more purposeful work. Instead, individuals who connect what they do to helping other people are happier. That's why Wrzesniewski's advice for an unhappy employee is not to quit one job and find another with a better purpose but to consider "*how, in small but meaningful ways, you can change your current work to enhance its connection to your core values.*"[46] She calls this approach to workplace fulfillment "job crafting." We believe our students can make similar small adjustments to the way they view their major and their potential careers that cause a significant shift in their drive and sense of purpose.

Wrzesniewski and her colleagues tested out their job crafting ideas at Google with an intervention as straightforward as the exercise Yeager used with high school students. Employees from a variety of departments, including marketing, finance, and accounting, were randomly assigned to participate in a job-crafting workshop. In the seminar, employees generated their own ideas for tweaking their daily responsibilities to create more meaningful and enjoyable work. Six weeks later, "managers and coworkers rated the employees who attended this workshop as significantly happier and more effective."[47] Similarly, we can help our students be happier, grittier, and more intrinsically motivated by guiding them in discovering a meaningful purpose for applying what they learn in our courses.

Give Students More Choice and Control

Maryellen Weimer, the eloquent champion of learner-centered teaching, explains that students are "very much turned on when they are involved in making the decisions that affect them. The converse is especially poignant. They are turned off when someone else makes their decisions for them."[48] One study found that when students were given a choice about what to do for homework, they were more interested, enjoyed it more, and had a greater sense of competence than students who weren't given a choice. And they "tended to complete more of the homework when it was of their choosing."[49] Other studies have shown that teachers who facilitate student choice rather than seeking to control it "catalyze in their students greater intrinsic motivation, curiosity, and desire for challenge."[50] The students we surveyed about important elements of a class ranked student choice in how to demonstrate outcomes relatively high at a mean response of 5.19 on a scale of 1 to 7.

Conversely, according to Deci and Ryan, students taught by more controlling teachers "not only lose initiative but learn less effectively, especially when learning requires conceptual, creative processing."[51] By limiting choice and leaning too heavily on grades as motivation, Weimer fears we have created "token economies where nobody does anything if there are not some points proffered." Sure, such techniques work in the short term, "but are they creating intellectually mature, responsible, motivated learners . . . ? Are they effectively piquing student curiosity—the kind of interest that drives student interest ever deeper into content and issues?"[52]

How can educators boost students' motivation by increasing their autonomy? "The most straightforward route to maximizing students' sense of control is quite simply to *give them control* by giving them choices in activities and assignments wherever possible," suggests Cavanagh. "To whatever extent you can, give them control of their own work, and treat them as the autonomous beings that they are."[53] Not only will greater student choice lead to "greater completion, interest, enjoyment, and perceived competence," Cavanagh argues, but there are other benefits. Perhaps one of the reasons students with more choice experience increased enjoyment is that they are "likely to choose activities for which they have the requisite skills. Having the skills to meet the challenge, they will be more likely to experience flow and all of its attendant benefits." [54]

It seems obvious that students are more likely to thrive with more choice, but the mental health benefits of allowing students to choose might be less clear. But just consider how much less anxious an introverted writer might be if she could choose to share what she has learned by creating a social media post instead of explaining a concept orally to someone else. Expanding student choice increases the odds that students will find a learning activity that works best for them, which increases their joy and sense of competence or self-efficacy, which increases their motivation, which, in turn, increases their learning—a marvelously virtuous emotional and cognitive cycle.

That said, a couple of cautions are in order when increasing student autonomy and control. First, if we move too far too fast, it rarely works. At least in terms of workplaces, Pink warns that "transitioning to autonomy won't—often can't—happen in one fell swoop. If we pluck people out of controlling environments, when they've known nothing else, and plop them in . . . an environment of undiluted autonomy, they'll struggle. Organizations must provide, as Richard Ryan puts it, 'scaffolding' to help every employee find his footing to make the transition." [55] In the classroom, research shows that "combining highly autonomy-supportive and highly structured teaching sessions bring about the best learning outcomes." [56] In other words, it's not unbounded student choice that optimizes intrinsic motivation, but student choice within the appropriate structure.

That's why we advocate an incremental approach—for the sake of both teachers and students. One easy way to begin offering students more choice is to give them more options about what to read or even which medium they use to study new material. Of course, there are some elements we need every student to cover, so here's a simple method we have used in some of our courses to provide some common consistency, along with choice, in preparing for each class: divide reading into a required portion (where all students read the entire passage) and a "digging deeper" portion (where students spend at least fifteen minutes diving into the content of their choice from a variety of sources, including articles, videos, and podcasts). The required reading contains essential ideas that every student must understand. Then we try to find a variety of sources in multiple modalities that relate to the topic of the day, albeit in very different ways. Not only does this approach give students more choice but it enriches the class discussion, since students collectively draw from a longer list of sources than we could have required them all to study. Because of its modularity, it's also easier to swap out old sources with more interesting or relevant new sources as they emerge, keeping the offerings fresh.

Another simple way to provide students with more choice—and a greater sense of ownership of the learning process—is to include a broad invitation like this one that Rob includes in his syllabi:

Choose Your Own Assignment

I've tried hard to create assignments that are meaningful and will actually help you learn stuff that really matters.

But maybe some assignments still feel like busywork to you. Or maybe you've got another idea for some assignments you wish you could do instead. So why not choose your own adventure?

Here's what you do. Propose your own assignment in place of any assignment on the syllabus and e-mail your proposal to me before the assignment is due. For me to approve it, your proposal needs to be something that helps you accomplish the same outcomes and involves at least as much effort to complete as the assignment you're replacing. Whether or not I accept your proposal, I'll let you drop your lowest score for a preparation assignment, just for making the proposal! Seriously. So propose away!

Even if students never take advantage of such a provision, it sends a message from the outset of the semester that they can exercise some control in the course. That knowledge alone can boost their sense of control and thus their motivation, even if they never take advantage of it. Incidentally, Rob has found that if he reminds students of this provision before a major assignment is due and even throws out a few possible alternatives, far more students choose their own project. And those who do, seem to put forth more—rather than less—effort than those who complete the assigned project.

Our second caution when increasing student choice is to be sure not to abandon accountability. "Encouraging autonomy doesn't mean discouraging accountability," Pink explains.[57] Many years ago, Rob failed to do this while providing a wide-open invitation for the final major project. One student submitted something he had painted about the text—quite poorly, in Rob's nonartistic estimation. But Rob had no rubric in place and no clearly established expectations he could reference. The student got a mercifully high grade, and Rob vowed never to increase student choice again without also creating flexible but clear rubrics. Another option for ensuring accountability is to invite students to create and propose their own rubric. Once accepted, a clear standard will be in place to guide students' efforts and your assessment of them. And creating their own rubrics increases students' sense of ownership.

Finally, we must acknowledge some tension between building in flexibility and keeping the course administratively manageable. The reality is that increasing flexibility for students sometimes results in more work for teachers. Consequently, it's important to create administratively sustainable opportunities for students to exercise more choice.

Make It Relevant

Of all the techniques Cavanagh has explored for generating and harnessing positive emotions, none is more important to her than relevance: "Choosing activities, readings, and assignments that are interesting, self-relevant, emotionally evocative, and/or deeply relevant to the future careers of students may be the most powerful organizing principle you have as a teacher."[58] According to Reinhard Pekrun's control-value theory of achievement emotions, if we can help students value what they learn more by connecting it to their lives, we can boost their intrinsic motivation.

In essence, if we can help students see how they can use what they learn in class today in their own lives tomorrow, its value will go up in their minds—and so will their inner drive to learn. Perhaps that's why, when we surveyed students about what was important to them, no variable received a higher mean response than "learning things that are relevant to your life" (6.08 on a scale of 1 to 7). That was closely followed by "connecting course materials to practical applications" at 5.77.

Two ways we can ensure what we teach feels relevant to our students are to (1) choose content and activities that truly are valuable and relevant to students and (2) help students understand why they are relevant—help them connect the dots. Ambrose and her colleagues have urged teachers to assign "problems and tasks that allow students to vividly and concretely see the relevance and value of otherwise abstract concepts and theories."[59]

Here's one challenge we face in making material relevant, especially in our introductory courses. We traditionally front-load our curriculum with theory, building a conceptual foundation early in a program and reserving practical application largely for upper-division courses. One qualitative study of motivation among undergraduate students in Hong Kong calls out this problem bluntly: "The antithesis of establishing relevance is teaching abstract theory."[60] These researchers understood the need to give students some theoretical grounding before diving into application, but they argued that reserving all application for upper-division courses "removes the opportunity for students to undergo experiences which enable them to see the relevance of what is taught in class."[61] The solution is not to abandon theory altogether but to intersperse application with theory, even early on. "While every course we teach might have a theoretical or pure side to it," observes Lang, "connecting to the questions that students bring to our courses means thinking about the 'applied' nature of our disciplines and our courses."[62]

This is especially true when we teach an introductory

course in our discipline as a general education course, where the vast majority of the students will not major in our discipline. Too many faculty members continue to teach such classes as though they were teaching majors and providing them with the necessary theoretical foundation for the more enjoyable experiences they will eventually have in upper-division courses, when they finally put theory into practice. What we too often forget is that for nonmajors, these classes may be the only opportunity to bring our discipline to life and help them see why it really matters. Referring to a couple of mathematical principles he found difficult to grasp, one student interviewed in the Hong Kong study lamented, "I am sure most of the students who do not pursue their study in math will soon forget [them]. We are unable to put them into a real-life context. Perhaps we have to learn these things in order to fulfil the requirement of the syllabus. I wonder how important they are to me now." [63] Sacrificing some breadth for more application-oriented depth might well be a worthwhile trade-off for fostering intrinsic motivation.

Bonnie gives students in her Multivariate Calculus class an opportunity for in-depth application that helps them see the relevance of what might otherwise seem like purely abstract mathematical concepts. To boost student engagement, she decided to have students work in teams on a culminating project they design themselves. She gives them a choice between diving more deeply into the mathematical principles they have learned or applying these concepts to their own major in some way. No one starts their project until she approves it, which can sometimes involve a week or two of dialogue between her and the students. Since Bonnie has started letting students take more control of their learning and has trusted them to choose an application relevant to them, a different energy fills her classes. The difference between student engagement with these major projects and the more abstract tests and quizzes she gave before is dramatic. When students pick a project they believe in, it's hard to pull them away from it—a hallmark of truly intrinsic motivation.

Note the synergy between two of the key ingredients in the recipe for drawing out students' inner desire to learn. Making what we teach and what students do relevant is powerful, all on its own. But when we let students choose how to apply what they are learning, heightening their control simultaneously increases the value they see in what they do, because they choose applications that are relevant to them.

Once we ensure our courses are focused on material that truly is relevant to our students, we need to help them recognize its relevance. Sometimes mastery of our subject can make us oblivious to what our students don't yet know, as we discuss in chapter 4. Perhaps it's gaps in our awareness that lead us to believe that the relevance of what students are learning is more obvious than it actually is. One of our colleagues and friends, Scott Galer, discovered this painfully through midsemester course evaluation feedback from one of his students. He was teaching an interdisciplinary course on China similar to the one Rob and Steve taught about Pakistan. When asked how Scott could improve, one of his favorite students wrote, "One small suggestion I would have—perhaps the last few minutes could be used as a 'So What Does [This] Mean for You' time, assuming that all of the necessary content was previously covered. I myself . . . find it difficult to see the relevance of international affairs [in] my life." Scott is a great teacher, and he thought he had made it very clear how what they were learning related to their lives, but this feedback helped him realize that his students were somehow still not seeing the relevance of the course content.

Our students may be similarly oblivious to real-world connections that seem obvious to us, unless we help them connect the dots. Like stage actors and singers who over-enunciate so that audience members throughout the house can clearly understand the words, we may need to be more explicit and repetitive than seems necessary in order to ensure that students understand a topic's relevance. This applies not only to concepts within a course but also to how our particular course fits into a broader program. "If you make explicit connections between the content of your course and other courses to come," suggest Ambrose and her colleagues, "students can better understand the value of each course as a building block for future courses."[64]

This is true not only for content but also for skills. Ambrose and her colleagues suggest we can boost motivation in this context "by explaining how various skills will serve them more broadly in their professional lives."[65] Simply asking students a question such as "How could you use the skills you developed in this course in your career?" can broaden their perspective and help them realize the relevance for themselves.

Create Opportunities for Small Wins Early

One of the essential psychological needs that shapes motivation is competence or self-efficacy, a sense that we have the ability to perform a task. Think about being asked to do something that doesn't just seem challenging for you, but impossible. Challenging tasks engage and inspire us; impossible tasks overwhelm and agitate us. One of the reasons so many employees are disengaged in the workplace, Pink says, is because of "the frequent mismatch between what people *must* do and what people *can* do. When what they must do exceeds their capabilities, the result is anxiety." [66] This is true in the classroom as well and can be especially problematic for students who are already high on the anxiety spectrum.

At the other extreme, tasks that aren't challenging enough tend to bore us. Mihaly Csikszentmihalyi, who articulates the concept of flow, titled his first book *Beyond Boredom and Anxiety*. The ideal assignments for drawing out students' innate drive to learn are neither mundanely easy nor impossibly challenging. As the authors of one study about autonomy and intrinsic motivation conclude, "the challenges need to be optimal . . . , neither too difficult nor too easy, the idea being to make the students feel competent in their learning." [67]

Doing that with a class full of students with diverse capacities and knowledge bases can be challenging, no doubt. But we can start by determining whether our assignments are either too challenging or too boring for the majority of our students and then adjust them accordingly. Gauging for understanding can help us know whether we're hitting the mark.

Another way to ensure that students are doing assignments that challenge them appropriately is by increasing choice, as discussed earlier. Frankly, the students in Rob's classes who most often take advantage of his invitation to create their own assignments tend to be his most engaged students. The opportunity for such students to propose their own assignment enables them to find opportunities to challenge themselves in ways the standard assignment might not.

Of course, what constitutes the sweet spot for students

should change over time as their knowledge and capacity increase. But sequence matters—a lot. According to Pekrun and his control-value theory of achievement emotions, students' early appraisals in a class are especially important. If students have "several positive experiences in a given classroom," they start expecting more of the same. And if their early experiences are negative in terms of control and value, then that's what they expect going forward.[68]

Not only will assignments early in the semester shape students' perceptions of how worthwhile the work is, but they will also affect students' sense of self-efficacy. When a quarterback is injured in a football game and his backup suddenly steps into action, wise coaches don't call for a high-risk long pass on the next play. They know the damage that immediately throwing an interception could have for their new quarterback. Instead, they call a few runs or screen passes to let him get his feet under him, before gradually escalating the complexity and risk of what they ask him to do. Such coaches are carefully crafting the backup quarterback's experience so that he will taste some initial success to boost his confidence and reduce his anxiety—confidence he'll need when he's asked to do more.

Harvard Business School professor Teresa Amabile would call completing a short pass in this situation a small win. And she believes that effective managers in the workplace can use small wins to boost engagement, creativity, and even joy among those they lead. Amabile and her colleague Steven J. Kramer have extensively studied the psychological experiences and performance of people in the workplace. In one study, they asked hundreds of employees to respond to daily end-of-the-day emails over the course of their project. The result was nearly twelve thousand diary entries describing how employees felt. What Amabile and

Kramer noticed in plowing through these journal entries was, not surprisingly, that "people are more creative and productive when their inner work lives are positive—when they feel happy, are intrinsically motivated by the work itself, and have positive perceptions of their colleagues and the organization."

More specifically, Amabile and Kramer discerned a phenomenon they call "the *progress principle*: Of all the things that can boost emotions, motivation, and perceptions during a workday, the single most important is making progress in meaningful work."[69] They found a strong correlation between whether people made what felt like progress and how positive they felt on a particular day.

Of course, it's possible that we simply accomplish more on days when we're in good a mood, and Amabile and Kramer acknowledge this. But their analysis of diary entries like this one led them to conclude that the causal arrow between small wins and upbeat attitudes points both ways: "I figured out why something was not working correctly," wrote one study participant. "I felt relieved and happy because this was a minor milestone for me." Not surprisingly, the converse is also true: "Small losses or setbacks can have an extremely negative effect on inner work life. In fact, our study and research by others show that negative events can have a more powerful impact than positive ones."[70]

What does all this mean for us as architects of learning experiences? Recognizing the positive and negative impact that minor accomplishments and small setbacks can have on people leads us to want to be more intentional in how we design the early parts of our courses. Ambrose and her colleagues write that "early success can build a sense of efficacy." Doing that "is incredibly important . . . for students who come into your course with anxiety for whatever reason." A simple way to accomplish this is to "incorporate early, shorter assignments that account for a small percentage of the final grade but provide a sense of competence and confidence before you assign a larger project."[71]

Reading that advice hit home for Rob. For years he taught a New Testament course and required students to take a multiple-choice test on twenty-five important factual terms. He placed the test in the second week or so of the semester, so students could benefit throughout the course from this foundational knowledge. Frankly, students did worse on this assessment than any other in the semester. And because it was the first major assessment in the course, the grade students earned on the test was usually what their overall grade was, until they completed some other major assessments. Rob tried to assure his students that they weren't really going to fail the class—that their scores on other assignments would bring their grades up.

Several years ago, Steve told Rob about spaced learning, and Rob decided to try a different approach. He offered the same test three times, each spaced one month apart. He also promised that if students scored better on a subsequent test, he would replace the lower score on the first test with their subsequent higher score. And he weighted the last test most heavily. Rob made this change to improve retention of knowledge. Only once he began working on this project did he realize that his course design had been sending the message early in the semester to far too many of his students that they were failing his course (a required religion course, no less).

The result was certainly negative for all the students who did poorly, but for those already struggling with higher levels of anxiety or depression, seeing a disappointingly low overall grade just two weeks into the semester must have been especially disheartening. Instead of building in small wins early on, Rob had inadvertently built in a big defeat for many of his students. And, contrary to what we recommend in chapter 3, he had given students no incentive or assistance to revisit and master important geographic and biographical facts. If they hadn't already grasped the geographic differences between Judea and Galilee or the biographical distinctions between Matthew and Mark, that was it—the class was moving on.

When we design our courses more intentionally, we can help students generate emotional momentum by first introducing a number of smaller assignments on which students are likely to do well—opportunities for small wins—before tackling more daunting tasks. And by building in opportunities to master concepts students don't initially grasp and complete assignments on which they don't initially do well, we can mitigate the disappointment that comes from failures, whether they are small or big. Taking such an approach helps fulfill the psychological need of competence—a sense that performing a task successfully really is possible.

What makes sense for individual courses also makes sense for programs. Especially in competitive majors, introductory classes have long been used—both intentionally and inadvertently—as weeder courses. The *Urban Dictionary* provides this telling definition of the term: "A weeder class is a class (typically in college) that is characterized by having a large dropout rate due to rigorous expectations, such as hard tests, impossible studying requirements (15 hours a week or more), and homework up the ***. These classes 'weed' out those who lack the motivation to

keep going. . . . Note: Weeder classes can seriously trauma-
tize an individual, destroy any ounce of confidence they
have, and make them seriously reconsider majors[,] as
most weeder classes are required."

There's something of a tradition of taking this approach
with introductory computer science courses, and until recently, BYU-Idaho was no exception. According to department chair Scott Burton, BYU-Idaho's computer science
program had enough students in their introductory course
to fill fifteen sections. But as if on some kind of cruel
reality TV show, only enough passed the initial course—
Introduction to Software Development (CSE 124)—and
continued with the major to fill six sections of the next
course. Students were literally leaving the introductory
course with *less* confidence in their ability to code than
when they began. By the fourth course in the sequence,
surviving students made up only four sections—a great
result for reality television perhaps but an incredibly ineffi-
cient process for the university and a thoroughly demoral-
izing experience for students.

Burton and some of his newer colleagues weren't content with this approach, however common it might be in
the field. "We feel like there is a large set of students who
could be successful in some kind of software engineering role. But when they got in the first course, it was too
much, too fast." The department had been hemorrhaging
students from their major, as students bailed out in search
of a different course of study where they felt they could
succeed. Under the direction of former department chair
Richard Grimmett, associate chair James Helfrich undertook a major effort to overhaul the curriculum in their
program. Together with several colleagues, Burton tackled

fundamentally restructuring the first twelve credits of the program. "We felt like if we could get them in there and get them some small wins, we could keep them throughout the whole program," explains Burton.

The faculty made a number of changes, significantly reducing the slope of the learning curve over the twelve credits. With the old design, learning had been front-loaded, making the curve steepest at the beginning and more gradual in the final semester. Burton describes the philosophy for the new approach: "We're gonna help you get there, but we're not gonna do it all in the first course." Students then began learning much more gradually, mastering essential skills in a supportive curriculum. In the end, students achieved the same level of mastery after twelve credits but with much of the steeper learning coming in the last four credits, once they had gained essential competence, skills, and confidence—that is, self-efficacy.

Burton and his colleagues began by repackaging what had been taught in four three-credit courses into a sequence of four two-credit courses, followed by a culminating four-credit, team-based course that functioned almost like a mini-internship. Today, students who feel well prepared can take the two-credit courses on a block and move through them quickly, if they prefer. But most students begin with a semester-long two-credit course, taking on far fewer concepts than they had been required to master in the three-credit course. That change alone significantly increased the odds that students begin their study of computer science with a small win rather than a big defeat.

Burton and his colleagues didn't stop there. The new introductory course—Programming Building Blocks (CSE 110)—streamlined what had been a long list of outcomes down to two. And the second outcome is simply to "develop confidence in learning new programming skills." Burton explains this narrow focus simply: "We wanted to help light the fire."

In the traditional weeder course, some of the first assignments had been entirely autograded and were pass/fail. If students didn't nail the code perfectly, the grading program simply told them they failed, with no indication of why or by how much. "Students would get it mostly right, but they'd be off by a space or a blank line," recounts Burton. While students were able to resubmit assignments until they passed, without any useful, specific feedback they had often spent many frustrating hours trying to discover their mistakes. Burton and his team replaced those assignments with projects where students first provided themselves with formative feedback by comparing their initial efforts with a successful program. "We wanted them to get feedback really quickly," notes Burton. "At some point they're going to turn in some code, and we have an instructor or TA look at it." But they begin with instructional scaffolding that builds confidence.

Every other week along with their assignment, students answer a question that fosters academic stamina, boosts self-efficacy and competence, or helps students connect the dots to see the material's relevance. For example, one week, students are asked, "While working on this assignment, you had to overcome some challenges. Why do you think you were able to overcome them?" Another week they are asked, "How could the topic of this lesson be applied to a real-world problem in your area of interest?" And at the conclusion of the semester, they complete a reflection assignment with three questions:

1. What is one program you wrote that you were particularly proud of during this course? Why were you proud? Explain.
2. How might you use the skills you learned in this course in the future? This might include skills such as programming, problem-solving, debugging, etc.
3. Describe an experience from this class that has given you confidence that you can learn new programming skills in the future.

Collectively, all these changes transformed a course that had routinely been an early, soul-sapping big loss into a confidence-boosting small win. Now it serves not only as a much more welcoming gateway course for future majors but also as an inviting, horizon-expanding course for students from any major who would like to better understand the world of computer science and how it relates to their discipline. That certainly wasn't true of the weeder course. "It was designed for people who were serious computer scientists," explains Burton. So when sociology or history majors seeking to branch out took the course, "It just wasn't a good fit. They'd drown." Not with the new course. "In [CSE] 110, we want everybody to be successful." The experience of Burton's team shows just how much less stress, anxiety, discouragement, and depression students experience with a curricular approach focused on lighting a fire instead of requiring students to pass through one.

Conclusion

We wish we had space to explore many more techniques teachers can use to awaken students' inner desire to learn, including building courses around beautiful questions (as educator Ken Bain suggests), using appreciative inquiry, inspiring students to take ownership of their learning, and employing the kinds of authentic assessments Lang describes in *Cheating Lessons.* In many ways, the particular techniques we choose to awaken students' innate desire to learn are much less important than keeping our eyes—and our students' eyes—on that loftier aim. As Lang urges, "Find ways to remind your students, as often as possible, that what your course has to offer them is more than just the extrinsic reward of a grade." [72] Throughout the course, we can help students see why what they are learning matters for reasons so much greater than the grade they earn.

Here's one final catchall: the more we do to improve our courses and our teaching, the more intrinsically motivated our students will be. In their study of junior high classrooms, Ferguson and his colleagues found that when students considered their teachers more captivating, they said they exerted more effort. Granted, their study was of junior high school classrooms, but we suspect their conclusions are quite applicable to higher education as well.

> When learning is more stimulating, students feel cheerier and less irritated. They are also more punctual, better behaved, more mastery oriented, and they feel more efficacious. They exert more effort, seek more help, and engage less often in disengagement behaviors. . . . They report more learning and they feel more satisfied with their achievement. In addition, they develop more growth mindset, conscientiousness, and future orientation. Generally, it seems that [teaching in captivating ways] has no downside. [73]

CHAPTER 5

....

FOSTER EMOTIONAL RESILIENCE

....

There's some debate about whether it's better to help students with mental health challenges by reducing unnecessary stressors or by building emotional resilience. We view these two approaches as complementary rather than mutually exclusive. Without some scaffolding and a bit of sensitivity, many of our students won't stay in college long enough to develop emotional resilience. Yet if we don't help them eventually build that resilience, many will struggle to succeed, not only in college but also in employment and other critical aspects of life.

We reiterate what we discuss in the introduction: our aim is not to remove all anxiety, stress, despair, or difficulty from students' lives by creating some kind of emotional plastic bubble for them. "We'll never eradicate negative emotions from our lives or those of our kids [or our students]. Nor should we," observes Marc Brackett, a research psychologist and the founding director of the Yale Center for Emotional Intelligence. Brackett freely acknowledges that "moderate levels of stress—feeling challenged—can enhance our focus. It's chronic stress that's toxic and makes it biologically challenging to learn."[1] But we can simultaneously seek to reduce the amount of stress and despair we unintentionally create for students while taking steps to bolster their emotional resilience.

The benefits of fostering emotional resilience in students are considerable. "Resilient students are happier, less overwhelmed, and more likely to succeed, in college and beyond," argues Gary Glass, director of counseling and career services at Emory University's Oxford College. "Finding ways to integrate resilience into the curriculum reflects a holistic approach to education that blends learning and personal growth. Instead of focusing on diagnosing and treating mental-health disorders, colleges should pay more attention to developing healthy mind-sets."[2]

In this chapter, we explore why and how professors can help students build more emotional resilience. To repeat, we do not advocate usurping the role of mental health professionals. Nor do we suggest simply throwing students in the emotional deep end of the pool and hoping they learn to swim. Instead, fostering emotional resilience requires thoughtful, intentional design of learning experiences. To keep our recipe for resilience simple, we'll focus on just two of many possible ingredients: fostering a growth mindset and increasing emotional intelligence, or the ability to regulate emotions. As usual, we begin by exploring the theoretical foundation and then turn to a discussion of some practical ways to apply these theories for building emotional resilience. Those applications include personally buying into the concept of growth mindset, teaching students about growth-mindset, helping students better cope with academic emotional triggers, being purposeful in how we praise students, helping students fail fruitfully, normalizing getting help, and harnessing the power of peers. Taken together, we believe these steps can help create a culture of growth and emotional resilience in our classrooms and perhaps even across our campuses.

That said, we also want to be very clear that simply reading a book like *Mindset* or focusing on increasing students' capacity for emotional self-regulation will not magically jolt students out of serious bouts of anxiety or depression. Professional help and medication are often required and, even then, sometimes not sufficient to help those with more severe cases of anxiety and depression to improve. We hope that nothing we argue in this chapter gives the misimpression that if our students will just do more to develop emotional resilience, their mental health challenges will evaporate.

Theoretical Foundation

Growth Mindset

At the heart of Carol Dweck's *Mindset: The New Psychology of Success* is the premise that *"the view you adopt for yourself profoundly affects the way you live your life."* Many people buy into a fixed mindset, the notion that their qualities and capacities are "carved in stone." [3] But some adopt a growth mindset, believing that "abilities can be cultivated." [4] Those with a growth mindset don't necessarily believe that we are all given the same intellectual gifts in the same measure, but they do believe "everyone can change and grow through application and experience." [5] Growth mindset is fundamentally based on a belief in neural plasticity.

It doesn't take a clinical psychologist to see how having a fixed mindset can create stress, anxiety, discouragement, and depression—especially in college, where students are literally graded on their cognitive performance. To students with a fixed mindset, a bad grade is terrible news—a confirmation that they just aren't cut out to succeed in higher education. Imagine the anxiety, then, that assessments produce if students believe those grades are a revelation of exactly where they stand—and will always stand—intellectually.

This is precisely what Dweck's research on college students and depression has found: students with a fixed mindset experience higher levels of depression. Why? Dweck theorizes that "they ruminated over their problems and setbacks, essentially tormenting themselves with the idea that the setbacks meant they were incompetent or unworthy: 'It just kept circulating in my head: You're a dope.' 'I just couldn't let go of the thought that this made me less of a man.' Again, failures labeled them and left them no route to success."[6] Of course, it's possible that some other independent variable caused both the rumination and depression. Still, the correlation between a fixed mindset and depression is compelling.

A fixed mindset not only leads students to taking disappointing academic news hard but to dealing with it in ways that are counterproductive. Dweck explains that "the more depressed they felt, the more they let things go; the less they took action to solve their problems."[7] Much like the negative snowballing effect we discuss in chapter 3, when students with fixed mindsets do poorly on an assignment, it can lead them to pull back rather than push forward academically. For some students, the downward spiral that starts with a poor performance on one assignment leads all too quickly to poor performances on subsequent assignments and failing grades in classes. In other words, a fixed mindset can create a sort of negative self-fulfilling prophecy in which discouragement and depression play a critical role.

By contrast, those with a growth mindset see academic

failures through a completely different lens. For them, a low grade on a test early in the semester is valuable information about where they need to target their efforts to improve. They are more prone to see a disappointing grade as part of the journey toward realizing their full potential rather than as an announcement that they've reached the end of their academic road.

Dweck and her colleagues found that students with a growth mindset were by no means immune from depression. But the "more depressed people with the growth mindset felt, the *more* they took action to confront their problems, the *more* they made sure to keep up with their schoolwork, and the *more* they kept up with their lives. The worse they felt, the more determined they became!"[8] We certainly don't suggest that only people with a fixed mindset suffer from debilitating depression, but for those who do have depression, having a growth mindset increases the odds of being able to cope more effectively. Just as a fixed mindset can lead to downward emotional and cognitive spirals, a growth mindset can lead to a virtuous upward cycle of development. As Angela Duckworth points out, "a growth mindset leads to optimistic ways of explaining adversity, and that, in turn, leads to perseverance and seeking out new challenges that will ultimately make you even stronger."[9]

Dweck's research also shows that students with a growth mindset learn more and earn better grades. That's not because they are smarter than their fixed-mindset peers but because they approach learning in an altogether different way. Generally, they are more self-aware, modeling the kinds of metacognitive skills we'd like all our students to develop. Explains Dweck: "The students with

growth mindset completely took charge of their learning and motivation. Instead of plunging into unthinking
memorization of the course material, they said: 'I looked
for themes and underlying principles across lectures,' and 'I
went over mistakes until I was certain I understood them.'
They were studying to learn, not just to ace the test. And,
actually, this was why they got higher grades—not because
they were smarter or had a better background in science." [10]

Research shows that people generally do not have accurate perceptions of their own performance and ability. [11]
Thus, having a growth mindset makes it much easier for
students to find and fill in their own knowledge gaps. If
you've got a normal ego and a fixed mindset, you have every
incentive to explain away a low test score by blaming it
on anything other than your own lack of understanding.
By contrast, if "you believe you can develop yourself, then
you're open to accurate information about your current
abilities, even if it's unflattering. What's more, if you're
oriented toward learning, as they are, you need accurate
information about your current abilities in order to learn
effectively." [12]

Emotional Self-Regulation

Helping students consider how they learn best and take
ownership of their own learning—metacognition—has appropriately become a hot topic in recent years in the scholarship of learning and teaching. What's gotten less attention
in higher education circles is an interesting extension of or
analogue to metacognition: emotional self-regulation and
emotional intelligence. Just as metacognition involves becoming more aware of how we learn effectively, emotional
self-regulation involves becoming more aware of how various

stimuli affect us so that we can better manage our reactions to them.

James Gross is a Stanford University psychology professor whose research focuses on emotion regulation. He defines it as "the process by which individuals influence which emotions they have, when they have them, and how they experience and express these emotions."[13] Similarly, emotional intelligence is "the ability to regulate emotions to promote emotional and intellectual growth."[14] We recognize that emotion regulation and emotional intelligence are two related yet distinct strands of thought that seem to have developed independently. But at least one article argues that both approaches "stand to benefit substantially from greater integration."[15] In this section, we'll draw on language and ideas from both lines of thinking, perhaps more freely than purists would prefer.

Licensed clinical social worker and therapist Andrea Bell says that someone with "good emotional self-regulation has the ability to keep their emotions in check. They can resist impulsive behaviors that might worsen their situation, and they can cheer themselves up when they're feeling down." Whatever life throws at them, they "have a flexible range of emotional and behavioral responses that are well matched" to the challenges they face.[16]

Paradoxically, when Rob was preparing to give his first presentation to colleagues about one of the chapters in this book, he had an opportunity to engage in emotional self-regulation. Somehow, he had in his mind that the presentation was at 1:30 in the afternoon, leaving him ample time to complete his presentation and take care of a number of other tasks. But when he checked his calendar, he discovered the presentation was much earlier—in less than an hour. He rushed to finalize his slides and take care of last-minute technological challenges. By the time he finished, just five minutes before the presentation was to begin, his heart was literally racing. Then he remembered some breathing techniques he'd learned and used on occasion. After just two or three minutes of using this simple coping strategy, Rob felt far calmer and much more emotionally prepared to give his presentation. Brackett explains why: "Pausing and taking a deep breath activates the parasympathetic nervous system, which reduces the release of cortisol, a major stress hormone, and naturally lowers our emotional temperature." [17]

The point of emotional self-regulation is to apply coping strategies to help people "reduce 'excess activation in the nervous system.'" Traumatic events or any overwhelming circumstance can trigger excess activation. Emotional self-regulation is more than just learning self-control, although that's part of it. Psychologist Stuart Shanker explains that self-regulation is about "reducing the frequency and intensity of strong impulses by managing stress-load and recovery." [18]

We reiterate that our aim is not to try to eliminate all the stressful experiences from our students' lives. "We'll never eradicate negative emotions from our lives or those of our kids [or our students]. Nor should we," observes Brackett. "But we need to attend to the play of positive and negative emotions, which is out of balance for too many of us." [19] We simply advocate being more intentional about our tactics so that we can reduce unnecessary anxiety in students. Even if all the professors at a university implemented every one of our suggestions, college life would still be stressful for students. And that's not necessarily bad. As we discuss in chapter 1, some stress can be positive. For example, the stress Rob felt as he rushed to finalize his presentation probably helped him focus and work with a burst of intensity. But as Brackett and others have pointed out, chronic stress can be cognitively debilitating.[20]

Moreover, because encountering stress and anxiety in life is inevitable, developing the capacity to recognize, regulate, and even harness our emotions is an important part of becoming emotionally resilient. In *Permission to Feel: Unlocking the Power of Emotions to Help Our Kids, Ourselves, and Our Society Thrive*, Brackett argues that "if we can learn to identify, express, and harness our feelings, even the most challenging ones, we can use those emotions to help us create positive, satisfying lives."[21] Indeed, according to Brackett, among "adolescents, higher emotional intelligence is associated with less depression and anxiety and may be a protective factor against suicidal behavior."[22]

Numerous studies show that a greater capacity for self-regulation correlates with greater well-being, life satisfaction, and happiness. Conversely, inability to self-regulate corresponds with poorer psychological health overall. According to psychologist John Gottman and his colleagues at the University of Washington, researchers "have found that even more than IQ, your emotional awareness and ability to handle feelings will determine your success and happiness in all walks of life, including family relationships."[23]

Emotional intelligence emphasizes recognizing how our emotions affect us and making the most of them. In *Permission to Feel*, Brackett posits that "our emotional state determines where we direct our attention, what we remember, and what we learn."[24] For example, strong "negative emotions (fear, anger, anxiety, hopelessness) tend to narrow our minds—it's as though our peripheral vision has been cut off because we're so focused on the peril that's front and center." [25] Thus, he suggests that whenever "we notice that we're suddenly having difficulty paying attention, or focusing, or remembering, we should ask ourselves: What emotion information is there, just beneath the surface of our thoughts? And what if anything can we do to regain a handle on our minds?" [26]

At the heart of emotional intelligence is the belief that we "can learn to identify and understand all our feelings, integral and incidental, and then respond in helpful proportionate ways—once we acquire emotion skills." And just as natural capacities in other areas may vary, "we can all increase our emotional intelligence." [27] Brackett uses a simple mnemonic to help readers remember what he sees as some critical steps in developing emotional intelligence: RULER (recognize, understand, label, express, and regulate).

To those who might question the appropriateness of teachers and schools helping students with such touchy-feely matters as developing emotional intelligence, Brackett responds: "The promotion of social, emotional, and academic learning is not a shifting educational fad; it is the substance of education itself. It is not a distraction from the 'real work' of math and English instruction; it is how instruction can succeed." [28] Similarly, Lisa Nunn argues that learning "how to manage stress is not just a good life skill to have; it is an essential element of academic survival for first-year students." [29]

Building on the pioneering work of earlier scholars in social and emotional learning, Brackett and his colleagues have created an entire program that many K–12 schools have implemented. For those schools who adopt the program, Brackett says, "It has to become part of the school's DNA. . . . Every adult walks the walk—not just teachers, principals, and guidance counselors but also security personnel, cafeteria workers, janitors, and bus drivers."[30] We see implementing a systematic approach like this as much more challenging in the college setting, especially with the central role played by independent-minded professors like the three of us. Still, in the latter half of this chapter, we explore some ideas for how individual professors can draw on the ideas of Brackett and others to help our students develop greater emotional stamina.

Putting Theory into Practice

How can we best promote emotional resilience in our students? We suggest seven principles: (1) develop your own growth mindset, (2) teach about growth mindset and harnessing peer support, (3) help students cope with academic emotional triggers, (4) praise intentionally, (5) help students reframe challenges, (6) match high expectations and concern with high support, and (7) destigmatize asking for help.

Develop Your Own Growth Mindset

One of the most intriguing aspects of growth and fixed mindsets is that they shape not only how we perceive our own potential but how we view others' potential as well. And when we are in positions of authority in the learning process, our mindsets as teachers can have a significant impact on our students. A German researcher studied this impact by identifying whether teachers had a growth or fixed mindset. Among those who had a fixed mindset, he encountered comments along these lines: "If I know students' intelligence I can predict their school career quite well." Not surprisingly, with such teachers, "the students who started the year in the high-ability group ended the year there, and those who started the year in the low-ability group ended the year there." On the other hand, the researcher found that some teachers had a growth mindset. They believed all their students had the potential to grow intellectually, and they treated them accordingly. In those classrooms, regardless of where students were academically at the beginning of the year, they all ended the year in the high-ability group.[31]

From the perspective of fixed-mindset teachers, their students' poor performance merely confirms what they perceive as their students' permanent lack of ability. By contrast, growth-mindset teachers respond more generously and humbly to disappointing student performance. They might start by wondering what knowledge gaps students have and how they as teachers can help fill them. They heed Dweck's advice to teachers to "try to figure out what they don't understand and what learning strategies they don't have."[32] A belief in their students' innate capacity to learn may also lead teachers with a growth mindset to wonder whether their own pedagogical approach was part of the problem, causing them to look for more effective ways to teach the concepts in question.

All this research has compelled the three of us to take a hard look at our own mindsets. It's one thing to adopt a way of thinking that limits our own growth. It's quite another to persist in such a mindset when it holds back our students, especially those who could most use our help. And faking a growth mindset isn't enough. Our students can read us. Duckworth cautions against making the mistake of "changing what we say *without* changing our body language, facial expressions, and behavior."[33] And the only way to ensure our body language changes is to make sure our mindsets have truly changed.

Teach the Concepts of Growth Mindset and Harnessing Peer Support

In an unprecedented experiment remarkable for both its scale and its methodology, cognitive psychologist David Yeager and his platoon of twenty-four credited coauthors (including both Dweck and Duckworth) used a simple, well-tested intervention to help students adopt a growth mindset. In the context of neuroscience, they taught students how the brain is like a muscle that "grows stronger and smarter" when we exercise it. They then "reflect[ed] on ways to strengthen their brains through schoolwork." Finally, students internalized the message by "teaching it to a future first-year ninth grade student who is struggling at the start of the year." The whole exercise took less than an hour.[34]

One of the principal hypotheses of Yeager and his colleagues was that for students whose academic performance was below average, this simple, one-time intervention would significantly improve academic performance. The rationale was that "a growth mindset should be most beneficial for students confronting challenges" because they might benefit most "from a growth mindset that alters the interpretation of these difficulties"[35]—a relevant insight as we explore ways to help students facing mental health challenges.

The results supported the team's hypothesis. The growth-mindset intervention slightly yet significantly improved the grades of lower-achieving students and increased overall enrollment in advanced mathematics courses. For a one-time intervention implemented in the real world on a massive scale, the impact was impressive. In fact, Yeager and his colleagues extrapolate from their data that if this simple intervention were adopted throughout the United States, it would prevent about 5.3 percent of the 1.5 million ninth graders in the United States *each year*— 79,500 students—from falling "off track" for graduation at a pivotal point in their schooling.[36]

When we teach growth mindset in a way that changes our classroom culture, that culture becomes part of a "virtuous cycle of skill improvement" that one social scientist calls the "social multiplier effect."[37] As a critical mass of students develop a growth mindset and greater emotional intelligence, their thinking rubs off on other students. Yeager and his colleagues documented this positive peer influence in their notable study. The intervention had a significant positive impact on the target students in all schools, but it had an even greater impact in schools where "the behavioural norm that surrounded students was supportive of the growth mindset belief system."[38] Yeager and his colleagues conclude that "sustained change" might require both the "high-quality seed," or the intervention, and the "conductive soil in which that seed can grow," or a supportive peer environment.[39] Thus, the more success teachers have in creating a culture of growth mindset in our classrooms—and that universities have in creating a culture of growth mindset on our campuses—the more likely individual students are to succeed in adopting a growth mindset.

For students with mental health challenges, we suspect a key aspect of peer support for adopting a growth mindset is hearing from other students with those same challenges who have benefited from adopting a growth mindset. Bonnie experienced the power of such support in her own battle with depression. She could not see a way out of the darkness, pain, and despair that engulfed her. But a friend who had been through clinical depression told her,

"You will get through this. This will not last forever." Those words gave her a small strain of hope with which she began to weave a rope that helped pull her out of her depression. Of course, for Bonnie and others with mental health challenges, it took much more than just peer support to get out of her dark place, but it can play a helpful role.

Help Students Cope Better with Academic Emotional Triggers

Educational psychologist Barry Zimmerman has developed self-regulated learning theory to apply self-regulation to the learning process. Zimmerman notes that self-regulation comes into play for learners at three junctures: before performing a task (for example, when the mere thought of writing a term paper might paralyze a student), while performing the task (as when writer's block can send a student into a panic), and when the student gets the results (especially when a student earns a disappointingly low grade). When students seek to proactively manage the emotions that might trigger negative reactions, "they gain deeper insights into how they learn, what works best for them, and, ultimately, they perform at a higher level." Zimmerman suggests three things teachers can do to help students cultivate the capacity to self-regulate:

- Give students a choice in tasks, methods, or study partners as often as you can.
- Give students the opportunity to assess their own work and learn from their mistakes.
- Pay attention to the student's beliefs about his or her own learning abilities and respond with encouragement and support when necessary.[40]

We're not suggesting that professors create calm corners for students, guide them in mindfulness meditations, or try to teach them everything about emotional self-regulation that a counselor would. Still, with a bit of effort and intentionality, resourceful teachers can find opportunities to help students recognize how they naturally react to certain emotional triggers in their classes and adopt coping strategies for dealing with such stressors more productively. If nothing else, we can encourage students to appreciate that when it comes to mental health challenges, they can help regulate their own emotions by becoming proactive agents rather than merely reactive objects. One study involving university students and professors suggests that teachers' approaches are "just as important as the university student's own [self-regulation] for predicting emotional behaviors of learning and ways of coping." The authors conclude that "it is essential that university teachers be trained to minimize stress factors through the design of their teaching process." [41]

For example, consider taking what Brackett calls a "Meta-Moment" at strategic points in the course, such as at the beginning of the semester, at midterms, on the day after students receive their scores on a major assessment, or as finals approach. When Rob paused to engage in a breathing exercise, he was taking such a moment. "In simplest terms, it's a pause," explains Brackett. "The Meta-Moment involves hitting the brakes and stepping out of time." [42]

While Brackett applies the term to pausing individually in the heat of an emotional moment, we also like the idea of teachers inviting students to take a Meta-Moment at those junctures in the semester when emotions may not be near the point of eruption but are percolating mightily beneath the surface. Teachers might begin by simply asking students in small groups—a less intimidating and more intimate setting—to describe how they are feeling emotionally and then share with each other some strategies for coping with the stress or discouragement they might be experiencing. Similarly, after students receive their grades on a midterm or other major assessment, we might give them an opportunity to reflect in writing on this question from Brackett: "What would my *best self* do right now?"[43] Or to invoke the mastery mindset, growth mindset, and grit, we would add, "What can I do to fill in some of my knowledge gaps and cracks so that I can truly understand some of the concepts I haven't fully mastered yet? What resources are available to help me?" We could even offer credit to students for submitting a plan to master the concepts they didn't fully understand in the assessment. Or as midterms or finals approach, we might ask them to reflect on one thing they can do during this critical time to boost their mental health and reduce their anxiety.

With less than two weeks left in the semester, Rob recently conducted a brief but animated class discussion he introduced this way: "Some of you have been at college a bit longer than others. As we approach finals, it can get pretty intense. What are some keys you have learned to avoid exploding?" No further explanation was necessary. Students volunteered a variety of comments with a slew of useful ideas for their classmates to be able to regulate their emotions—lessons they had gleaned from their own experiences.

Finally, we might ask students what kinds of negative thoughts come to their minds when they get a discouraging grade, fall behind in their courses, or worry in anticipation of a test. Brackett notes that especially in Western cultures, "our inborn negative bias contributes to our negative self-talk, not to mention all of the negative talk we've picked up from our parents and peers." Brackett argues that we need to replace such negative self-talk with positive self-talk. Doing so even creates positive physiological effects.[44] Because many of our students might be experiencing similar negative thoughts—"I'm just not good at math," "There's no way I can get everything done in time," "Maybe I'm just not cut out for college"—we can help them discover some useful retorts to such doubts. We might even post some of those thoughts and ask students to role-play how they would respond to a friend or sibling who articulated them. As they step back from the situation for a moment to think of helping someone else, students are soon sharing some of the very responses they need to hear themselves.

Praise Intentionally

It's a sad paradox that sometimes in the very act of trying to build students' confidence by praising them, we are actually setting in mortar the bricks of a fixed-mindset wall that impedes their growth. When we praise based on *who students are* instead of *how much effort they exert*, we send the demotivating message that success—and implicitly, failure—is based solely on innate ability rather than effort. That may seem like good news when you're succeeding, but it's terrible news when you fail.

Moreover, whether students are doing poorly or well, when we talk about student performance in terms of innate ability, we give them no incentive or inspiration to try to improve. Telling them that they are naturally gifted writers may make them feel good for a moment, but it takes away any reason to work at improving their craft. And when they later encounter a writing challenge they can't immediately conquer—and they eventually will—such praise has conditioned them to give up rather than work harder. Conversely, complimenting students on how many drafts they completed before submitting an assignment fuels growth.

Dweck and her colleagues tested out the effect of these competing types of praise with hundreds of children. They praised some students for their ability but others for their effort. When students were later given the chance to undertake a challenging new task, those who had been praised on ability declined. "They didn't want to do anything that could expose their flaws and call into question their talent. . . . In contrast, when students were praised for effort, 90 percent of them wanted the challenging new task that they could learn from."[45] For Dweck, the implications of fixed-mindset praise is clear: "Praising children's intelligence harms their motivation and it harms their performance."[46]

If praising students in a fixed-mindset way inhibits their growth, our hunch is that criticizing them or even talking about failure in fixed-mindset terms hinders their growth even more. One reason for our hypothesis is that so many students suffer from imposter syndrome—where, despite their capacity and accomplishments, individuals are racked with "persistent self-doubt and fear of being exposed as a fraud or imposter."[47] Imagine the impact of professors saying that students who did poorly on a test just aren't cut out to succeed in that major or field. For students already grappling with imposter syndrome, such statements from an authority figure serve only to reinforce their worst fears, potentially triggering further anxiety and depression.

That makes it critical that we decouple student scores and student worth—in both our minds and our students'. One way to do that is to remind students, before returning their graded assignment, that their scores do not define them, their potential, or their value. These numbers represent only the teacher's assessment of the students' proficiency on this particular assignment. With a bit of intentionality in our rhetoric, we can do a lot to help students counteract the natural tendency to equate their value as a human with their GPA. That's not to say students should never feel bad about a low score on an assignment. If they bombed a paper because they partied all week and then threw together at the last minute a half-hearted attempt to get some credit, frankly, we hope they feel some regret—enough to learn from their mistaken priorities. But if they study earnestly and receive a low grade, disappointing scores are no reason for guilt or shame.

If we're not careful, even the way we talk about a growth mindset may send the message to students that how they perform in any endeavor is *solely* a function of how hard they try. That's a dangerous oversimplification of these two theories, but it's what students might hear if we aren't precise in the way we teach about growth mindsets and emotional regulation. Although we genuinely believe we can all improve in every aspect of our lives, it's also important to acknowledge that we each have fundamentally different life circumstances. While those circumstances don't define us, they certainly affect us. In his formulation of growth mindset, James Lang adds an important nuance we appreciate: "We can get better at math, or writing, or whatever else we want to learn. The potential is not unlimited; it is more likely the case that we each have an intelligence range within which we fall, but that range can be very broad and our effort and attitude help determine whether we are growing within that range or remaining stuck in the same place." [48]

Moreover, our students have undoubtedly been influenced by just how much parental support they had, the discrimination they encountered, the quality of K–12 education they enjoyed, and the socioeconomic support they were given. While we don't want to define or limit our students by their life circumstances, it's unrealistic to pretend they are unaffected by them. This is especially important for college professors to recognize, given how many of us benefited systemically from certain advantages that many of our first-generation college students did not.

In fact, when we fail to acknowledge the profound impact of students' socioeconomic circumstances or racial realities—sometimes quite different from our own—it's both insensitive and unrealistic. For example, some students may have a keen growth mindset but need to work twenty hours a week to put themselves through school. Others might be wonderfully resilient emotionally, but they speak English as a second language, so reading the assigned material takes them much longer. Our rhetorical and even attitudinal challenge, then, is to be appropriately sensitive to such differences while still inspiring students to do all they can going forward to grow and persist, whatever their life circumstances.

We must also be clear in our own minds and with our students that sometimes, despite our best efforts to grow and be gritty, mental health challenges can still get the best of us, at least for a season. While becoming grittier will improve life for most students with mental health challenges, it's not nearly enough to lift some students out of debilitating depression or overwhelming anxiety. If we inadvertently send the message that our mental health is purely a function of our willingness to grow and our ability to regulate our emotions, we're implicitly telling students who struggle with severe anxiety or depression that they must not be trying hard enough. That certainly wasn't the case for Bonnie when she was battling her depression, and it's not the case for a number of our students. Simply acknowledging that could go a long way in helping students feel understood.

We can emphasize the difference that having a growth mindset and grit can make in students' lives without claiming too much or unduly minimizing the different hands our students have been dealt. The motto "Be appropriately sensitive to students' widely different life circumstances while giving them as much hope as possible going forward" does not make for a great meme or inspirational poster for teachers. But tempering our zeal for growth mindset and emotional intelligence just a bit can help us avoid unintentionally sending students the discouraging message that the only reason they haven't accomplished more in life is because they haven't made enough effort.

Help Students Reframe

One of the techniques Brackett recommends for regulating emotions in *Permission to Feel* is *reframing*. In a nutshell, he describes reframing as "transforming our perception of reality as a way of mastering it." [49] More specifically, psychologists call cognitive reframing strategies *reappraisal*. The technique is a way to "reimagine or reframe whatever is triggering an emotional experience and then react instead to that new interpretation. . . . The basic principles of reframing are that we consciously choose to view a situation in a way that generates the least negative emotion in us."[50] For example, when we experience affliction in life, our natural tendency might be to ask, "Why me?" We can reframe our perception of a challenging situation by looking back on how we have grown from the trial. Instead, we might ask, "What can I learn from this situation?" Such a simple change of perspective can prove enormously useful in regulating our emotions.

Reframing or reappraisal could be an especially powerful tool for helping students regulate their emotions in college. For example, experiencing some anxiety before tests is entirely natural and perhaps even helpful. Yet, paradoxically, for students with high anxiety, rising stress might trigger more anxiety, much like the fear of not being able to fall asleep can make it even harder for someone with insomnia to fall asleep. What if we encouraged students experiencing stress to lean into it? Brackett cites one study out of Harvard in which students "who were asked to think of pretest anxiety as being beneficial performed better on exams than a control group."[51] Imagine encouraging students who are feeling stressed out about an upcoming test to harness that cortisol—like we harness the wind when flying a kite—as something to power us to study more intensely.

Similarly, we might help our students view some stressful emotions as useful messages from the brain that they need to pick up the pace a bit or work on important assignments they have been neglecting. Brackett argues that all "emotions are an important source of information about what's going on inside us. . . . We need to access that information and then figure out what it's telling us."[52] Encouraging students to ask questions like these when they are feeling stressed out might help them reframe at least some of their anxiety as helpful reminders:

- Which classes or assignments are causing me this stress?
- What is my plan for preparing for or completing those things? Is there something more I could reasonably do?
- Have I written down the things I need to get done or created digital reminders on my phone so that I can worry less about missing deadlines?
- Could I do better if I got some help? Where could I go to get that help?
- Have I taken on too much or not allowed myself enough time to get it all done? If so, how could I cut back?

Few stressors trigger more emotions for college students than academic failures—getting lower grades on assignments or in courses than they had hoped for. As one student acknowledged, she was "always feeling depressed" when she failed an exam. One of the most powerful opportunities for helping students become more emotionally resilient is to change the lens through which they see failure. We can help students see disappointing scores as opportunities for growth rather than certification of intellectual ineptitude. One student who had learned about growth mindset and grit through BYU-Idaho's College Success course explained, "I tend to have thoughts like 'I'm not good enough' or 'That's too difficult for me.' This makes me feel like there is no point in even trying. Grit and growth mindset help me push forward even when I have these thoughts. It helps me to understand that even if I struggle with a task it is always worth it to try. Even if I fail in my attempt I will have grown and learned from it. Grit and growth mindset helps [sic] me to *accept failure but to reject quitting*" (italics in original).

A growth orientation helped another student learn that "failure isn't the end but something I can use for my benefit." That's a far cry from the attitude of many of the students Duckworth encounters. She calls them "fragile perfects"—students who have always worked hard and succeeded academically but are often thrown completely off balance when they encounter academic setbacks in college. "Sometimes I meet fragile perfects in my office after a midterm or a final. Very quickly, it becomes clear that these bright and wonderful people know how to succeed but not how to fail." [53]

That may be why Doug Lemov advocates taking "actions that build, over time, a classroom culture that makes errors visible, normal, safe, and even positive." [54] As psychologists Elena Bodrova and Deborah Leong have pointed out, "learning from mistakes is something babies and toddlers don't mind at all." Unfortunately, that changes around kindergarten for most children as they notice how adults react to their mistakes. To counter this development, some psychologists encourage teachers to "model emotion-free mistake making." [55] Humbly sharing our own mistakes and growth with students shows them that making and overcoming mistakes is inherent in lifelong learning. Our examples can help students learn, in the words of leadership expert John Maxwell, to "fail forward."

Conversely, when students and organizations fail to learn from shortcomings, they often mushroom into much bigger failures. Getting a low grade on an assignment early in the semester is like getting a dashboard warning that we're almost out of gas. That's no cause for despair. It's a merciful warning that we need to get more gas before things get worse—or, in the case of grades, that we need to fill a gap in our knowledge. When students adopt that kind of mentality about low grades, they reframe failure and engage in cognitive reappraisal, a coping strategy "where we try to look into a stressful situation from a whole new perspective." [56]

Certainly, failure alone doesn't help us grow. Instead, to fail fruitfully, we have to add some intentional reflection. Here are three critical questions students might ask themselves to reframe failure in a way that promotes growth:

1. What don't I understand as well as I would like to?
2. How can I strengthen my understanding or mastery of that concept?
3. How can I change the way I prepare or practice that will help me do better in the future?

Such introspective metacognition helps students take ownership of their learning by finding their own knowledge gaps and then taking steps to fill them in. Students who develop a mastery mentality will come to view low scores on assignments as helpful data in their journey to mastery rather than as depressing validation of their inferior intellect. The same student who acknowledged that failing tests made her feel depressed explained that learning about the growth mindset and grit helped her see that "failure is part of learning," something that allows her to see "where our weaknesses are" and "what actions she needs to take to improve."

As this student's comments demonstrate, students with a mastery mindset are eager to learn from their mistakes; they care more about learning than status. And such students will become extraordinarily valuable employees, citizens, friends, and family members. As Maxwell contends, "The difference between average people and achieving people is their perception of and response to failure." [57]

Indeed, the willingness and ability to learn from mistakes is at the heart of a growth mindset.

Two BYU-Idaho biology professors, John Fisher and Caleb Bailey, have found some simple and effective ways to cultivate gritty growth mindsets in their students through customized but automated feedback. With technological acumen that exceeds the three of ours (but certainly not that of technology-support experts on your campus), they use Outlook's mail merge function to automate sending personalized messages to students after each major assessment. Harnessing data such as how much time each student spent on the exam—a rough measure of their grit—John and Caleb fill their emails with useful data and relevant admonitions. While setting up the emails takes an initial investment of time, sending them out takes the professors almost no time at all.

Caleb initiated this approach, and John has added his own twists. One email John sends after exams notes what grade students earned on the test and how long they spent on the test while encouraging them to spend at least one minute on each question. He also tells them he is interested in the student's "continual progress," even for those who mastered most of the material and earned a high grade. John then offers a deal to his students: if students earn a grade that's at least 10 percent higher on the next test, he'll award them a bonus of another 5 percent. Each email concludes with an invitation to come and meet with the teacher if they'd like some help.

For students who have done very well, John cautions against becoming complacent, warning them that the next exam is even more challenging. He then invites these students to reach out to help other students: "There are a lot of students in the class who could benefit from your skills and understanding." After suggesting some ways to do this, John then challenges these high-performing students to do even better on the next test, reminding them that it "will require time and effort, but your hard work will pay off in the end."

The first semester that John tracked the impact of his emails, he sent messages to 210 students. Sixty-seven students responded, leading to 125 subsequent email conversations. Nine students came to his office for help on a recurring basis. The next semester, John sent 215 students emails after the second exam, leading to individual visits with 37 students who had earned a C or lower on the first exam. Altogether, 118 students met with him, either individually or in groups—a measure he needed to implement after he was flooded with students finally taking advantage of his office hours.

Among the email responses they received from students, this one from a first-year student was typical:

> I am a brand new freshman and all of this stuff is so new, exciting, scary and some more challenging then [*sic*] others. I really would love to succeed in this class, but I haven't found what the best way for me is yet. I also really struggle with test taking in general and I learned that the music testing room is not the place for me.
>
> I would love to get a chance to meet with you to go over my test and maybe you have some studying insights that would better work for me?

Note how John's growth-mindset email seems to have cultivated a growth mindset in the student.

Even more gratifying than the initial emails of thanks

and vows to improve are those John and Caleb receive when students put in the work and see growth:

> I just wanted to update you and let you know that this second test went a lot better! *I got a 92%.* I did many of the things that you suggested and I feel like they worked. I studied really hard, went to tutors every day, asked for help when I didn't understand something, and even went to that drop in tutor lab. But most importantly I made sure to include Heavenly Father in my daily prayers and ask for his help. I think all these things combined is how I was more successful.
>
> Thank you for being willing to give me another chance and ultimately believing that I can be a successful student. I feel like I had a rough start but am starting to understand how to be successful.

Such student responses verify that through purposeful praise and reframing failure, teachers can help students develop growth mindsets and emotional resilience.

Finally, even as we encourage students to reframe failure, it would be a mistake to gloss over the very real heartache and disappointment students experience with some failures. "Embracing failure without acknowledging the real hurt and fear that it can cause, or the complex journey that underlies rising strong, is gold-plating grit," argues Brené Brown, a research professor at the University of Houston. "To strip failure of its real emotional consequences is to scrub the concepts of grit and resilience of the very qualities that make them both so important— toughness, doggedness, and perseverance."[58] In practical terms, "our job is not to deny the story, but to defy the ending."[59]

*Match High Expectations with High Concern
and High Support*

Kim Clark, former dean of Harvard Business School and president of BYU-Idaho, introduced faculty members to a simple but powerful construct in the form of a diagram in which the x-axis represented the amount of love or concern teachers have for their students and the y-axis is the level of their standards or expectations. He argued that the most effective teachers are those who have both high levels of love or concern and high expectations for their students. Growth-mindset teachers who foster emotional resilience clearly fall in the high-concern, high-expectations quadrant. Precisely because they believe all their students are capable of intellectual growth and academic achievement, they avoid a shortcut that would appeal to high-concern, low-expectations teachers: simply lowering the bar so that more students can clear it. "Lowering standards," warns Dweck, "just leads to poorly educated students, who feel entitled to easy work and lavish praise." [60]

Based on data from their massive study of junior high classrooms, Ferguson and his colleagues are also emphatic about the need for teachers to have both high levels of concern and high expectations. Among many benefits, they found that when teachers challenged students to think more rigorously, students were better oriented, showed greater effort, had more of a growth mindset, thought more of attending college one day, and showed more conscientiousness. [61] Yet Ferguson and his team also demonstrated that students with teachers who are concerned about them are happier and have higher future aspirations. [62]

Thus, the researchers don't perceive having high expectations and having high concern as mutually exclusive, competing traits. Yet there are some tradeoffs, to be sure: "When teachers insist on rigorous thinking they risk at least slightly diminishing students' happiness in class, feelings of efficacy, and satisfaction with what they have achieved." Acknowledging the slight emotional costs of teachers' high expectations on students, Ferguson and his colleagues conclude that these "slightly dampened emotions in the short-term seem small prices to pay for the motivational, mindset, and behavioral payoffs we predict to result from requiring rigorous thinking." [63]

Despite those minor trade-offs, Ferguson and his colleagues found that in classrooms the team had categorized as ideal—those that fell in the top quartile on seven criteria—far more students simultaneously agreed with these statements than disagreed with them:

- "Class is a happy place for me to be."
- "[My teacher] really cares about me."
- "[I'm in a class where] students learn to believe that they can get smarter."
- "[My teacher] accepts nothing less than our full effort."
- "I have pushed myself hard to completely understand my lessons in this class."
- "Students learn to try harder when the work becomes difficult."
- "[One of my goals is] to learn as much as I can."
- "[My class] stays busy and doesn't waste time." [64]

In other words, the attributes of caring teachers and rigorous teachers were complementary rather than competing. In the best classrooms, students sensed both that their teachers cared about them *and* that they expected a lot of them. In fact, Ferguson and his colleagues conclude that a combination of concern and rigor is necessary to create the ideal classroom: "For happiness, learning, and high aspirations, we need high performance on multiple teaching components."[65] Their advice to teachers is to be "attentive and sensitive but avoid coddling students in ways that hold them to lower standards for effort and performance and may thereby undermine agency. At the same time, express interest in students' lives, activities, and aspirations so they will feel known and inspired to follow your example."[66] In other words, when it comes to the battle for student success, if we fight prudently, concern for students and concern for academic excellence are allies, not competitors.

These researchers further warn that "in an effort to be emotionally supportive, some teachers may be especially accommodating," with concern morphing into counterproductive coddling.[67] But too "narrow a focus on *sensitivity* as an aspect of caring may include a type of accommodation to students' feelings that fosters slightly less orderly classrooms, less persistence in the face of difficulty, and less development of agency."[68] On the other hand, growth-mindset teachers avoid the other extreme employed by coaches or executives who believe the best way to improve performance is to just shout more loudly or simply mandate improvements. Instead, these teachers lovingly establish high expectations for their students and then provide a path and resources that make it possible for willing students to rise up to those expectations. As Dweck explains, they recognize that just as lowering standards doesn't really boost students' self-esteem, "neither does raising standards without giving students ways of reaching them." Indeed, one of the great benefits of a growth mindset is that it gives teachers "a way to set high standards *and* have students reach them." [69]

As we look for the most effective ways to raise students' sights, it's also worth noting that different types of students might respond to various types of feedback in different ways. For example, in a famous study, a trio of Stanford University professors conducted an experiment and found that "Black students who received unbuffered critical feedback responded less favorably than White students both in ratings of the evaluator's bias and in measures of task motivation. By contrast, when the feedback was accompanied both by an invocation of high standards and by an assurance of the student's capacity to reach those standards, Black students responded as positively as White students and both groups reported enhanced identification with relevant skills and careers." [70] Note how with the more effective approach identified by the Stanford researchers, teachers simultaneously hold students to high expectations while also providing support by assuring students of their ability to meet those high expectations. We would love to see this same study replicated with an analysis of how students with higher levels of anxiety respond to the various types of feedback. We suspect they would also benefit disproportionately from some assurance of their capacity to succeed.

High expectations and high concern are critical to fostering emotional resilience and student achievement, but we suggest adding a third component: high support. Support is critical; even teachers' high concern and high expectations don't do much good if not accompanied by some practical resources. Ferguson and his colleagues note the importance of providing "curricular supports to accompany demands for rigor."[71] From an emotional standpoint, providing the resources that make growth possible is critical, because seeing a plausible path forward gives students hope.

Here's a concrete example of what the high-expectations component of growth-mindset teachers might look like. Professors at the University of California, Davis, conducted a straightforward experiment highlighting the support available to students. Seeking to boost the self-efficacy of students in a large economics course, they used a very scalable intervention. They sent students in the experimental group an email twice a semester, letting them know how they were doing in the course, sharing some strategies that could help them learn, and informing them of resources available for help, including the professor. Students who received the email "scored higher on exams, homework, and final course grades than students in the control group who did not."[72]

Another intriguing way to implement high expectations with high concern and high support is what have become known as "honors contract courses." Professors transform courses into honors courses when students enter into a contract, agreeing to engage in a higher level of work. Gary Wyatt, a professor of sociology at Emporia State University and dean of ESU's honors college, is a big believer that "feelings of belonging are a function of relationships," and he sees honors contract courses as a marvelous vehicle for better connecting students and professors. According to Wyatt, such courses allow students and their professors to create "close, meaningful, and supportive relationships." At ESU, part of the contract for such courses requires students to meet with their "professor one-on-one to develop a high-impact learning experience that the student and professor will work together on during the semester." As a result of these courses, students and faculty members "have formed strong and lasting relationships in those courses, relationships that extend beyond graduation. While contract courses are not unique to ESU, the design of our contract offerings are. They truly promote a sense of belonging as students and faculty work together one-on-one throughout the semester." [73]

Making the kinds of changes we have described in other chapters gives teachers greater ability to establish high expectations with high support and high concern. Choosing to allow students to resubmit work or retake tests for additional credit can allow teachers to be more adamant about quality. Breaking large tests up into smaller components makes it easier to insist on students mastering every concept in a course. And developing meaningful relationships with students who most need our help gives us the goodwill in the bank we need to effectively expect more of them.

In sum, Ferguson and his colleagues urge teachers to improve along all three axes of expectations, concern, and support. As we teach in more engaging ways and show more care for our students, concludes Ferguson, we "mitigate the tension" that comes from high expectations and "make the experience more enjoyable." [74] High concern and high support from teachers make their high expectations inspiring rather than discouraging, achievable rather than overwhelming.

Destigmatize Asking for Help

David Latimer spent five years supporting students at New York City College of Technology. One theme he heard in speaking with students was their fear of seeking the help they needed—a fear that was especially pronounced in those who needed it most: "They fear talking to a professor because a professor represents an intimidating authority figure. They are not sure how to approach them. They also resist asking for help or asking for a tutor, because utilizing a tutor is perceived as not being smart. They do not want to go to counseling when they have emotional problems, because that's for people who are weak. The fear of shame is everywhere."[75]

In *Relationship-Rich Education*, Felten and Lambert find that the same psychological barriers holding students back from getting help are sometimes reinforced inadvertently by institutional indifference or insensitivity: "This message echoed across every institution we visited; many students of all backgrounds are hesitant to ask for help, and institutional environments often reinforce this tendency to believe that college is a solo endeavor. Students are ashamed to admit what they do not know and are embarrassed to let others know that they are confused or uncertain or struggling with a personal issue."[76] Such a mindset leads too many students to "see college as an individualistic, anxiety-inducing slog."[77]

One powerful way to help students develop emotional stamina along with a growth mindset, then, is to help them see seeking help as a sign of wisdom rather than weakness—whether it's academic or emotional help. Nunn suggests that we can help students change the way they perceive such resources by our own attitude and behavior: "We can make resources such as tutoring and study groups seem normal if we talk about them as routine parts of successful students' habits in front of our classes, rather than letting students believe the common perception that tutoring and the like are courses of action that failing students ought to take."[78] In that spirit, one online instructor at the University of Nebraska tells her students each week, "College will not get the best of you if you have the courage to ask those you trust for assistance."[79]

We suspect that being concrete and explicit in connecting students with resources is especially important for students feeling overwhelmed by mental health challenges. As a student who has struggled for years with mental health challenges observed about students trying to cope, "There is already so much on their plate from the negative pressures they already are dealing with in their mental health. They don't know where to begin to ask for help because they already are quite overwhelmed." So instead of just telling students you're always willing to help during your office hours, it's better to send students a reminder with detail about where your office is and when your office hours are. (Better yet, as we discussed in the chapter on natural mentoring, you might take your office hours to them.) Similarly, instead of just telling students about the counseling center, give them its phone number and web address.

Creating a culture where asking for help is seen as courageous rather than weak can help students overcome one of their most dangerous inhibitions: getting professional assistance with their mental health challenges. As we discussed in the chapter on mentoring, a surprisingly high percentage of students who experience depression and even suicidal ideations do not or would not seek help.[80] As we normalize and even promote the idea of seeking academic help, we may help students adopt a mindset that makes them more willing to also seek clinical help for their mental health challenges.

Remember that roughly three-quarters of college students indicated they wouldn't seek help even if they had a serious mental health condition. The leading causes of their reticence included feeling like they could handle such problems themselves and being too embarrassed to ask for help. Perhaps that's one reason why the Jed Foundation, an organization focused on preventing suicide among college students, lists increasing help-seeking behavior as one of its seven tenets: "Work to destigmatize mental-health issues and raise awareness of the resources available to students." Fortunately, it's not our job as teachers to also become our students' counselors. However, when we develop a relationship of trust with our students, we are often uniquely positioned to encourage them to obtain the help they need and to connect them with the appropriate resources.

How can we help? In addition to making students aware of academic support resources, we can make them aware of campus and other resources for mental health challenges. Sarah Ketchen Lipson, coprincipal investigator of the national Healthy Minds Study and assistant professor of health law, policy and management at Boston University, encourages faculty members to include information about on-campus resources in their syllabi and "at stressful points of the semester, such as during midterms and finals."[81] We can also mention the importance of talking with classmates, friends, or us when students find themselves struggling.

Rob has added a module in the learning management system for his courses titled "Need help?" He then includes a list of resources for both mental health challenges and academic support, with this introduction: "One of the hallmarks of gritty and successful people is that they are willing and able to get help when they need it. They realize that taking advantage of helpful resources is wise, not weak. And at BYU-Idaho, there are some great resources available to help you succeed!"

Sometimes despite our best efforts to destigmatize getting support for mental health challenges, students will still feel embarrassed about talking to another person for help. And even for those willing to seek help, as the mental health crisis has swept across college campuses, far fewer learning institutions are equipped to provide the level of counseling support to students they have in the past. Those two factors combined make online self-help resources, for which many colleges are now contracting, a particularly valuable option. Filled with videos and interactive modules, these programs can help students better cope with mental health challenges and develop important life skills. At critical junctures, professors could put in a plug for such resources—including sharing a link to the website. We might even show students a bit of the content from the site to help draw them in and lower emotional barriers to entry.

We can't wish our students' mental health challenges away. But we can help them adopt a healthy philosophy of using help from a variety of resources to improve and conquer every challenge—whether it's not completely understanding an algebraic concept or feeling the urge to cut themselves. And by giving all our students the details they need to connect with resources from tutoring centers to counseling centers, we increase the odds that those students who need help the most will get it.

Conclusion

As important as it is for teachers to remove and reduce unnecessarily vexatious obstacles on the path to learning, helping students develop greater emotional stamina may be even more important. Introducing students to the concepts of growth mindset, emotional intelligence, and self-regulation can benefit them far beyond the walls of our classrooms. As we find ways to help them believe they really can grow intellectually and to cope productively with emotions, we can eliminate the hopelessness that fixed-mindset students have when they encounter failure. Finding creative and compelling ways to cultivate such emotional resilience in our students can help most of them find more hope, peace, and perseverance.

In our classes and colleges, we can create growth-oriented cultures in multiple ways. For starters, it's critical that we genuinely adopt a growth mindset about our students' potential. Otherwise, our attitudes tend to limit their growth. When we praise students for their effort rather than their innate ability, we help them focus on their ability to improve. And helping students reframe failure can change the narrative from one of negative validation to hopeful opportunity. Ideally, they will begin seeing low scores on assignments as important data to help them find and fill in their own knowledge gaps.

None of this requires us to lower the bar for our students. On the contrary, to create a genuine culture of growth, it must be clear to our students that we expect a lot of them. But the most effective teachers combine those expectations not only with great concern for their students but with the support that makes it possible for students to succeed. They are high-concern, high-expectations, and high-support teachers.

Finally, another critical aspect of a growth-oriented culture is that students feel safe asking for help, whether it's going to a math tutor or a counseling center. Being able to encourage students to seek help with their mental health challenges requires us to become aware of the resources available to our students, especially on our own campuses.

And as we discuss in the chapter about being natural mentors, helping students overcome embarrassment and false notions of self-sufficiency so that they are willing to ask for help in times of crisis may be the single most important thing we can do to assist in saving a life.

CHAPTER 6

·················

BUILD COMMUNITY

·················

In an essay published in 2019, Gabriella, a first-year student at Loyola Marymount University, describes her struggle to find friends and adjust to college life. "So far," she says, "college has been lonely." She continues,

> It is the loneliest I have ever been, in fact. Lonely in a "what if I'm always lonely" or "I don't think I'm cut out for this" way. . . .
>
> I am constantly told that "everyone is having a hard time," but I don't believe it. I see kids from orientation at parties and spending time in each other's dorms, and I admire their confidence and ability to acclimate. I do not believe that everyone cries in their room every day. I believe some people are built to belong immediately. And I believe that some are not.
>
> I am not built to belong.[1]

Gabriella's difficult start at Loyola Marymount is a sharp reminder that amid the excitement and energy that often accompany meeting roommates, learning how to get from your apartment to your classrooms, buying books, and all the other activities that mark the traditional start of a new academic year, there is also pain. For any number of reasons, and despite all the energy and excitement around them, some students simply don't acclimate easily. In all cases, feeling lonely and isolated hinders adjustment, while feeling connected helps students to learn and to thrive.[2]

Figuratively, we believe there are times when students like Gabriella need a warm blanket around their shoulders. Happily, Gabriella appears to be one student who has survived early stresses and challenges and who is now thriving. She maintains a website (https://www.gabriellajeakle.com/about), writes for the *Los Angeles Loyolan*, and gives every indication that she has found a sense of belonging. Although Gabriella probably couldn't have believed it was possible when she wrote her essay on belonging, her initial struggle appears to have led to strength. Her pattern of finding success only after struggling through early discouragement is experienced by millions of students every year.

In *The Years that Matter Most*, author Paul Tough stresses the ubiquity of challenges and successes like Gabriella's. Tough introduces us to students who succeed only after overcoming formidable obstacles—including significant mental health challenges. Among those challenges, Tough emphasizes the "often intense anxiety about *belonging*. Do I fit in? Can people like me feel at home here?"[3] On the other hand, Tough describes a student who "experienced debilitating episodes of depression and insomnia and anxiety" but who also "eventually found friends, developed strategies to manage his anxiety, and earned his BA."[4] Wherever they enroll, whatever their major, each year millions of students find friends, manage anxiety, and discover a sense of belonging at their colleges and universities. And yet, thousands of others never make those personal connections, learn to manage anxiety, earn their degrees, or ever feel that they belong.

In this chapter, we explore students' need to find a

supportive learning community where they can thrive. We discuss the importance of friends and their role in helping college students to develop a genuine sense of belonging wherever they complete their studies—a sense vital to both emotional health and academic success for all students and student groups. The final section of the chapter is dedicated to introducing steps professors and instructors can take to help students of varied socioeconomic classes, gender identities, sexual orientations, and ethnicities believe that they do belong and that they can be successful.

Theoretical Framework

Students who struggle with social isolation may face a challenge even greater than the shrinking probability that they will persist and complete their degree. Recent work in public health stresses that there is "evidence that social connection influences a variety of mental and physical health outcomes," such as depression, cognitive decline, and dementia.[5] It is only logical that while all our students need help to cope with emergencies, students of color and those of other underrepresented groups who may encounter difficulty finding a supportive social community are particularly vulnerable to mental health challenges during times of crisis. Frankly, raising these challenges is somewhat awkward for us as authors, when we know that we have a lot of progress to make at our own university to better welcome students who might be marginalized. But rather than ignoring an important issue for which we are far from a perfect messenger, we felt it better to raise the issue while acknowledging our own need to improve.

This survey of challenges faced by groups vulnerable to marginalization in higher education should inspire careful reflection regarding ways we can help rather than hinder learning.

- People who are marginalized or stigmatized within society, such as members of underrepresented groups, were at a significantly higher risk of experiencing mental health problems.
- Mental health issues vary by student demographics. For example, compared with heterosexual students, bisexual and gay/lesbian students had a substantially elevated risk for mental health issues.
- Students of color and students with current or past financial difficulties were found to have a substantially higher prevalence of depression.
- Researchers have paid attention to the lower graduation rates seen among students belonging to minority groups, but less attention has been given to graduation rate differences in students with mental health issues, although research has indicated that depression predicts lack of persistence in college. To be clear, these inequities not only appear in higher education but also may have affected students long before reaching settings of higher education.[6]

The anxiety experienced by students, already alarmingly high before the pandemic, isn't likely to dissipate soon. Furthermore, our students and colleagues of color and those from other historically marginalized communities are likely to continue to bear a disproportionate burden of police brutality,[7] unemployment,[8] poor access to online education,[9] and pandemic-related deaths.[10] A cruel irony that compounds these challenges for these students is that while they tend to face more stress, they are actually less likely to seek counseling.[11] "There's a high level of students of color suffering in silence," according to Annelle Primm, the senior medical director of the Steve Fund, a nonprofit mental health advocacy group that focuses on equity and young people of color.[12]

And it's not just dealing with the repercussions of past discriminations that can affect the mental health of students of color. Many continue to experience racism today from classmates and even professors. As Greta Anderson writes in *Inside Higher Ed*:

> Black students at many predominantly white colleges have long complained of the racial hostility, subtle and blatant, that they regularly encounter on their campuses. Whether victims of constant microaggressions or outright verbal or physical assaults, many have stories of being called a racial slur directly or seeing it scrawled on a campus wall, viewing racist posts by classmates on social media, or sitting through a presentation by a classmate professing a white supremacist conspiracy.[13]

As students cope with and fight against such discrimination and injustice, they "have less time and emotional bandwidth to dedicate to typical student experiences, such as creating and maintaining personal relationships and a social life, performing academically and navigating what is likely their first time living away from home."[14]

Imposter Syndrome

All of this upheaval leaves many students feeling profoundly isolated and vulnerable. Even before we were asked to practice social distancing, social isolation was a major problem for many college and university students. Far too often, students live in close physical proximity to their peers but simultaneously in social isolation from them. Also discussed in chapters 2 and 5, one aggravating factor in students struggling to connect with others is imposter syndrome, the student's own belief of being a fraud and at risk of being exposed at any moment. According to psychologist Arlin Cuncic, "Imposter syndrome is the experience of feeling like a phony—you feel as though at any moment you are going to be found out as a fraud—like you don't belong where you are, and you only got there through dumb luck." [15]

Student Experience Research Network characterizes the impact of the syndrome this way: "When students are uncertain about whether they belong, they are vigilant for cues in the environment that signal whether or not they belong, fit in, or are welcome there. They may also be concerned about confirming a negative stereotype about their group. This hyper-vigilance and extra stress uses up cognitive resources that are essential for learning, diminishing their performance and discouraging them from building valuable relationships." [16] While imposter syndrome itself isn't a disorder, we are aware of the close association between this syndrome and anxiety and depression. "Though the impostor phenomenon isn't an official diagnosis listed in the *DSM* [*Diagnostic and Statistical Manual of Mental Disorders*], psychologists and others acknowledge that it is a very real and specific form of intellectual self-doubt. Impostor feelings are generally accompanied by anxiety and, often, depression." [17] Indeed, there is a whole literature on the phenomenon. It's rampant among college students, with 25.8 percent of students experiencing it, according to one study.[18]

Not surprisingly, those with depression and anxiety often struggle with imposter syndrome as well. Studies have found significant positive correlations between imposter syndrome and anxiety, insomnia, social dysfunctions, and depression; high school students with a history of attempting suicide were significantly more likely to suffer from imposter syndrome; and imposter syndrome is especially prevalent among African American, Asian American, and Latino/a/x American students.[19]

This harmful belief can strike students of all backgrounds, but it takes a particularly harsh toll on women and students of color in STEM (science, technology, engineering, and math) and members of other underrepresented or marginalized groups. These students often conclude that they aren't university material and should have stayed home. "Questions about belonging are most common among students from negatively stigmatized groups. These students are aware that they are underrepresented in a particular environment and recognize that negative stereotypes exist about their group. . . . [C]ompare this to the feeling of being told there is a snake in your house. It could be anywhere and it could harm you, but it also might not; regardless, you are constantly on the lookout." [20] The emotional cost of knowing that we might be surprised at any minute by a slithering intruder emerging from under a pillow or hiding under a blanket would make it next to impossible to relax on a sofa to read a book or to lie down in bed. Likewise, the fear of being exposed as a fraud can exhaust students with imposter syndrome and, consequently, deplete their cognitive capacity to learn the material in their classes.

Relationship-Rich Education authors Peter Felten and Leo Lambert explain why students who may feel on the margin of college life are at particular risk for imposter syndrome and doubt about whether they belong:

Although isolation, shame, and imposter syndrome are common among college students, these feelings are not necessarily evenly distributed, nor are all identity contingencies equivalent. Our students are products of educational, cultural, and economic systems that are highly inequitable, preparing them differently for the demands of higher education and perpetuating stereotypes of who is or is not likely to succeed in college. For instance, the racial-ethnic achievement gap in US higher education is well documented, but research also demonstrates sharp psychosocial disparities between white and black students, including more "belonging uncertainty" and more pervasive feelings of imposterism among black undergraduates.[21]

Uri Treisman is a mathematician and master teacher who was a first-generation college student. He worked for years cleaning chicken coops and mowing lawns before enrolling as a university student. Treisman had to learn to overcome imposter syndrome, beating back fears of inadequacy despite evidence of immense talent. Tough describes Treisman's struggle with imposter syndrome as follows:

> That fear—what psychologists sometimes call impostor syndrome—is not unusual among college students and graduate students, especially first-generation college students like Treisman was. He sees it all the time today among his Math 408C students. Even when he was a student, he was able to recognize, on one level, that his doubts about his ability were irrational. But identifying a problem and naming it doesn't make it go away. "These were forces that were dark and amorphous," he explains. "They are not amenable to rational counterargument. They permeate you like a fog, like a mist of self-doubt."

In every way that the outside world could perceive, Treisman's first few years at Berkeley were a success. He passed his qualifying exams. He served as a teaching assistant for advanced courses. He helped other students with their dissertations. But all the while, he felt profoundly stuck, like he wasn't in the place he belonged, like he wasn't doing the work he was supposed to be doing.

"At Berkeley, you were supposed to be great," Treisman says. "And I felt certain that I would never be great." [22]

Treisman went on to become a legendary teacher and mathematician. We'll end the chapter with a few inspiring words from him.

The Sense of Belonging

The sense of belonging is the opposite of the imposter syndrome. It is an empowering belief that enables students to see themselves as worthy to be at the institutions where they are enrolled and capable of succeeding there. Sociologist Vincent Tinto argues that students' feeling of belonging is a consequence of learning to see themselves as members of "a community of other students, academics, and professional staff who value their membership—in other words, that they matter and belong." [23]

There is broad consensus in the literature on the importance of social connection for a student's mental health and well-being. Having supportive friends and a robust sense of belonging is important for all college students, and it is especially so for students with mental health challenges. Tinto suggests that "a student's sense of not belonging, of being out of place, leads to a withdrawal from contact with others that further undermines motivation to persist. As importantly, feeling one does not belong in the classroom or program can lead to withdrawal from learning activities that then undermines not only the motivation to persist but also the motivation to learn."[24]

It follows, then, that we would do well to be clear about what belonging means. Educational researcher Nicholas A. Bowman and his colleagues explore the concept, identifying two strands of scholarship. The second strand is more relevant to our discussion, as it stems from studies of higher education. Research in this tradition typically views belonging "as a perception of one's own positioning in relation to—or a sense of affiliation with—a group or college community."[25] According to Bowman and his coauthors, belonging in a college community can lead to resilience, life satisfaction, and improved cognitive and affective response. On the other hand, they cite studies that attribute physical pain, emotional distress, mental illness, physical illness, anxiety, low self-esteem and reduced motivation to "alienation or absence of belonging."[26]

Student Experience Research Network supports the contention that belonging is vital for student success: "Students who are confident they belong and are valued by their teachers and peers are able to engage more fully in learning. They have fewer behavior problems, are more open to critical feedback, take greater advantage of learning opportunities, build important relationships, and generally have more positive attitudes about their classwork and teachers. In turn, they are more likely to persevere in the face of difficulty and do better in school."[27] On the other hand, failing to find this belonging can hurt a student's chances of succeeding academically. Bowman and his colleagues similarly observe this phenomenon: "In the college setting, a lack of belonging predicts less social and academic engagement, lower academic achievement, and ultimately departure from the institution." [28]

The Role of Friends

Perhaps unsurprisingly, given the great importance of positive peer relationships, friendship—or the lack of friendship—plays an outsize role in the process of gaining a sense of belonging. Frankly, the claims for the centrality of friendship to student success presented in Daniel Chambliss and Christopher Takacs's *How College Works* caught Steve off guard, perhaps because he was fortunate enough to have very few moments in his university years when he felt that he didn't belong. In speaking about patterns of success in college, the authors claim, for example, that most students "need only a few people—two or three good friends and one or two great professors—to have a rewarding, even wonderful, college experience." [29] Steve had one or two truly influential professors as an undergraduate and the two or three friends Chambliss and Takacs identify as necessary. Had he been asked to rate the level of the importance of those friends at the time, Steve is sorry to say that he would have underrated their contribution to his success. He didn't see things this way at the time, but according to Chambliss and Takacs, those relationships alone were sufficient to produce a wonderful college experience. That's a startling statement. In still stronger phrasing, they reaffirm the importance of friends, saying that college students "face a roughly chronological sequence of predictable major challenges. . . . First, they must successfully enter the social world of college, most importantly by finding friends. Failing that, little else matters." [30]

Chambliss and Takacs go further, with the contention

that friendships are essential for student success. They argue that "going to college" is much more than moving into a dorm room, "pulling all-nighters" to finish term papers, and putting up the Che Guevara poster. They use the term *entering* as a metaphor for the whole social and emotional process of "entering a new community, stepping into the exhilarating but sometimes frightening world of incipient adulthood. When students successfully enter this community of young adults, it can—potentially—energize and motivate them for learning, for excelling at athletics, for socializing (yes—for partying, drinking, hooking up), for giving tremendous loyalty to the institution, for pursuing careers, and sometimes even for becoming, as the cliché has it, 'lifelong learners.' When they don't successfully enter socially or academically, students often become lonely, demoralized, and even depressed. They may well drop out psychologically, if not physically." [31]

Entering, then, is about joining a community and sharing an experience; it is a matter of developing a sense of belonging. According to the authors, when a student is unable to enter the community, loneliness, demoralization, depression, and dropping out follow. This notion, along with a brief mention of "some very unhappy social isolates," links friendship in *How College Works* to mental health issues. Although their use of the word *friend* is ultimately vague, Chambliss and Takacs see friends as vital for the well-being of college students, even as a prerequisite for their success.

For her part, in *Connecting in College*, Janice McCabe takes us on a deep dive into the subtle differences between three varieties of friendships, but her analysis is ultimately ambivalent on their importance to student wellness. Though *How College Works* and *Connecting in College* appear to talk at cross-purposes regarding friends and their importance for student well-being and eventual success, the apparent contradiction is easily resolved. Good friends are vitally important in the process of entering and belonging in college, Chambliss and Takacs say. McCabe, examining friendship from a different angle, warns against confusing tight connections for quality friends. Their common message for students is, in short, your friends will have an enormous effect on your success in college and beyond. Choose them with great care.

To make the point somewhat differently, loneliness hurts. And connectedness helps all college students in important ways. Further, building strong connections with other students has a particularly strong positive effect on mental health. As a result, friends are a vital element of belonging, and belonging is a key component of mental health among college students. And what about Gabriella? Was she right in asserting that she was not "built to belong"? Are some people just unluckily wired to suffer a while in alienated disconnection before they can connect and belong? What did Gabriella's professors and mentors do to help her when she came to Loyola Marymount feeling friendless and fearing that she didn't belong? Are our attitudes and behaviors unintentionally making it harder for students like Gabriella to believe that they, too, can belong, and that they, too, can succeed?

Putting Theory into Practice

We as professors can offer no universally applicable advice for students who haven't yet connected with others, but we can do many things to make the challenge of entering college less daunting. If our readers will indulge us in an extended metaphor, we'd like you to think about warm blankets.

Steve, like many of our readers, has experienced the disorientation and even dehumanization that precede surgeries. In the surreal minutes before those surgeries began, in those moments when he was at his most vulnerable—sporting a hospital gown that didn't fully cover everything to his satisfaction, tethered to an IV tree by a large needle in a vein, connected to various blinking and beeping monitors, about to fade out as he succumbed to anesthesia—in those moments, a kind soul on the surgical team invariably asked him, "Would you like a warm blanket?" Steve always found that those warm blankets had an instant calming, soothing, and reassuring effect that was almost—but not quite—enough to compensate for the indignities of the gown.

Among the very last observations in *How College Works*, we find this hopeful nugget: " 'Warm blankets' make a difference." The authors continue, reminding us of the power of "even a tiny bit of high-quality human contact, applied at the right moment in a student's career, to restore confidence and drive." Further, "a helpful resident advisor in the first few weeks, an engaging teacher in a single introductory class, a writing instructor who sits with a student one-on-one to go over a paper, one field trip with a congenial group—with a regular smattering of such lucky breaks, a willing student can have a very satisfying and educationally productive college career." [32] It doesn't have to be a big deal, it doesn't need to take a long time, and it doesn't need to take us away from teaching, service, and research. But if we open our minds to the possibilities, we will find opportunities all around us to share warm blankets and high-quality human contact.

As Felten and Lambert say in *Relationship-Rich Education*,

> Doing this work well is not easy, but is possible at every institution and for every student. Individuals and institutions will need to rethink practices, policies, and priorities. The mantra echoing through this volume is that higher education must act so that all students experience welcome and care, become inspired to learn through interactions in and out of the classroom, cultivate constellations of important relationships, and use those relationships to begin to explore the big questions of their lives. To influence every student in these ways is an enormously aspirational goal, but if students are to achieve the promise of higher education, no one in higher education can settle for anything less than relationship-rich experiences for all.[33]

Remembering that these tactics and approaches are neither silver bullets nor panaceas, a quick tour through some pedagogical practices might help us all to see ways we can offer a warm blanket to a struggling student. With some creative adjusting, these activities can be as useful in remote or hybrid environments as they are in traditional classroom settings.

Warm Blanket 1: Foster Collaboration Rather than Competition among Students

A wonderfully warm blanket we can provide our students is learning environments that are more collaborative than competitive. We recognize that competition in education is a hotly debated subject. In certain circumstances, it appears to energize students and improve academic performance. We've used it ourselves to jolt a lethargic class to life. Perhaps that's why competition is a favorite technique of so many teachers. But when we create classroom environments students perceive as highly competitive, we may also experience psychological blowback—unanticipated, negative mental health consequences.

In many ways, relying inordinately on competition for motivation is like drinking soda to quench our thirst. In the short term, it seems to get the result we hope for. But in the long run, soda actually dehydrates us and makes us thirstier. Similarly, using competition can temporarily spark energy in a class, but using it chronically sends the message to students that they are competitors rather than collaborators in the learning process. While we don't argue for complete abstinence from this pedagogical soda, we do caution against making it a steady part of our teaching diets. Like other activities that generally generate stress, competition may be best employed only in small doses. Or as education scholars Julie Posselt and Sarah Ketchen Lipson assert, competition is a "double-edged sword. It can drive [students] to high levels of effort, but it can also create unhealthy levels of stress and discourage persistence." Like them, we do not argue that we need to "erase competition from education altogether. Rather, we need to address 'the kind that spurs more anxiety than it does motivation.' "[34]

One challenge to pitting our students against one another in the classroom is that they have already been swimming in a sea of zero-sum activities—applying to colleges or graduate schools, seeking scholarships, or pursuing admission to highly sought-after programs. Such constant competition can lead even the mellowest of students to begin to see college life as one big contest. This is especially true as a growing percentage of students view higher education as having more to do with getting ahead than finding meaning in life. As Posselt and Lipson put it,

"Many young adults today are raised in a culture of competition that leads them to approach education with instrumental motivations and to think of their peers as a source of social comparison rather than of support." [35]

Unfortunately, when students view each other as rivals rather than allies in learning, it may undermine their ability to connect and collaborate with each other in ways that would improve both their learning and their mental health. Drawing on data from the Healthy Minds Study, Posselt and Lipson conducted "the first major study of competition in college classes, depression, and anxiety, using a large, diverse sample and widely validated screening measures for depression and anxiety." [36] They found that when students perceived their class environments as highly competitive, they were more likely to experience anxiety or depression. To be more exact, in "multivariate models, perceptions of competition within the academic environment increase the odds of screening positive for anxiety by 70.0% and for depression by 40.0%." They also found that highly competitive environments did not affect students uniformly: "College students from underrepresented or marginalized backgrounds who perceive their classroom environments to be very competitive are particularly vulnerable to depression and anxiety." [37]

Of course, as the authors acknowledge, the nonexperimental nature of their study and data "prohibit causal arguments." Does competition increase the odds that students are diagnosed with anxiety or depression? Or do anxiety and depression increase the odds that students will perceive their classrooms as highly competitive? Either way, to Posselt and Lipson the implications for those of us in the college classroom are clear: "For educators concerned with developing inclusive learning environments, our results highlight the need for pedagogies and interactions that challenge tendencies toward intense competition and conventional status hierarchies based on social identities."[38]

As professors, we are uniquely positioned to reduce the competitiveness both in our classrooms and in students' minds. Indeed, numerous studies show that teachers' "instructional decisions help shape whether collaboration, support, and/or competition characterizes classroom interactions."[39] Not only can we nudge our classroom environments away from being highly competitive, we can move them toward being more collaborative. As one study notes, "Several decades of empirical research have demonstrated the positive relationship between collaborative learning and student achievement, effort, persistence, and motivation."[40] Moreover, as a fascinating study of Google's employees found, among the most important characteristics of successful employees were "communicating and listening well; possessing insights into others (including differing values and points of view); having empathy toward and being supportive of one's colleagues"[41]—all collaborative skills that ranked higher than having STEM expertise. Helping our students see classmates as collaborators rather than competitors is preparing them to see their future professional colleagues in the same way—a critical soft skill.

One simple way to help students view each other as allies in learning is to avoid creating token economies characterized by a scarcity of high grades. One study found that "college students' greatest source of academic stress was competition for grades."[42] Perhaps the best way to reduce the level of competitiveness in our courses is to kill the curve. We recognize that many professors have department or university mandates that limit our grading flexibility in this regard, but where we can, per-haps nothing can do more to facilitate a shift in student thinking than eliminating a zero-sum grading scheme—a system that literally incentivizes them to *not* help their classmates. From a grading standpoint, when students can succeed only if other students are less successful, it's hard for them to regard each other than as anything but rivals.

We can also design course structures and use language that lets our students know we perceive them as a commu-nity of learners who work together and assist each other. Each of the techniques we discuss in this chapter subtly sends that message to students. Beyond that, though, we may want to be explicit in inviting students to help each other learn and succeed. For example, after Rob establishes partnerships in his classes, he invites the students of each class to help everyone pass the course, with a special focus on helping their partner be successful.

David Miller, a professor of computer information tech-nology at BYU-Idaho, creates community scaffolding into his courses by asking students who are feeling comfortable with their mastery of the content to volunteer to help their classmates during labs. These students continue to do their own work during class, but their classmates know they are available for assistance as needed. Junior, one of Miller's students who has ADHD, explained how being part of such a community of learners helped him overcome inhibitions about asking for help:

> I've always had a ton of issues asking for help if I get stuck because I feel like I'm stupid for not getting it, and I don't want to be that annoying student that asks dumb questions to the TA and the professor all the time when I don't under-stand, and I'm sure that I'm not the only one. I'm extremely

sensitive to what other people think of me, so having a group that's designed solely to answer questions that other students have, it take[s] a lot of pressure off because if I get stuck, I can totally ask for help, and I can switch which groups I go to so I don't feel like I'm bothering one person too much.... I think this is a really unique way to have students interact and help one another and develop soft skills that are mandatory in the workplace, and it should be helpful to students with mental health disorders like mine with the class, which can feel a bit overwhelming sometimes.

We can also be careful in how we word our praise. Just as some praise fosters a fixed mindset, some fosters a competitive mindset. For example, instead of telling a student that her essay is the best in the class, we can compliment her on writing an especially illuminating, well-organized essay.

Finally, one implication Posselt and Lipson note about their research on competition and anxiety is that professors should "encourage students to think critically about generational norms that lead to unhealthy social comparisons."[43] In a world where students see education in increasingly utilitarian terms already, we may be able to help them adopt a different, more collaborative view of the world. One way to do this is to lead by example: if we choose to see others within *our* spheres more as allies in accomplishing good things than as rivals competing for limited resources, our more community-oriented worldview just may become a part of our students' worldviews.

Warm Blanket 2: Use Team-Based Learning

One of the most effective ways to establish a sense of connectedness and community among students is team-based learning (TBL). Pioneered in the 1970s by Larry Michaelsen, TBL is supported by a rich body of research, including 140 journal articles published between 1996 and 2013.[44] Multiple books also explore and advocate this technique, including the seminal *Team-Based Learning: A Transformative Use of Small Groups in College Teaching* by Michaelsen, Arletta Bauman Knight, and Dee Fink. Here, we provide only a brief summary of TBL and how it benefits students.

Like other active-learning methods, TBL encourages students to become agents in the learning process rather than passive observers. But TBL is distinctive in several ways. First, teachers create teams of five to seven members, taking a variety of factors into consideration to ensure balance and diversity. Having students complete questionnaires at the beginning of the semester can provide the information necessary to create balanced groups. Professor-created groups also avoid awkward dynamics that can arise when some subset of a student-created group is already friends.

Incidentally, even with diverse groups, teachers may need to play an active role in monitoring to ensure that some students aren't being ostracized, inadvertently or otherwise. For example, literally the week before we wrote this, an international student in one of our colleague's courses asked to be able to work alone instead of with his team. He felt uncomfortable speaking up because he spoke English slowly. Our colleague began monitoring the teams more closely and discovered other students in a similar situation. He didn't grant this student's request, but he did provide some scaffolding, requiring that a different team member lead the discussion and serve as the spokesperson each day.

While team makeup is important, continuity and

longevity are critical. In fact, what distinguishes a team from a group is that in teams, participants establish lasting relationships—something not possible in a four-minute, small-group discussion whose members have just met. Students in teams work together throughout the entire semester. "Although even a single well-designed group assignment usually produces a variety of positive outcomes," acknowledge Michaelsen and his coauthors, "only when students work together over time can their groups become cohesive enough to evolve into self-managed and truly effective learning teams."

Second, individuals and teams must be accountable. With TBL, students prepare before class by reading or viewing assigned material. In class, readiness is assured by taking a multiple-choice test, first individually and then as teams. All team members must agree on each answer. Teams also receive feedback immediately, allowing them to recognize and learn from their mistakes. Furthermore, students are required to evaluate each team member's contributions, often at midterm and the end of the semester.[45]

Third, students apply the knowledge they have gained to some kind of case. All teams work on the same case and have a specific choice to make and defend. When possible, teams report their recommended solution or choice simultaneously.[46] While the multiple-choice tests help ensure students master core facts and ideas, it's the application phase of TBL where higher-order learning takes place.

TBL has proven to be beneficial in numerous ways. First of all, students benefit from the collective wisdom of a team—and get a dramatic object lesson in the advantages of tackling difficult problems together with others who have different perspectives and strengths. To any of us who prefer to be loners, we should pause and think carefully about the following fact: "In the past 20 years, over 99.9+% of the nearly 1,600 teams in our classes have outperformed their own best member by an average of nearly 11%. In fact, in the majority of classes, the lowest team score in the class is higher than the single best individual score in the entire class."[47] In other words, TBL isn't a touchy-feely left-over of freethinking approaches to overhauling education; it results in students learning more.

Through repeated practice and peer evaluations, students also learn interpersonal skills necessary to more successfully collaborate with others. "Many students gain profound insights into their strengths and weaknesses as learners and as team members," report Michaelsen and his coauthors.[48] One quasi-experimental study showed that students who were in team-based learning sections of a course experienced significantly more "intrinsic motivation, identified regulation, perceived competence, and perceived autonomy" compared to students in lecture-based sections. Moreover, their engagement and perceived learning increased significantly. Of particular note, given the additional challenges faced by students who might feel they are on the margins of college life, Michaelsen and his colleagues find that "TBL enables the 'at risk' students (probably because of the increased social support and/or peer tutoring) to successfully complete and stay on track in their course work."[49]

Advocates of TBL encourage professors to build their courses around the TBL model. Most teachers who have adopted this approach embrace it wholeheartedly and implement it systematically. But for those who are overwhelmed by the notion of completely revamping their curriculum, we believe it's possible to harness some of the benefits of TBL, even with incremental implementation. For example, consider establishing teams in which students participate in their small-group discussions throughout the semester. Even without implementing other aspects of TBL, we suspect that students will feel more connected—and be more productive—if they can establish deeper relationships with the few other students in their small groups.

Warm Blanket 3: Create Opportunities for Connecting

One of the most effective things professors and instructors can do is to provide opportunities for students to connect with each other. Far from feeling that these opportunities were a waste of time, the students we spoke with found great value in having the space and time to connect. One young man observed that the sense of community in a course "all depends on the personality of the professor." When professors get right to business at the start of each class, there's not much community building. But when professors appropriately open up about themselves, ask students questions about their lives, or give students a moment to get to know the person sitting next to them, the students we interviewed felt it began to create a sense of community in a class. "It makes a whole different atmosphere . . . , which I feel like helps everybody," explained a young woman with anxiety. "You can just kind of tell but everybody else's like less tense and willing to actually communicate." Another student added simply, "If you ask about me, it makes me like your class even more. If you care about individual students, that's just very important."

Like many others at BYU-Idaho, David Miller encourages students to create connections with other students through something we call "running buddies." These partnerships are a variation of the more common idea of a study buddy. Interestingly, the *Oxford English Dictionary* cites the first known use of the term in a 1946 *Cedar Rapids Gazette* article in which the author calls on readers to avoid the ignominy of not participating: "Don't be a fuddy-duddy—be a study buddy!"

Distance and online education seized on this tactic as a way to help students connect with and support each other, despite being physically remote. Expanding on that early idea, David and Rob have successfully experimented with trios, and at least one BYU-Idaho colleague uses, in the rhyming spirit of 1946, "quad squads." Whatever the configuration, these teachers usually create groups on the first day of class and ensure that at least one member of each group has already read the syllabus. Rob even allows and encourages students to schedule a time to take the syllabus quiz together as partners or a group. These instructors also invite students in these partnerships or groups to exchange phone numbers and become one another's first contact when questions come up. They encourage the students to help their running buddies if they start to slip academically and to reach out to them if they miss class. And they have the students work together in these same configurations throughout the semester in a variety of ways.

One of David's students thanked him for how running buddies had benefited her:

> I became . . . buddies with someone I previously worked with in a different class. I know I can count on him if I run into any trouble during this class. I was nervous that I would be able to do well in this class, but now that I have somebody I can work with and knowing we have so many resources to help us, I believe I will do well in this class. Throughout the semester my . . . buddy [and I have gotten

together for labs] and we have taught each other. Not only are we [running buddies] but we have become friends. We are taking some class[es] together next semester that we both need, and I think that having a . . . buddy really helps. Thank you for making it possible for us to make a new friend.

Running buddies is just one example of scaffolding that can enhance connectedness and reduce loneliness among students. In *33 Simple Strategies for Faculty*, Lisa Nunn offers a rich store of pedagogical tactics that are, in our judgment, as helpful for students who are living with anxiety and depression as for first-generation and first-year students. For example, after describing a low-pressure and informal way to share contact information with classmates, Nunn then invites teachers to encourage their students "to reach out to classmates whom they don't know well. This is a chance to get to know someone new—who knows, they just might meet their new best friend today. I like to remind them that it is okay if they try studying together once or twice and it doesn't click. They should still try it. No hard feelings." [50]

Warm Blanket 4: Create a Departmental Safety Net

Students sometimes feel like they are building a tall tower alone in a rainstorm, with no safety net to catch them should they slip and fall. As the tower of their education and future career grows, it may be difficult for them to believe that they would survive a fall as they scramble upward. Most students find building their future exciting, engaging, and fulfilling, but understandably, they also need to feel safe. A net of many strands can catch a student who falls, but that same falling student might not be able to see or grasp a single rope. Together, peers, professors, and departments can create a safety net of belonging.

Mike Sessions, chair of the department of design and construction management at BYU-Idaho, leads a group of faculty that is impressively focused on student success. Mike considers the cooperative creation of a "net of belonging" through the joint efforts of the department, the faculty, and the students a very significant achievement. Reflecting on how his department developed their focus on belonging, Mike notes that several "years ago, our administrative and faculty team recognized that our department citizens form a unique community that exists within the larger university society. . . . With this awareness, discussion turned to fostering students' awareness that they belong to something that is greater than self."

The first strand in their departmental safety net is student-to-student relationships. "One of the initiatives we undertook to develop a sense of belonging focused on the power of cohorts," explains Mike. The department's aim was to build on cohorts within classes to create "larger cohorts leading towards a cohort for each major, and eventually for the department." They used large department-sponsored events, such as career fairs, industry competitions, special training or certification events, and student societies to foster student identification with those larger cohorts. They even gave students hats and shirts with department branding, which they proudly wear still.

Friendships develop as students work together to complete assignments and as they seek emotional support from peers who understand their academic challenges. In friendships, students often become aware of things about their classmates that faculty members may never see. That relationship sometimes puts a student in a prime position to help another who is in danger of a perilous fall in the form of anxiety, depression, or even suicide. Creating opportunities for student-to-student relationships to develop, such as TBL, is not only good pedagogy; it also strengthens the safety net.

Mike recalls a time when two students came to his office near the end of the semester. They had been working on a team-based assignment that took several weeks to accomplish, and they were concerned about one of their teammates who had let them know he was struggling with depression. They had become concerned when they couldn't find him to complete the project. Mike sprang into action. "I made a call to student support, and they made a home safety check. The student was experiencing suicidal ideation, but working together, professionals, his peers, and I were able to help him avoid a dangerous fall and safely continue."

Mike's department provides a vital second strand in a strong and enduring safety net. Department leadership initiates, inspires, recognizes, and rewards a culture of caring. Their focus is creating a safe environment for students to interact with teachers through respect, approachability, authenticity, and genuine concern. They emphasis many of the principles we discuss in our chapter on becoming natural mentors. Caring faculty members welcome students into class discussions, hold students to high standards of classroom conduct, know their students' names, and have an open-door policy. Some teachers even list their cell phone numbers in their syllabus—with specific directions on when and for what reasons it is appropriate to use them. Most of the professors use project-based learning to do away with the defensive turret podium, circulate to mentor students on the project and, more importantly, get to know students better. Many of the program faculty also coach student teams in preparation for industry competitions. And many attend those competitions with their students to intentionally create additional mentoring opportunities. When a culture of caring begins to emerge throughout a program or department, department citizens—students, faculty, and administrators—develop a sense that they belong, that they are wanted, needed, have value, and are part of a unique community.

Mike's department also uses their student society as a vehicle for cultivating community by increasing "the student society's leadership role in what had been faculty-led events." Intuitively, Mike and his colleagues sensed that relinquishing control would create students' sense of ownership and lead to meaningful leadership opportunities. Now, explains Mike, "student society leaders organize academic, social, career promoting, and community service events. Faculty work in an advisory role supporting and guiding students." The work of the student society has grown so much in managing activities, such as industry-student golf outings, recruiting events, industry-specific résumé workshops, weekly industry seminars, and community service outreach projects, that they have had to create subcommittees of students. "We take advantage of these committees to foster personal relationships among students, to provide mentoring opportunities between faculty advisors and students, and to create a sense of belonging to something that is larger than self."

Mike's faculty colleagues find that caring about students' needs for living a good life brings focus to the profession of teaching. Faculty with this focus want to support students as they discover their next steps upward. Faculty teach students to build buildings, and they also teach those students how to build lives by taking them as apprentices under their wings. When they do that, they foster a culture of caring that supports students and helps catch the ones who fall.

Warm Blanket 5: Tell Students They Belong—and Mean It

Kurt Baker, a professor of psychology at California State University, Stanislaus, observes that "almost all human beings—and students are a subset of that category—need some sense of belonging." [51] Uri Treisman, the legendary math professor at the University of Texas we met earlier, recognized that need and created a celebrated program that boosted the achievement rates of Black students at the University of California at Berkeley. The key element in that program? Community. A 1992 article by Claude Steele in the *Atlantic* summarizes Treisman's work in this way:

> In the mid-seventies black students in Philip Uri Treisman's early calculus courses at the University of California at Berkeley consistently fell to the bottom of every class. To help, Treisman developed the Mathematics Workshop Program, which in a surprisingly short time, reversed their fortunes, causing them to outperform their white and Asian counterparts. And although it is only a freshman program, black students who take it graduate at a rate comparable to the Berkeley average. Its central technique is group study of calculus concepts. But it is also wise; it does things that allay the racial vulnerabilities of these students. Stressing their potential to learn, it recruits them to a challenging "honors" workshop tied to their first calculus course. Building on their skills, the workshop gives difficult work, often

beyond course content, to students with even modest preparation (some of their math SATs dip to the 300s). Working together, students soon understand that everyone knows something and nobody knows everything, and learning is speeded through shared understanding. The wisdom of these tactics is their subtext message: "You are valued in this program because of your academic potential—regardless of your current skill level. You have no more to fear than the next person, and since the work is difficult, success is a credit to your ability, and a setback is a reflection only of the challenge." The Black students' double vulnerability around failure—the fear that they lack ability, and the dread that they will be devalued—is thus reduced. They can relax and achieve.[52]

Hear the community language in the passage: *group study, working together, shared understanding.* Now at the University of Texas, Austin (home of the Longhorns), Treisman continues to take a very direct approach to building community, opening each semester of Math 408C, Differential and Integral Calculus, with a lecture filled with hopeful messages about belonging. "You're a Longhorn. You're a mathematician. You're a future leader. You're one of us."[53]

If we can adopt an equally heartfelt message for our students ("You're an Aggie, a Husky, a Nittany Lion, a Hilltopper, a Cougar, a Banana Slug. You're an engineer, a linguist, a political scientist, a graphic designer, a philosopher. You're a future leader. You're one of us.") and then commit to be there for them as Treisman has been for his students, we, too, can become legendary in our efforts to promote a sense of belonging on our campuses and in our classrooms. Treisman's pep talk doesn't shield his students from the rigorous work necessary to master calculus, and his standards don't slip downward when a student from a group that continues to face inequities shows up in class. Treisman's work clearly shows that rigorous standards and a sense of belonging are essential precursors to strength, health, and achievement.

················

CHAPTER 7

AVOID PITFALLS WITH ACTIVE LEARNING

················

All three of us are big proponents of active learning, which has been defined as "a process whereby learners deliberately take control of their own learning and construct knowledge rather than passively receiving it."[1] It's at the heart of our university's learning model. Yet, over the years, we have discovered some important pitfalls to avoid when engaging in active learning, especially when it comes to unduly creating anxiety. In this chapter, we explore some of the stress-inducing downsides of four active-learning techniques that involve student interaction: cold calling, using graded polls or quizzes in class, small-group discussions, and group projects. We then suggest some modifications to temper their emotional impacts while preserving their pedagogical benefits. We also suggest some ways teachers can engage individual students in active learning, without necessarily having them make comments in class or participate in groups.

Shift from Cold Calling to Warm Calling
···

For a certain generation, a twisted model of the Socratic method was epitomized by the erudite, impassive, intellectual snobbishness of a fictional Harvard Law School professor, Professor Kingsfield, in the 1973 film *The Paper Chase*.

Kingsfield infamously declares to students in one scene that they "come in here with a skull full of mush and leave thinking like a lawyer." The movie opens with Professor Kingsfield imperiously cold calling the film's young protagonist, who is so flummoxed by the grilling from the law professor that when the class ends, he bolts to the restroom and throws up.

Technically, such pedagogical bullying is a form of active learning. But if it were a medication, that strain of the Socratic method ought to come with a warning that side effects may include nausea and vomiting. Knowing their professor might call on them and engage them in intellectual battle at any given moment certainly creates incentive for students to prepare and be alert in class. But it does so by instilling fear. As we discuss in chapter 4, fear definitely has its distinct limitations as a source of motivation.

Rob attended law school in the late 1980s and early 1990s, in the aftermath of *The Paper Chase*. Fortunately for him, professors at his law school made a conscious effort to be more humane than Professor Kingsfield. One professor in particular stood out, with a simple twist she employed on the usual approach of cold calling. Barbara Babcock regularly let three or four students know a couple of days in advance that she would be calling on them in the next class. When she called on them, her questions were analytically rigorous and thought provoking, yet there was something slightly but profoundly different about the tone of Professor Babcock's questions: she was more intent on helping students discover their capacity than the flaws in their thinking. Rather than testing students' intellectual mettle, her unwritten goal seemed to be to help those three or four students realize that they belonged, that they could make worthy contributions to the class. And by and large, the featured students shone in each class. More importantly, they came away with an extra bounce in their step.

Of course, like all professors, Professor Babcock also called on students who raised their hands. By the end of the semester, a fascinating pattern had emerged (as well as Rob can recollect decades later): in a typical class, only about a third of students volunteered comments, but in Professor Babcock's class, it was closer to 75 or 80 percent. Even at a place like Stanford Law School, a majority of students chose not to regularly volunteer comments—except in Professor Babcock's class. Having enjoyed success making comments on their designated day, most of Professor Babcock's students gained the confidence to speak up regularly. Professor Babcock's approach illustrates the finding from one meta-analysis of classroom participation: "A supportive classroom climate is critical to higher levels of participation." Conversely, studies have shown that when professors put down students, are overly critical or sarcastic, or even just have a negative personality, students are less likely to participate.[2]

Not surprisingly, Professor Babcock's students loved her: she was awarded the John Bingham Hurlbut Award for Excellence in Teaching four times. Her simple innovation—which Rob thinks of as the "friendly hot seat"—helped her generate tremendous participation in class without generating tremendous anxiety. Babcock sensed intuitively what our surveyed students told us about how anxious a variety of teaching practices made them. They indicated that they experienced much less anxiety when being called on to make a comment in class when they had been given some time to prepare than when they were cold called—a mean of 3.11 on a scale of 1 to 7—compared to 4.88 when there was no preparation time.

A trio of biology education researchers at Arizona State University, Katelyn Cooper, Virginia Downing, and Sara Brownell, wondered how various active-learning techniques affected their students. They conducted detailed, structured interviews with fifty-two students, asking each student which active-learning techniques heightened their anxiety and which ones reduced it. Asking open-ended questions, the interviewers did not suggest any possible practices by name. Of the fifty-two students, thirty-two brought up the practice of cold calling, and all but one of them said it increased their anxiety levels.

The common theme running throughout their comments about cold calling was that students feared looking foolish in front of their peers—what psychologists call fear of negative evaluation. "Overwhelmingly, students' anxiety seemed to be rooted in a fear of negative evaluation," observed Cooper and her colleagues.[3] Feeling like they might be judged academically and found wanting—by either their professor or their peers—is a major stressor for many students. Paradoxically, that acute anxiety often clouds students' ability to think clearly, leading to the very outcome they dread: not being able to remember the correct answer or articulate a solid response in front of the class.

Cognitive load theory suggests that our limited amount of working memory capacity is divided among three activities: those that are germane (the kind we need for new learning), those that are intrinsic, and those that are extraneous—in essence, distractions. It's a zero-sum game, so the more time we spend doing things like worrying about whether we're going to get called on and what other students or the teacher will think of our answer—or, as we discuss in earlier chapters, where to find assignments—the less working memory we have to focus on the task at hand.[4] Students in the ASU study "ultimately struggled to pay attention in class because once the threat of cold call or random call was introduced, they were preoccupied with worrying about how others might perceive their intellectual capability if they were to be called on."[5]

It's precisely that cognitive quagmire that Celeste, one of the ASU students, described when she said, "My brain stops. [If the instructor] asks me a question, I have no idea what the answer is. If you were asking me in a small group, yes, I'll tell you the answer and get it. If in a large group, my brain just stops. I have no idea why." Although Celeste doesn't consciously know why, the rest of her answer gives us a pretty good idea of the reason she freezes up: "That's what I'm afraid of when getting called on in front of the whole class, getting it completely wrong, or not saying anything. . . . Not knowing the answer makes me feel anxious, makes me feel like I'm the outcast, the stupid one."[6] Lidia echoed Celeste's sentiments: "Having to speak in front of a large group of people makes me anxious. It's the fear of being wrong or sounding dumb—being embarrassed."[7]

Cooper and her coauthors noted that such feelings are consistent with what previous studies have found: students who fear being negatively evaluated tend to focus much of their cognitive energy on "a possible threat of evaluation, such as the threat of being called on in front of the whole class, and therefore, have less cognitive capacity to engage in other activities, such as thinking through a science problem."[8] The acute stress that fear of negative evaluation creates can be especially problematic when students are trying to articulate concepts: "High levels of anxiety have been predicted to be especially detrimental to learning when students are required to hold and manipulate speech-based information . . . and can prevent students from clearly articulating their thoughts in front of others."[9]

The stress of cold calling not only undermined some students' ability to think clearly in class on the days when they were asked to comment but also had a chilling effect on students voluntarily participating in and sometimes even attending future class discussions. Many of those interviewed by the ASU researchers indicated they were "less likely to want to participate in the future." That sentiment jibes with research that suggests that "if students have a negative experience in class, then their fear of negative evaluation, and consequently their anxiety, is only going to be exacerbated in future situations."[10] Another study found that while students admitted that cold calling kept them alert in class, it came at quite a cost: "frequent absences from class."[11]

On the other hand, in a 2013 study, Northeastern University professors Elise Dallimore and Marjorie Platt saw evidence that cold calling increased both the percentage of students who voluntarily participated in class discussion and the frequency with which they commented—all without increasing their discomfort with class discussion. Their robust, observational study involved 632 students in sixteen sections of a course with seven different instructors.[12] Moreover, another study found that "the frequency of a student's participation is positively associated with learning and that the participation of other students increases learning." And when teachers rely solely on voluntary participation, a relatively small percentage of students raise their hands: according to one estimate, five to eight students typically account for 75 to 95 percent of the comments in class discussion.[13]

How can the findings of the research teams led by Cooper and Dallimore be reconciled? It's entirely possible that cold calling increases overall student participation and learning while also causing consternation among a subset of students with higher levels of anxiety. It's also worth noting that all seven instructors in the study by Dallimore and Platt scored high on student evaluations on the metric of treating students with respect: "All instructors in this study were considered to provide a supportive learning environment."[14] Thus, when cold calling students, these teachers were more like Professor Babcock than Professor Kingsfield.

In fact, Dallimore and Platt make it clear that they do not argue that "any and all cold-calling by instructors would produce the same results as those shown in this study." In earlier research, they note the power of "instructional strategies used by experienced instructors to 'warm up' cold-calling so that it is effective and nonpunitive. These strategies include establishing the expectation of participation (e.g., stating expectations in the syllabus, telling students you will cold-call, cold-calling in first class), providing opportunities to reflect and respond (e.g., give them time to think and prepare, let small groups of students discuss the answer first), and creating a supportive learning environment (e.g., encourage with body language, reinforce any reasonable attempt)." Dallimore and Platt recommend gradually escalating cold calling—much like Professor Babcock did—in a way that creates "a series of successes through which a student can develop the skills to participate more substantively and the confidence to participate voluntarily."[15]

Other scholars have referred to such techniques as *warm calling*, which Harvard's School of Education calls "a less intimidating take on cold-calling in which students are given advanced warning before being called on." [16] It's entirely possible that the cold calling experienced by the ASU students was more toward the cold end of the spectrum than the warmer version the Northeastern students likely experienced. In any case, we believe a great way to preserve the benefits of cold calling while avoiding the negative side effects for students with mental health challenges is to employ warm-calling techniques that knock the rough emotional edges off cold calling.

Anytime we give students some advance notice and a chance to formulate their thoughts before requiring them to articulate those thoughts before their classmates, we are engaging in warm calling. For example, we could post a few key questions in advance of class and let students know we will be calling on some of them to answer these questions. We can invite them to engage in a think-pair-share exercise or a writing exercise before cold calling. By letting students know in advance that they would be on the hot seat, Professor Babcock was engaging in a form of warm calling, which was enhanced even more by her desire to help students succeed rather than merely to expose the flaws in their thinking.

Rob had a unique experience one year when he taught an online course that included Danielle, a student who had taken his course on campus the previous semester. In the face-to-face course, she had rarely volunteered a comment. But in the online course, she made multiple insightful comments in the discussion board every week, often citing other resources she had found. Rob asked her about the difference between her participation in the two types of classes, and her explanation was simple: she needed time to gather her thoughts before answering. In a face-to-face class discussion, she felt like the discussion always moved on before she was able to adequately formulate her thoughts. In the online discussion board, she was able not only to gather her thoughts but also to buttress them with quotes from her own research. Giving her notice provided her the time to process her thoughts, identify supporting evidence, and make important contributions to the class discussion.

Teaching via videoconferencing during the pandemic helped Rob embrace a technique he calls "ponder and post." He gives students time to reflect and write about a question and then has them post their responses on a digital blackboard. Sometimes he also asks students to peruse their classmates' responses and reply to or upvote them. Whether he wants to highlight a thought a student shared or help a reluctant student develop the capacity and confidence to participate in class, he then warm calls a few students to elaborate on what they posted. Virtually all the students contribute a written comment. Rob has noticed that when he calls on students after they have already reflected on the question and posted a comment, they are almost always willing to and quite capable of elaborating successfully on their written comments. Granted, we haven't yet done or seen the research to verify the impact of such practices, but our hunch is that warm calling techniques such as these preserve and may even enhance the benefits Dallimore and Platt noted in their cold-calling research while mitigating the negative effects Cooper and her colleagues observed in their focus groups, especially among students with higher levels of anxiety.

Warm calling has another distinct advantage over cold calling. When we ask the entire class to reflect on, write about, or discuss with a partner a question as a prelude to a general class discussion, the relative percentage of students who engage skyrockets compared to when we put a single student on the spot. This is what educational innovator Doug Lemov refers to as *ratio*—how deeply students are thinking and what percentage of students in the class are participating.[17] Warm-calling techniques tend to engage the entire class in cogitating on the question at hand. By contrast, as Northeastern's Center for Advancing Teaching and Learning through Research points out, with cold calling, "one person is singled out with a question, putting them in the position to think quickly and speak publicly while the rest of the class may or may not be also thinking as hard about the question."[18]

If we focused solely on short-term anxiety in students, we might be tempted to abandon any form of calling on students who have not volunteered. But preserving the benefits of cold calling may be important, because when we help students successfully participate in class discussion, we may well help them reduce their anxiety level in other courses where they are required to participate. We also help them develop an important skill for succeeding in most workplaces. And as Dallimore and her colleagues suggest, "The more a student practices participating in class discussions (even if via cold-calling), the more skilled the student becomes, and the more comfortable he or she becomes when using this skill."[19]

Finding ways to mine the insights of our more reluctant students can also improve the quality of classroom discussion, since research has shown that introverts tend to be particularly knowledgeable. One study tested college students on their knowledge of twenty different subjects ranging from statistics to art, and "introverts knew more than the extroverts about every single one of them."[20]

Susan Cain writes that introverts "often work more slowly and deliberately." [21] When in-class discussion with no advance notice of the questions is the only mechanism for students to hear from one another, we miss out on the important insights of students like Danielle. Consequently, giving students time to formulate their thoughts before answering a question is critical. Providing some thinking time before discussion also provides a corollary benefit to extroverts who may be quick to opine: developing the skill of being more thoughtful before speaking. Adding *think* to the beginning of a pair-and-share activity not only provides introverted students a chance to collect their thoughts before pairing up but also helps extroverted students learn the benefits of quietly pondering and organizing their thoughts before sounding off.

Another option to consider is creating ways for more students to contribute without having to orally articulate their thoughts. We've sometimes caught ourselves equating active learning with students commenting in a class-wide discussion. When we do that, we've probably succumbed to what Cain calls the "Extrovert Ideal"—the "omnipresent belief that the ideal self is gregarious, alpha, and comfortable in the spotlight" [22]—as if getting students to be able to articulate ideas coherently in front of big groups were always the ultimate aim. One simple way to help more students engage in active learning is to bust the monopoly that class discussion sometimes has in our minds on active learning. By providing a variety of methods by which students can share their thoughts, we democratize opportunities to participate.

From our perspective, the bottom line is that used wisely, kindly, and in moderation, cold calling poses much less risk to mental well-being than if used exclusively and antagonistically. As with many other strategic suggestions we offer in this book, the key here is not to abandon a potentially stress-inducing practice altogether but to provide students some scaffolding to help them succeed.

Use Graded In-Class Quizzes More Wisely

A slew of apps have made it possible for teachers to quiz students in class using their smartphones. We can see students' aggregate responses to any question we ask, automatically grade individual responses, and feed the results into a learning management system. Such tools provide powerful ways to quickly measure students' understanding in real time. And unlike asking students to simply raise their hand, the privacy of these assessments ensures that students don't change their answers to conform with other students' choices. Assessing students in the moment also enables teachers to make well-informed adjustments in our teaching, using data from the quizzes to decide whether to proceed to the next concept or to further review the current concept.

Such quick assessments also let students know when they are on track and when they need to keep studying a concept. Confirming that they actually understand a concept can reduce stress for students by removing uncertainty. As one of the ASU students who was interviewed commented, "If anything, I feel like the active-learning part reduces my anxiety. . . . The clicker questions really helped me feel like I'm getting a more complete understanding of [the material]." Even when a clicker quiz revealed that students didn't fully grasp an idea, some students found such knowledge helpful in reducing their stress. Celeste appreciated how clicker questions help "you

know what you understand and what you don't understand. . . . In traditional lecture courses, you're just given
the material, and [the instructor says,] 'I'll see you during
the test. Let's see what you get wrong or right.' " In essence,
low- or no-stakes clicker quizzes are a form of formative
feedback that reduces uncertainty and students' anxiety as
they prepare for higher-stakes assessments.

Still, the ASU student reviews of clicker use and anxiety
weren't all positive. In fact, while only six students indicated that the use of clickers decreased their anxiety, fifteen
said it increased theirs. Another five felt it both increased
and decreased their anxiety. Students who participated in
the study also completed a survey to determine their general anxiety level, and eleven of the fifty-two students had
severe levels of anxiety. Of those eleven students, seven
commented on clickers, with six of the seven indicating an
adverse effect. In short, using clickers raised the stress of a
number of students, but its impact was disproportionately
negative on students with high levels of anxiety.

Cooper and her colleagues sifted through the comments of these students and identified which aspects of
clicker use decreased anxiety and which increased it. For
example, seeing results that showed other students also
struggled to understand the same concept decreased some
students' anxiety. Having the opportunity to clarify their
understanding also reduced anxiety for some students, especially when they received points simply for completing
the quiz.

On the other hand, clickers increased anxiety under
three circumstances, which were often combined in the
responses of interviewed students. First, timed clicker
quizzes—often with deadlines that made students feel
rushed—tended to increase their anxiety and, as we

examine in chapter 3, thus interfered with their ability to learn. Lindsay explained, "Clicker questions are stressful. . . . I'm a very slow thinker. I don't know what is wrong with me, but I'm a very, very slow thinker. I'm rushed into things. Being rushed causes me anxiety."

Second, when students were awarded points based on the correctness of their answer rather than for participation, those higher stakes often compounded the anxiety induced by time pressure. Taylor articulated this source of anxiety: "If [clicker questions] are timed, it causes me to feel anxious. Because [when the question is for points], it's like I need to get something in, and I'm going to get it wrong." As with the anxiety students experience when anticipating being cold called, fear of not being able to respond with the right answer on a timed, graded clicker quiz becomes a sort of self-fulfilling prophecy.

Finally, knowing that the aggregate results of the quiz would be published and fearing that they might end up being in the incorrect minority again triggered the fear of negative evaluation. Parker explained, "If I really tried on the question and really don't understand the concept and see that on a graph, 90% of the class knows this and I'm in the 10% that got the question wrong. I guess I'm not doing great. Then especially for me, with my anxiety, it can really affect me." Lindsay had similar feelings: "I feel anxious when . . . everyone else understands [the concept], and I don't. When [the instructor] puts up that graph . . . and says 'All these people say C, and this majority says D,' or something. *I'm usually the B people.* In that moment, I'm like, 'How are people understanding it?' I feel so dumb. I don't understand how people get it, and I can't." [23]

How can we preserve the active-learning benefits of clickers while knocking off the rough edges that unnecessarily include stress? Cooper and her colleagues recommend posing a clicker question that students answer individually and then allowing them to discuss it together in groups before answering again individually. They suggest grading the first attempt only for participation and the second attempt on accuracy. They also recommend not displaying "a histogram when all but a few students selected the correct answer."[24] If lots of students didn't understand the concept, it reduces stress for students to know they're not alone. But when they see they are among the few who didn't understand the concept, students get discouraged in counterproductive ways.

We add another recommendation of our own for teachers using clickers: loosen the time limits, especially if giving points for accuracy. Aggressive time limits can enhance the pressure students feel, creating the kind of acute stress that impairs working memory. Thus, giving graded quizzes with a relatively short period of time for answering creates a less than ideal learning environment. Megan articulated how some students feel under those circumstances: "When I feel anxious, it's almost that I can't solve the problem or answer the question clear-mindedly because I'm so scattered and worried about getting my answer in on time. . . . I can't think clearly . . . because I'm so worried about getting my points that day that I feel that I don't know. I'm not always having the clearest mind."[25] Ultimately, with timed quizzes we may be measuring students' ability to perform well under pressure rather than their mastery of a concept. But when we use in-class quizzes without unduly rushing students, these assessments can be powerful tools for gauging student understanding and focusing discussion and follow-up instruction.

Make Small-Group Discussions More Fruitful and Less Stressful

Cooper and her colleagues acknowledge multiple studies showing benefits of students working together during class in small groups. These include helping students achieve more through collaboration and allowing them to hear diverse viewpoints. However, their focus groups with students demonstrate that small groups are not without their risks, especially for students with mental health challenges. Of the thirty-six students who mentioned small-group discussions affecting their level of anxiety, they were almost perfectly split on how it affects their anxiety. Fifteen students said small-group discussions reduced their anxiety, but sixteen students said it increased their anxiety. Another five felt it both increased and decreased their anxiety.

At first glance, such results appear to suggest only that small groups work better for some students than others, and that's certainly a possibility. But as Cooper and her colleagues scrutinized the comments students made, some common threads emerged. Students generally indicated that working together in groups in class reduced stress when it confirmed what they did or didn't know or helped them clarify their understanding. It also reduced anxiety when they could see that other students were also struggling with concepts. Getting along with their partner or others in the group also decreased anxiety.

Felicia appreciated the way peers explained scientific concepts in terms she could understand: "The professor might be not saying it in 'English,' but your classmate might say it in 'English,' so for sure, definitely the active learning style was so helpful in decreasing my anxiety."

Antoinette said that when she doesn't understand something the professor said, her anxiety "comes down when
I talk to the students around me. Then we talk about the
concept, then I'm like, 'Okay. I understand this. It's not
that hard.' . . . I really like group work, to be honest, just
because we all just teach each other, that helps a lot."

It was also easier for students to clarify misunder-
standings and get customized explanations in these small
groups. Quinn said that discussing science helped lower
his anxiety quite a bit, "because once you get the input of
other people, even if you are wrong, it does change your
answer, and you're like, 'I can see how they got there or
why they got there.' . . . Then you feel extra good because
you're like, 'I can recognize what I don't know and what I
do know.' "

Yet here's where things get a bit complicated. As helpful
as having small groups discuss quiz questions right after
taking a clicker quiz can be, the threat of negative evaluation—the fear of feeling judged academically—fuels anxiety for many students. In particular, when students had
just answered a quiz question in a biology class—a question
with definite right and wrong answers—and they were one
of a few students who got the wrong answer, some felt negatively evaluated. "If I realize that I answered a question
wrong when talking with people in my group, it makes
my anxiety a little worse," explained Craig, another ASU
student. "I'm sitting there thinking, 'Oh man, the person
next to me probably thinks I'm dumb because I just shared
with him the wrong idea.' " Other students echoed his
concern.

It's quite possible that this particular challenge is
more prevalent in STEM classes, where the subject of the

small-group discussion is often about questions that have incorrect and correct answers. In the social sciences and the arts, groups might be more likely to explore questions that can be answered fruitfully from a variety of perspectives, making it less likely that a student will ever have a demonstrably "incorrect" answer, let alone have it known that they were among only 13 percent of students in the class who chose the incorrect answer.

Still, in any small-group discussion, some students may worry about how others perceive them. "In active learning I worry, 'What are [other students] going to think of me?'" admitted Alana. Parker ruminates over what he says in small-group discussions: "[My anxiety during group work] goes back to the central theme of being judged. Some things I'll say will keep me awake at night. It's like, 'Did I overshare? Did I not talk enough?'" Students working together in groups also experienced more anxiety when they struggled to get along with others in their group. Rodger shared this fear: "I think a lot of the anxiety in classes comes from the people around you—trying to find someone that you're comfortable with or can talk to."

Cooper and her colleagues suggest counterbalancing the problem of students feeling more anxiety when they don't get along well with their partners by letting students choose their own working groups. Studies have shown that doing so can reduce anxiety for students generally and especially reduce anxiety for female and LGBT+ students.[26] As students get to know one another better, it seems likely that they feel less stress. Noted one student in the study, "I feel less uncomfortable bouncing ideas off of [my friend in class], because I guess when you say something to someone, and it's the first thing you've ever said to them, it's like a big impact. It makes a big impression, or it feels that way. Whereas, [my friend] has known me for a year, so I feel like even if I say something stupid, she still knows that I'm smart."

However, other students have seen some benefits from instructors assigning groups to distribute academic strength and other qualities. The students we interviewed weren't especially anxious about participating in small-group discussions in class, but those we surveyed much preferred for professors to assign their groups, experiencing anxiety at a mean of 4.25 on a scale of 1 to 7 when they had to choose their own groups, compared to 2.91 when the professor assigned the groups. Perhaps some students dread the higher education equivalent of the childhood nightmare of being the last person chosen for a team—or the adolescent nightmare of asking someone out, only to be told no.

When professors do assign groups for our students, there's no clear consensus on the best method. One issue to weigh as we seek to create diverse groups is that when some students find themselves as the only member of a particular identity in their group, it can adversely affect their influence and willingness to participate in the group. For example, a multiyear study of undergraduate accountant students found that when randomly assigned groups of five included only one woman, she spoke far less than her proportionate amount of time. In fact, only in groups with a female supermajority did women speak a proportionate share of the time.[27]

According to the surveyed students, participating in the same group throughout the semester is even less stressful, with a mean response of only 2.57. Trisha, a student in one of our focus groups who describes herself as an introvert and also has anxiety and depression, explained, "If you work with the same group every time, I think that sometimes that can help you because you kind of start to get to know each other . . . because group work can be kind of awkward at first. Nobody wants to look up, because we don't know each other. . . . [W]hen you know the people that you're working with, group work can be a lot more successful." In addition, the fear of getting a wrong answer or saying something embarrassing is much more stressful when interacting with a brand-new group of peers each class than when talking with classmates you have built up some rapport with over the course of the semester.

Even if teachers choose to use different groups each time, Cooper and company recommend "allowing students to have sufficient time at the beginning of class to introduce themselves and try to quickly establish a level of comfort with each other."[28] And regardless of how the group is created, teachers can also share some basic ground rules about how to share ideas respectfully, which further reduces anxiety.[29]

In sum, small-group discussions have great potential to increase learning and decrease anxiety in the process. But some students may struggle with fear of negative evaluation. By establishing continuity in groups, we can diminish that risk. When students participate in the same small group over time, it gives them a chance to develop relationships with the same students and become more comfortable interacting with them. Finally, as teachers become more mindful of students' fear of negative evaluation, we can provide valuable coaching to students as they embark on small-group discussions.

Take Some of the Anxiety out of Group-Based Assignments

Having students work together on assignments in groups—
or better yet, in teams—is one of the best ways we can help
students develop critical collaborative skills they will need
in the workplace. Done poorly, however, it's also a surefire
way to frustrate students and heighten their anxiety.

BYU-Idaho has engaged fairly extensively in online
learning since at least 2009, offering courses both to our
campus-based students and to students living in over
one hundred countries. From the outset, a critical component of our online courses has been to engage students in
teaching and collaborating with one another. However, in
the early years, despite many positive student comments
about group-based assignments, a few common concerns
emerged. According to Peter Williams, an administrator
for the online team who participated in the online team's
analysis of the challenges, students had three principal
sources of frustration: difficulty in coordinating schedules
to meet (especially with students who worked during the
day and lived in time zones across the globe), disorganiza-
tion within groups, and frustration with a lack of individual accountability for freeloaders. On campus, Steve and
Rob noticed these same issues in a group assignment that
students completed in their Pakistan course.

In our focus groups with students who experience anxiety or depression, participants echoed these frustrations.
One young woman whose principal mental health challenge was anxiety said she'd never had a positive experience with group projects. "It always seems so stressful to
me because your grade is based off of everyone's efforts."
Her experience was that every group had freeloaders, and
she found herself focusing on whether they would deliver

on their portion of the project. Just as cognitive load theory would predict, she said, "Emotionally, it makes the project a lot harder than it needs to be because instead of just worrying about the project, you end up worrying about others' efforts too."

While this student's teachers had often promised to dock the points of team members who did not do their part, she said they rarely did. Consequently, even before she begins work on a group project, she finds that the anticipation about such team dynamics increases her anxiety. On the other hand, another young man who agreed with this perspective said that he had taken a class where the professor had devised an effective mechanism for holding every member of a team accountable. The professor's method resulted in everyone on the team contributing, which was "such a huge relief of the anxiety."

For either face-to-face or online learning, the solution is the same: provide some scaffolding. STEM professors Jeremy Hsu and Gregory Goldsmith point out that "instructors may be able to lower student stress by assigning roles for students in groups; providing clear expectations with specific goals, objectives, and deadlines; and structuring activities so that students bring different pieces of expertise to the project."[30] When creating groups in a class, teachers might have students sign up for their groups by time slot, asking them to choose a group scheduled to meet at a time that works for them. Similarly, we can create rubrics for grading group work that include individual performance as a key component, perhaps even creating a mechanism by which students hold each other accountable for their efforts. Another issue is that students often need help getting organized initially, or they flounder even before getting their team off the ground. Yunjeong

Chang and Peggy Brickman suggest another critical component for ensuring individual accountability from the outset: "Peer evaluations have been shown to reduce the incidence of free riding and to improve student attitudes toward groups and group projects if they are done early and frequently."[31]

Once we made such changes in our Pakistan course, including an opportunity for students to evaluate one another, it changed their behavior—and, we suspect, reduced stress—considerably. Brian Felt, one of our colleagues on that teaching team who created these mechanisms, explains, "Including this 'freeloader' mitigation system in the assignment's rubric helped our students feel confident and less stressed as they worked on their group projects. This was especially true for those students who had experienced group assignments where their grade had suffered due to others' lack of contribution. Our students knew that if they did their part and worked with the group, their ultimate grade would reflect their contributions."

Actively Learning Alone

As we consider less stressful alternatives to some traditional active-learning techniques, it might be useful to broaden our understanding of what those may include. While discussion and group work are important tools for active learning, many others are available to us. If we use only class discussion and groupwork or teamwork for engaging students in active learning, consider the constant psychological strain that creates for students who naturally prefer working independently. The very act of producing this book has required a combination of solo and collaborative work. Both were necessary—and both involved active learning.

Cain reminds us that "solitude can be a catalyst to innovation." She argues persuasively that neither "$E = mc^2$ nor *Paradise Lost* was dashed off by a party animal."[32] While working in solitude may come naturally to introverts, it's an acquired taste for others—or at least a taste Cain argues we should acquire: "If solitude is an important key to creativity[,] then we might all want to develop a taste for it." She fears that we have "come to overvalue *all* group work at the expense of solo thought."[33] Maybe college teachers can play some part in righting the balance. Just as it is important for us to provide scaffolding that helps our quieter students develop the capacity to articulate their thoughts, we can also provide scaffolding that helps our extroverted students develop the capacity to quietly think while relieving a bit of the sometimes unrelenting emotional pressure on introverted students to make comments in class or collaborate in groups. Simply replacing a few of our pair-and-share or small-group discussions with a ponder-and-post activity can create a healthier tactical mix.

Incidentally, we are not suggesting that introverts are more prone to having problems with mental health. However, it seems fairly safe to assume that when the only outlet we allow for student contributions to the class is through comments made to groups or the whole class, introverts are more likely to experience higher levels of stress. As we level the playing field by providing multiple avenues for active learning and participation, we create opportunities for introverted students to shine. Perhaps doing so can help undo a little of the societal infatuation with the Extrovert Ideal that Cain laments, since "the bias against quiet can cause deep psychic pain."[34] Finally, because those of us who aren't naturally introverts may not realize just how much anxiety some of our activities might create for those who are, it's all the more important for ex-troverted professors to be intentional—to step back and consider what kind of stress a tactic or assignment might create for students who are much less outgoing than we are by nature.

Conclusion

Even though it can create undue anxiety when implemented poorly, active learning has well-documented benefits in help-ing students gain and retain new knowledge. Thus, as the three of us conduct pedagogical-psychological cost-benefit analyses for active learning techniques, we're definitely bi-ased toward finding adjustments that allow us to preserve their benefits while minimizing their negative emotional im-pact on students—because active learning works. To aban-don such techniques altogether because some versions of them increase anxiety would be to throw out the pedagogi-cally beautiful baby with the psychologically dirty bathwater. The key is to choose the most appropriate active-learning practices or to find ways to temper the anxiety-inducing as-pects of certain active-learning practices.

Being intentional about how we approach active learn-ing can help us preserve its benefits while reducing its psychological disadvantages. We can begin by shifting from cold calling to warm calling, looking for ways to help students succeed when they raise their hands, especially early on. Techniques such as providing students with notice of our questions and an opportunity to reflect on them and even research them briefly can improve both the quality and breadth of class participation. If teachers avoid using in-class quizzes with tight timelines and lowering the stakes of such quizzes, we can eliminate some of the anxiety-inducing aspects of small-group discussions. And providing some scaffolding for group projects can reduce floundering, freeloading, uncertainty, and anticipatory anxiety—all while improving both the work process and the work product.

CHAPTER 8

....

PROMOTE WELLNESS PRACTICES

....

John was late—*again*. When he finally slipped into his seat during calculus class, he laid his head down in his arms and did not look up for another twenty minutes. Was he asleep? He didn't start snoring, so Bonnie wasn't certain. After class, she caught up with him and asked how things were going. John told her that he'd been up all night working on a computer program for another class. His programming class was keeping him up into the early morning hours, and it was starting to take a toll on his other courses. He explained with frustration—even sadness—that the help lab for his programming class was never open when he was free. John spent hours at night creating code that would not run, and he was getting more and more discouraged.

As the semester wore on, John started to look more disheveled, until he finally dropped Bonnie's calculus class. She wanted to call his programming teacher to see what was going on with the assignments giving John so much trouble. Was John just unprepared for the course? Was he unaware of resources he could have used to help him through this homework? Bonnie started to wonder if her own students could be going through similar obstacles with the homework she assigned. Did she have the resources in place to give them the help they needed when they needed it? Were they, too, sacrificing their sleep and well-being to get through her class?

At the beginning of a semester, we often see students bright eyed and ready to learn. However, as the workload increases and students strive to balance the many demands on their time, some students lose their enthusiasm. Additionally, students may even neglect self-care as they ignore sleep and exercise to meet deadlines. For a student like John in the thick of a challenging semester, reminders of the importance of getting enough sleep, eating well, connecting with nature, and exercising might seem laughably out of touch. Yet wellness practices like these can be key to academic success as they provide a means for students to successfully handle the stress and pressures of college. Such wellness practices can also play an important role in avoiding difficulties with mental health, or at least making them more manageable. In our role as teachers, we can connect our students to practices that promote wellness by making a few intentional tweaks to our classroom discussions, assignments, and curriculum. Such practices can not only help reduce the incidence of depression and anxiety among students but also nudge students—wherever they are now—closer to the wellness end of that spectrum.

How do we keep our students and ourselves from feeling overwhelmed as we strive to adopt wellness practices into our busy lives? With schoolwork and financial concerns, adding wellness habits may not be a priority. One student in our focus group emphasized the importance of just getting started. "It doesn't have to be like I have to exercise for this amount of time. I don't stress out about having to get a certain amount of time in every day. It can even be as short as five minutes. Even that gives me the boost of energy I need. . . . It can also impact my sleep as well. I fall asleep quicker. I sleep longer. . . . I'm more ready for the next day."

The idea of starting small was reinforced by Kristie Lords, the student well-being managing director at BYU-Idaho. She shares that when she started getting back into exercise, she had to be willing to be bad at it. Kristie says, "Once we allow ourselves to be bad at something, we actually free our inhibitions and start to see small success. If we can admit we are bad at exercise (or at eating vegetables, at math, etc.) and just do it anyway, we have started down the path to achievement." It's the regular everyday practice—running three miles or for just five minutes—that makes the difference. This pattern of accepting imperfection and moving forward with small steps can be applied to every other activity our students engage in. The repetition produces the change. As professors, we can apply this principle as we seek for manageable ways to promote wellness in our courses and our own lives.

Theoretical Framework

In this chapter we explore the theoretical underpinnings and research relating to wellness, followed by a few practical ideas to work into courses to support our students' well-being. As we sought to identify practices that promote wellness, we found a growing body of books, articles, and research emphasizing a number of wellness principles that have been shown to mitigate mental health challenges and enhance well-being. We also scoured wellness information on college and university websites to identify the wellness practices they promoted. From all this, we selected the five wellness areas that appear to have the greatest impact for college students: sleep, diet, exercise, mindfulness, and nature. Connection and purpose are also very important wellness principles, but we've already covered these topics elsewhere in the book.

Sleep

Having gone without sleep a few times in our lives, we wholeheartedly appreciate the connection between good sleep and a positive outlook on life. Many psychologists have weighed in on the connection between sufficient sleep and mental health. Sarah Rose Cavanagh states that people who are better rested perform better on almost "any measure you can throw at them—from tasks of physical performance to mental acuity to the affective states they both feel and project outward."[1] Sleep impacts overall well-being, which in turn can affect academic performance. The lack of sleep diminishes academic performance and strains a student's overall well-being. Short sleep duration and poor sleep quality often have a negative influence on GPA.[2]

Patterns of sleep can play as important a role in wellness as sleep duration. Research has shown that consistent, high-quality sleep is correlated with improved academic performance, higher GPA, better student recall, and increased student retention.[3] Consistent sleep patterns also improve mood and well-being.[4] Thus, not only is getting enough sleep important for well-being, but a consistent pattern for sleeping also improves physical and mental health performance. In fact, one 2019 study of college students found that "sleep measures accounted for nearly 25% of the variance in academic performance."[5]

In *The Depression Cure*, clinical psychology professor Stephen Ilardi argues that adequate sleep is vital for both physical and mental well-being. He explains that it takes only a few nights of deprivation before "adverse effects start piling up: memory and concentration wane; mood turns irritable; judgment grows poor; reaction times slow; coordination deteriorates; energy dims and immune function declines." Moreover, "disordered sleep . . . plays a major role in triggering" depression.[6] On the other hand, anything we can do to improve our sleep can combat depression and act as a protective factor against it.

Where better to find a plethora of sleep-deprived individuals than on a medical floor full of future doctors? One observational study of almost eight hundred medical students found that sleep deprivation can cause depression, agitation, apathy, and poor academic performance.[7] Our own focus groups revealed similar findings. When asked how sleep affects their well-being, many of the students said that lack of sleep often makes their depression worse and makes it harder to deal with everyday stresses.

One of our colleagues sees firsthand the impact improved sleep has on his students. This professor sets aside a small percentage of the overall points in his class to account for a weekly wellness challenge. Students choose their own goal relating to wellness practices, such as sleep and others discussed in this chapter, and they account for how they did in a self-graded quiz each week. After just a week, several students who chose to improve their sleep shared these insights:

- "I felt more energized and happy. I've always been passionate towards exercising and nutrition; however, my sleep schedule is not always the best. This week I have been getting a minimum of eight hours of sleep, and I feel so much more awake and ready to 'take on the day.' "
- "I felt like the less sleep that I got, the more angry I was

around other people. When I got more sleep, I was able to focus more in school and able to do better in almost everything."

- "My goal this week was to get eight hours of sleep, and when I met my goal, I noticed the next day my level of energy and motivation was much higher and it made me more productive with my schoolwork."

Clearly, adequate and consistent sleep promotes wellness and health.

Diet

Along with sleep, food choices also impact overall wellness. Our friend and colleague Rachel Huber reflected on how her imbalanced diet in addition to her unusual sleeping habits jeopardized her physical and mental health as a young college student:

When I started my freshman year of college, my diet consisted mainly of carrots and diet soda. I had body image and food issues left over from my teen years, and this was the result. In addition, being a very diligent student, I kept odd hours. I would usually go to bed before anyone else in my apartment and get up about 2 a.m. to study. Lack of sleep and poor nutrition thus became my norm.

Not surprisingly, by midway through the semester, my mind began doing strange things, jumping from one idea to another, and it seemed like I had no control over my thoughts. I was unable to concentrate. In addition, my skin turned orange from all the beta-carotene in the carrots. I looked like I'd had a bad experience with a spray-on tan. I had always taken my mental and physical health for granted and had never associated health with nutrition. In addition, I am a very private person, and didn't want to talk to anyone about how I was feeling. But I was *really* scared because I thought I was losing my mind.

One afternoon, as I sat outside with my boyfriend, I blurted it all out. He probably wanted to say, "Duh! You don't eat and rarely sleep. Of course, you are falling apart." But he was more kind than that. He simply said, "I have read studies on people in the military, and when they don't have a balanced diet and don't get enough sleep, they quickly lose their ability to concentrate. Let's go get something to eat. And then maybe you should take a nap." I'm so grateful that I opened up to him and that he knew enough to steer me in a healthy direction.[8]

As our friend Rachel learned, diet and nutrition play critical roles in mental health. One recent study confirms that diet significantly influences mood, mental health, and well-being. While the study's authors recognize the complex task of trying to precisely identify all the factors that contribute to mental health, evidence indicates a strong association between a poor diet and the exacerbation of mood disorders, including depression and anxiety, as well as other neuropsychiatric conditions.[9]

Conversely, an improved diet may lead to improved mental health. One meta-analysis associates a healthy dietary pattern with a decreased risk of depression.[10] Diets high in fruit, vegetables, whole grain, fish, olive oil, low-fat dairy, and antioxidants are associated with a decreased risk of depression. This diet reflects similar eating patterns suggested for lowering the risk of heart disease and cancer. Can the same type of diet also affect mental health in a positive way? While acknowledging that additional randomized trials are needed, these researchers believe it can.

Many students in our focus groups pointed out that their diets often influence their moods and mental wellness. One student shared, "When I'm eating the way I'm supposed to, everything is better. My body works better. My mind works better. I feel better about myself in general." Monique Tello, a practicing physician and clinical instructor at Harvard Medical School, echoes this sentiment: "I am passionate about diet and lifestyle measures for good health, because there is overwhelming evidence supporting the benefits of a healthy diet and lifestyle for, oh, just about everything: preventing cardiovascular disease, cancer, dementia, and mental health disorders, including depression." [11] Healthy eating choices not only contribute to overall physical health, but nourishing choices can also promote balanced emotional and mental health. [12]

Exercise

It's hard to overstate the benefits of exercise on mental health. One of our friends experienced the healing effect of exercise in a very real way. For the sake of anonymity, we'll call her Pam. Within a short period of time, Pam experienced both a painful divorce and the untimely death of her son in a car accident. Suffocating darkness enveloped her, threatening to swallow her up. Despair and depression became constant companions. In this time of darkness, the one thing that kept her afloat was running. Pam ran and ran. Her daily workouts became her relief, her solace, the only place she felt she had control. Running brought back her hope, her perspective, and even her life.

Pam's story suggests that a good cardio workout may be

more than just invigorating and refreshing. Could it also be healing and mentally restorative? Research shows that aerobic exercise can reduce anxiety and depression. Exercise promotes blood flow, which in turn promotes psychological influences on the brain that help control motivation, mood, and other important factors that contribute to a sense of positive overall well-being.[13]

A 2008 report on exercise from the US Department of Health and Human Services concluded that "physical activity can protect against feelings of distress, enhance psychological well-being, protect against symptoms of anxiety and development of anxiety disorders, protect against depressive symptoms and development of major depressive disorder, and delay the effects of dementia and the cognitive decline associated with aging."[14] Ilardi claims that even small amounts of exercise—just "thirty minutes of brisk walking three times a week"—can actually help some patients with depression do just as well as those on medication. In fact, he argues, exercise changes the brain. "It increases the activity level of important brain chemicals such as dopamine and serotonin (the same neurochemicals targeted by popular drugs like Zoloft, Prozac, and Lexapro)."[15] He states that many of us see the direct benefits of exercise on our physical health, yet it is just as important for "preserving mental health."[16] Exercise is medicine.

Unfortunately, few of our students are taking advantage of this free medicine. Just over 30 percent of students we surveyed indicated that they hadn't exercised moderately to vigorously for 30 minutes even once in the last month. And about 24 percent reported working out only one day a week. Basically, more than half of the students surveyed were working out one day a week or not at all. Only a small minority—just over 16 percent—reported working out five to seven days a week. We can change this by starting small—even exercising just ten minutes a day to begin. We'll discuss a few ways we can invite our students to start exercising in the practical section of this chapter.

Mindfulness

In recent years, a growing body of literature has advocated another important wellness practice—mindfulness, or being present in the moment. In fact, there is an entire branch of positive psychology focused on improving health and happiness through mindful meditation.[17]

One purpose of mindfulness is to help practitioners live in the present rather than ruminating on things beyond their control in the past or future. Rumination is a fixation strongly linked to both causing and perpetuating depression and anxiety. When we ruminate, we replay a thought repeatedly in our minds, almost like driftwood churning around and around in an eddy. The object of rumination may be an interaction from the past or anticipation of what could happen tomorrow. Bonnie remembers cleaning out her son's room after he left for college. She thought it would be an uplifting experience to savor cherished memories as she sorted through his possessions. It wasn't. While every piece of his clothing, every award he had won, and every picture on the wall did lead her to the past, they also led to a sadness and longing that triggered deep depression and withdrawal. The ancient Chinese philosopher and writer Lao Tzu reportedly said, "If you are depressed, you are living in the past. If you are anxious, you are living in the future. If you are at peace, you are living in the present." Mindfulness promotes living in the present and finding peace there.

The literature suggests two general approaches to using mindfulness to avoid or overcome depression. The first is to practice simple meditation, using basic activities such as sitting for thirty to sixty seconds and paying attention to your own breathing. A student in one of our focus groups explained how a simple breathing exercise can help her focus on the present: "With my anxiety, it is hard for me to be present in the moment. So mindfulness helps me get present. . . . Just taking a moment to do breathing exercises can help. I can even just do a breathing exercise in class, and that helps calm down my body. My thoughts become more peaceful." A second mindfulness technique is tackling rumination by keeping the mind actively engaged. Ilardi suggests that people typically ruminate—and feel the worst—when they have nothing else to occupy their attention. The single biggest risk factor in rumination is simply spending time alone.[18] Employing both techniques in the classroom—meditation followed by intense engagement—may be the most effective approach.

Sunlight and Nature

One day during her junior year at college, Bonnie found herself resting on freshly cut grass under the blue sky. She breathed in the sweet air and just took a moment to be. Usually when she was outside, she was running from building to building to get to class on time, then on to the library or her apartment to study. There was no time for relaxing on campus. But this day, her English professor had cut his official lecture short and then split up the class into small groups. He gave each group a poem to analyze and then sent everyone outside to discuss it. This small anecdote is one of

Bonnie's favorite memories of her undergraduate education. Why? Because it was so simple. Looking back now, she can see that it was a change in the routine of her day. She was in the sun—soaking in the natural light that she rarely took time to enjoy.

Research shows that time in nature has a rejuvenating effect on attention and can relieve stress. It can also promote student self-motivation, enjoyment, and engagement.[19] Bonnie felt all of those on that day in the sun. According to an interdisciplinary Cornell University team, as little as ten minutes in a natural setting can help college students feel happier and lessen the effects of both physical and mental stress.[20] "There is mounting empirical evidence that interacting with nature delivers measurable benefits to people."[21]

Research in a growing scientific field called ecotherapy has also shown a strong connection between time spent in nature and reduced stress,[22] and Ilardi argues that sunlight can promote a positive outlook and can even turn a dark mood around. Sunlight can also reset the body clock and promote healthy sleep. He writes, "Bright light stimulates the brain's production of serotonin,"[23] which has widespread effects on mood and behavior. Thus, bright light boosts feelings of well-being. Some of our focus group students also agree. One said, "When I'm stuck inside with all the walls and barriers it is easier for me to start ruminating. You forget about the beauty in the world. Getting outside helps me to get fresh air . . . [and] is very calming." Another student shared, "Getting outside helps me see the big picture. When I'm inside my apartment, I'm just inside my head. I don't realize there is a whole life outside. Outside, the fresh air and the sunshine just help."

Practical Application

Having reviewed the research and some experiences with the positive effects of regular sleep, healthy diet, exercise, meditation, and time in nature, we now look at some small and simple ways teachers can invite students to add these practices to their lives. How do we do this without over-whelming ourselves or our students? The next sections offer a few ideas for you to consider. We encourage you to begin by trying just one or two.

Talk the Walk, and Walk the Talk

Research has shown that students' values can be influenced by those of their professors.[24] If they know that we think busy, successful people just don't have time for exercise, they may adopt that same attitude. However, if they learn how we overcame reservations about Idaho's cold winters and learned to embrace them by cross-country skiing, they may choose to bundle up and enjoy the wonders of exercising in nature themselves. As we intentionally share subtle plugs for getting enough sleep, eating well, exercising, enjoying sunlight and nature, and being mindful, we just may spark some positive lifestyle changes in some of our students. In particular, as we help them understand the emotional and cognitive benefits of such practices, we invite our students to rethink some of their routines.

Developing our own wellness habits has the dual ben-efit of helping us cope with our stressors while giving us credibility when encouraging our students to adopt these practices. Of course, few of us have ideal habits in each of the five areas. But trying to make even modest progress in an area may inspire students who also struggle to make efforts to improve. For example, a professor who has rarely exercised but decides to start taking a short walk each day may do more to motivate students to exercise than a professor who prattles on about training for an upcoming marathon. When we let students see both our weaknesses and our attempts to improve, the vulnerability can promote more personal connections as we model a growth mindset.

You can also promote balance and sleep by modeling healthy sleep practices yourself rather than answering emails at all hours of the night. Consider setting a time each day when you stop answering emails. You could even let students know that you will answer emails in a consistent window every day, promising to always reply within twenty-four hours. In doing so, you would be modeling the kind of time management that helps create balance in your own life and invites students to do the same.

Another one of our colleagues at BYU-Idaho, psychology professor Rob Wright, conducted an experiment in which students were encouraged to exercise more, sleep more, or eat more fruits and vegetables. In the six weeks of the study, students improved their overall wellness significantly more than students in the control group, who were not given any of the intervention materials—including an assignment to work on a goal for one of these behaviors.[25] Unfortunately, Wright's follow-up research showed that most students failed to sustain these changes once the scaffolding and support of the experiment and the class were withdrawn. This experiment illustrates the importance of shifting mindsets for sustained change as we work to alter our behavior. Most other pedagogical practices we recommend elsewhere in the book can be implemented successfully even if you're the only one at your institution who adopts them. But for promoting wellness practices, broader institutional efforts and a shift in culture may be required to help students make lasting changes. You can be part of this cultural shift by making some small tweaks to your course and intentionally promoting wellness with your students.

What are some small yet significant ways you can promote wellness in your courses? One option is to share thoughts like this one by the author of *The Power of Habit: Why We Do What We Do in Life and Business*, Charles Duhigg: "When people start habitually exercising, even as infrequently as once a week, they start changing other, unrelated patterns in their lives, often unknowingly. Typically, people who exercise start eating better and becoming more productive at work. They smoke less and show more patience with colleagues and family. They use their credit cards less frequently and say they feel less stressed. It's not completely clear why. But for many people, exercise is a keystone habit that triggers widespread change." [26]

Even more powerful than sharing the quote above would be to share an experience with one of the wellness practices you have implemented in your own life. For example, you might talk about and show a photo of a beautiful hike you went on over the weekend. When her students are struggling with difficult and new mathematical concepts, one of our math colleagues often shares a relevant graduate school experience. She had been struggling to finish a proof to a theorem she needed to complete her thesis. After much frustration and little progress, she was exhausted and mentally spent. She decided to go to bed. The next morning, she woke up early and went on her morning run. As she took in the fresh air and got her blood pumping, the missing piece of the theorem started to form in her mind.

She was surprised because she hadn't even been thinking about the theorem. Rest, fresh air, and exercise had all contributed to her being able to work through the problem in a refreshed state of mind.

One way Rob brings sunlight and the benefits of nature to his students is to meet them for office hours (which he now calls "student hours") at some beautiful gardens on campus. In doing this, he accomplishes multiple purposes. First, he gets to enjoy some time outside in the sun for himself. Second, he introduces many students—especially first-year students—to a natural sanctuary on campus, filled with flowers, trees, and fountains. Third, he mentions that he loves to spend a few minutes in the gardens whenever he can because it helps him deal with his own stress. That admission not only hints at this wellness technique, but it also reveals that Rob himself experiences stress and must do some things to regulate his emotions, which helps to destigmatize these challenges. Finally, students seem more willing to open up as they walk through the gardens than when they sit in Rob's office. As students not only hear us talk the walk but see us walk the talk, they will feel our authenticity and more likely believe that these practices can enhance their own well-being and college experience.

Create Dual-Purpose Assignments

We are not suggesting that every teacher try to promote each wellness principle in every course. And finding ways to nudge students to adopt any of these practices may be more difficult in some courses than others. But if teachers think creatively, no matter what our discipline, we can often find some way to link at least one of these practices to our course content, perhaps even in compelling experiential-learning ways.

In many disciplines, teachers need contexts in which to apply or transfer the concepts we are teaching. Writing classes need subjects to write about, language classes need topics to speak about, statistics classes need real-life data to analyze, and chemistry classes need opportunities to show the impact of chemistry in our lives. In many situations, teachers can have a two-fold influence on students simply by using the skills of their discipline to help students discover some of what researchers have already learned about the power of these wellness principles. Here are a few examples:

- A teacher in a nutrition course gives students a weekly wellness challenge, inviting students to set a concrete goal for eating more nutritiously each week and then requiring them to account for how they did in a weekly quiz.
- Students in a statistics course review the statistical analysis in any of the plethora of journal articles about the interaction between sleep and cognitive performance—or better yet, they analyze fresh data to determine whether there is a statistically significant relationship between the amount of sleep students get and their academic performance or mental health.
- Biology or chemistry students analyze the impact of high-intensity interval training on the body's metabolism.
- In a sociology course, students examine societal exercise trends and the kinds of factors that lead to a population exercising less or more.
- In a music class, a teacher discusses the work-enhancing benefits of listening to music during exercise or meditation.[27]

- Computer science students partner with psychology students to develop an application designed to help people exercise more.
- Students in an anatomy and physiology course conduct a short research project explaining how and why the way we eat, exercise, or sleep affects the way we feel.
- Psychology students do a research project examining the relationship between mindfulness and mental health.
- In a speech class, students give an oral presentation about some aspect of a wellness topic of their choice.
- Students in a social media class design a campaign promoting one wellness technique.
- Students in an English composition class complete one writing assignment while sitting somewhere outside in peaceful surroundings. In class, the teacher leads a brief discussion about how writing in that environment affected their creativity.
- A professor in a writing class assigns a creative writing assignment from two perspectives—one where the main character has had two hours of sleep the night before and another where the same character has had eight hours. How does the amount of sleep influence how the protagonist sees the world?

We can also change up a routine assignment to give our students a well-deserved break while also inviting them to rejuvenate. Every week, Bonnie's differential equation students take an individual checkpoint quiz to see how they are doing on the week's objectives. In the eighth week of the semester—when students traditionally hit a wall— she changes up the quiz. The first five questions assess mathematical outcomes from the week. The last five-point question reads, "Taking time to reconnect with nature can actually invite balance to your life and clarity to your mind. Thus, please choose an activity from the following options, and then write a 3–5 sentence paragraph describing your experience. Take at least 20 minutes to enjoy this activity in nature."

1. Take a stroll in a nearby park or in the gardens on campus. Take time to enjoy the intricacies of a leaf on a tree or the designs in a cloud, etc.
2. If you have a garden, take time to water it, weed it, and just enjoy the feel of the dirt and spray of the water.
3. Play with a pet outside.
4. Sit by the water. Find a nearby stream or a water fountain, and just enjoy the sound of the gurgling/splashing/movement of the water. Take note of the blessings in your life and list what you are thankful for.
5. Find out what fruits are in season. Purchase one of these fruits, and enjoy eating it outside at the park, in the gardens on campus, or somewhere beautiful outside.
6. You choose an outside activity in nature, and tell us what you did.

   Many of the students expressed their appreciation for this assignment and did find some time to reconnect with nature and reduce their stress. One student mentioned, "For this activity I went on a walk through the Ricks Gardens. I found this activity to be more than just peaceful, but also rejuvenating. By getting away from everything that was giving me stress, I was able to collect myself and bring peace to my troubled mind. I really liked this activity and will look for ways to do activities like this when I am feeling stressed or need to get away from schoolwork for a bit." Many of the other comments echoed this student's feelings. The assignment was simple. It did not take Bonnie long to implement, and her students recognized that spending time in nature is one way to help them regulate their stress while tackling a college workload.

As students discover the significance of each of these wellness areas for themselves through experience, research, analysis, and writing, they are invited to increase awareness of their own habits and be more likely to implement these practices. And given how much any of these practices affect overall academic performance, perhaps teachers could spare a small fraction of the overall grade to allot to some weekly wellness challenges that give students choice while encouraging them to take responsibility for improving their own wellness.

Lace Wellness Prompts throughout Your Course

There are many small ways we can integrate wellness and balance into our course routine. These include providing brief moments of class time for students to share ideas, promoting sleep by making wise decisions in designing our courses, integrating an actual wellness activity into class occasionally, and weaving wellness hints into our learning management systems or our course materials.

Just as the academic and emotional benefits of building community justify investing a bit of class time to promote connectedness, the benefits of wellness practices might also warrant our taking a couple of minutes periodically for some attention to our mental health and well-being. For example, consider taking two minutes at the beginning of each week to discuss how students are doing with their wellness habits. Those two minutes could raise enough awareness to inspire action. Or imagine letting students know about a study showing that sleep levels can account for up to 24 percent of the variance in grades and then leading a quick brainstorming session on keys to getting enough sleep. Or as the end of the semester approaches, you might use your weekly two minutes to ask students what they can do differently to get more sleep during this finals week than they did last semester.

We can also easily design a wellness moment in a way that builds community. Students may think we are doing an icebreaker with these prompts, but the discussions all relate to wellness:

- How many people can you find in this class who really enjoy doing the same kind of exercise you do?
- What is your favorite thing to do outdoors around here?
- Where are the best places and times on campus to play soccer, do yoga, or connect with other students who like to play board games?
- What are your favorite healthy things to eat, and where do you buy them?
- What's your favorite way to exercise around here?
- Who's on an intramural team? What has your experience been? How can others sign up?
- What are some of the best ways you have found to get more sleep?
- Find someone in class who has meditated, and ask them to tell you about the benefits.

Sometimes just recognizing that students have stressors outside of our classes can promote understanding and create a safe space for students to learn. One of our colleagues takes a few minutes of class time toward the beginning of the semester to acknowledge some of the stressful events happening in students' lives outside of school. She creates a Google Doc spreadsheet that lists all her students' names in the left-hand column. And in the heading in the right-hand column is the question, "What are some things besides school that are challenging for you right now?" The students then take a few minutes at the first of class to complete the form. The digital document helps speed up this collaboration while simultaneously validating the challenges students are going through. It helps put school into perspective, and the students receive a strong message that their teacher is aware of their challenges in life outside of school. Because students may hesitate to share their struggles with their classmates, teachers might instead use a digital whiteboard, such as Padlet, where students can choose to remain anonymous.

Obviously, you can't dedicate a significant amount of class discussion to such exercises or small-group discussions. But spending a couple of minutes periodically in class could be an investment that pays rich dividends for our students, academically and emotionally.

In addition to brief class discussions on wellness, consider adjusting assignment due dates and times to help our students get more sleep. Many students wait until the last minute to complete and submit assignments. If assignments are due or tests close at midnight, students end up working into the late evening hours, and today's assignments inadvertently affect tomorrow's productivity and feelings of restfulness. By assigning earlier deadlines, instructors can support healthy sleep habits. In recommending this, however, we add one caution: if most of your colleagues are using the learning management system's default deadline of 11:59 p.m., your adjusted deadlines will catch some students off guard. So if you change from your system's default time, be sure to highlight the different deadline. Clearly communicating the rationale behind the due dates will help students be more aware of their sleep schedules. They may actually take advantage of the adjusted deadlines to head to bed a little earlier than they normally would. Similarly, breaking up mammoth projects, such as a research paper, has the salutary benefit of promoting healthy sleep patterns and helping students avoid all-nighters. Breaking big assignments down into smaller components with spaced deadlines prevents students from leaving an entire project or paper until the last minute.

Some teachers choose to do more than just talk about wellness techniques by occasionally incorporating them into their class. As midterms or finals approach, teachers who sense their students are overwhelmed could take a couple of minutes to engage in a breathing exercise. Inviting students to join us in a breathing exercise on occasion not only can help students mentally reset themselves for class but also introduces them to a tool for regulating their emotions whenever they need it.

Similarly, some professors enjoy holding class outside periodically under the right circumstances or allowing students in breakout groups to meet outside for part of class. Of course, there are some risks with such techniques, like not getting everyone back into the classroom at the same time, so some carefully planning and scaffolding may be in order. For instance, you could keep students close enough that you can walk by to give them a one-minute warning when it's almost time to wrap up.

If you don't want to give up any class time—or if you want to supplement class time—an easy way to encourage wellness practices would be to take advantage of the learning management system. For your course's background image, consider choosing a picture of a waterfall, a sunset over the ocean, or a mountain against a sunrise. You can use the announcement feature to post a wellness quote or an invitation to participate in a particular wellness practice that week. You might create a shared getting-to-know you page where your students post pictures of their weekend adventures outdoors. All these techniques can have a significant impact on students' wellness practices and well-being—without taking any class time.

Conclusion

As we hope we have made clear by now, our aim with this book isn't to help students with mental health challenges succeed by lowering the bar academically or removing every potential obstacle. Nor are we trying to cure or diagnose students. True, we do want to remove or reduce some of the hurdles we unintentionally place in our students' paths. But we also want to help students develop the emotional stamina and strength that will help them better manage their mental health in college and throughout life. We want to help them take steps that lead to greater happiness.

In this chapter, we review several habits any of us or our students can adopt to help us better cope with stressors and move toward wellness. Remember, research shows that stress doesn't impair the academic performance of only students diagnosed with mental health conditions. The happier students are—the more wellness they enjoy in life—the more they tend to learn, and the more likely they are to persist academically. As we help students embrace the wisdom of eating well, sleeping enough, exercising regularly, taking advantage of the sun and nature, and becoming more mindful—regardless of where they may currently be on the mental health spectrum—we are helping them move toward the happier end of that continuum.

Frankly, depending on what discipline you teach, promoting these wellness practices is more pedagogically challenging than most of the ideas we share in this book. With some creative thinking, however, in many cases we *can* find ways to connect our curriculum with at least one of these potentially life-changing practices. And even when we can't foster such practices directly through assignments, we can take advantage of the influence we have on our students by engaging in and briefly sharing some of our own experiences. Finally, just as most teachers wouldn't hesitate to deviate from a lesson outline every now and then to plug a critical study skill when needed, occasionally spending a couple of minutes in class to promote a wellness practice is likely a very worthwhile investment of time in our students' academic and personal success.

CONCLUSION

....

To conclude, we share an illustration that integrates ideas from each of the strategies we examine in this book into one class—the first day. How might we change that day to improve learning for our students with mental health challenges in a way that benefits all our students?

A traditional approach to the first day of class is to cover the ground rules for the course, plowing through the syllabus with students to avoid the confusion that can lead to many emails and much frustration later in the semester. We might also hope to introduce students to the subject matter of the course in some exciting way, but because we spend so much time helping students understand policies, assignments, and due dates, students have come to know the first day of class simply as Syllabus Day.

What if we killed Syllabus Day—and in the process created a compelling beginning for all our students, especially those living with mental health challenges? If our aim were to create the best possible motivational, cognitive, and emotional climate for our students, how might we approach that first day of class differently? And how could we still make sure that students actually understand the course details we often spend so much time explaining? Here are a few ideas.

We'd begin by getting to class early, greeting as many

students as possible. In a smaller class, we'd have already studied their names and be able to name many of them before they introduced themselves. Once we began class, we'd introduce ourselves and follow James Lang's suggestion to share enough about who we are and why we love the subject to humanize ourselves and pique our students' interest in the subject of the course.[1]

We would then find a safe way to identify the students who have and have not read the syllabus, perhaps saying something like, "Some of you have had a chance to read the syllabus already, and some of you haven't," before asking for a show of hands. We'd then create complementary pairs or small groups of students—or let them create their own partnerships or small groups—that included someone who had already read the syllabus quiz. Then we'd give them a few minutes to introduce themselves, get to know each other a bit, and invite them to exchange phone numbers so that they can contact each other with any questions about the course. We would also invite them to spend a few minutes showing each other around the course in the learning management system and reviewing what assignments are due this week. After they've engaged in both these exercises, we'd open it up for questions. (We find they have surprisingly few they haven't already had answered in their group.)

Even this isn't enough to ensure students really understand the ground rules, so we'd create a syllabus quiz—and let students take it multiple times during the first week, with only the highest score counting for the grade. In fact, we'd encourage them to take the quiz with the help of a partner from the class. But we'd also remind students who have already taken it that the best way to help other students is to point them in the right direction, indicating the paragraph that contains an answer rather than simply giving them the answer.

Rob made this shift a few years ago, and he's been amazed at how dramatically it has changed the vibe in the classroom. Rather than him droning on about the syllabus, half the class is immediately tutoring the other half of the class. And courtesy of some strategic social scaffolding, students come away feeling connected to at least two or three other students whose contact information they have. The psychological barriers to entry to texting that classmate with a question are much lower than they are to emailing or calling their professor. And that increases the odds that students will get the help they need to fill in knowledge gaps or cracks they may have about the course. (A fortuitous benefit is that teachers also get far fewer emails from students confused about basic course mechanics.) Best of all, these pairings often lead to genuine friendships.

Covering the syllabus in this way, including using the syllabus quiz, also frees up time on the first day. Teachers can then engage in a more exhilarating introduction to the course material—the kind we always mean to undertake but often have to compress into a hurried lecture at the end of class. We can now better do what Lang suggests: "Consider the first day as your best opportunity to spark students' curiosity and invite them into a fascinating intellectual journey." [2]

After compellingly painting the big picture for the course, we would help students connect what they will learn in the course with ways they can help others. We might give our best five-minute pitch about what we hope students will gain from the course and then invite students to reflect and write their own purpose statement for the course—how they will use what they learn to make a difference for others. Rather than cold calling on four or five students to share their comments, we might use a ponder-and-post activity, with everyone writing their statements on the physical or digital whiteboard and then perusing their classmates' statements to find some ideas that inspire them to tweak their own statements.

This streamlined approach to covering the syllabus often leaves some time to lead a brief discussion about mental health challenges, which is especially helpful in courses with first-year students. We could clearly and succinctly acknowledge that many of us struggle with mental health challenges in various ways, and those challenges can sometimes make it difficult to succeed. We might then ask students who have gained some insights through years of experience to share some of what they have learned. When we do this, we're always impressed by how many students are willing to share comments and by the quality of their insights.

Note how we've applied each of the eight strategies not only to make life better for students with mental health challenges but also to improve the learning experience for all our students. As we greet them (possibly by name) and they sense our genuine concern, we lay the groundwork for becoming natural mentors. By tackling relevant and compelling content instead of just the syllabus, we've transformed the first day of class into an inspiring beginning rather than a necessary evil—starting the semester strong. By allowing students to take the syllabus quiz multiple times and partnering them with another student, we have intentionally built in incentives and opportunities for them to find and fill in their own knowledge gaps—gaps that often neither we nor students are otherwise aware of until they have significantly hampered students' success in the course. ("I was supposed to turn in a reflection journal every week? I didn't know that!") We've also subtly signaled that mastery matters and we want to help them achieve it. And we've built in an early win, allowing them to get help with the first assignment (the syllabus quiz) and to take it multiple times until they master the content.

Perhaps the most significant contrast between this approach and Syllabus Day is how the entire experience awakens students' inner desire to learn by creating a genuine excitement about the course. As we help them connect what they will learn to ways to help others, students can also develop a purpose that creates academic stamina and grit. The opportunity to hear from students who have learned some effective ways to cope with their mental health challenges also promotes grit and growth mindset, the notions that they can take action to improve their situations and persist in doing hard things. By acknowledging the importance of mental and emotional well-being and perhaps even sharing an insight of our own about managing stress, anxiety, discouragement, or depression, we also help destigmatize having mental health challenges and shrink the psychological gap between us and our students. And partnering with a classmate and exchanging phone numbers is a great first step in building community in the form of a supportive relationship with a peer.

Engaging students in active learning by reflecting, writing, and posting their thoughts avoids a potential pitfall. Rather than potentially intimidating students by cold calling them on the very first day, we show introverted students and those who struggle with anxiety that they will be able to contribute in multiple ways. Moreover, we dramatically increase the participation ratio in the class, as everyone writes an answer rather than just a few more outgoing students volunteering theirs. Finally, when students share what they have learned about how to cope with their mental health challenges most effectively, they invariably share a number of ideas related to wellness techniques, such as getting adequate sleep, exercising, and meditating.

And that's just the first day of class!

We hope this integrated illustration is illuminating rather than intimidating. In reality, neither Bonnie, nor Steve, nor Rob fully utilizes every one of the tools we suggest in this book. And if we think of trying to implement them all at once, it discourages *us*. Fortunately, like the changes Lang advocates in *Small Teaching*, our suggestions are modular. Making any of them will boost learning for students with mental health challenges, even if you don't make all of them.

In fact, we recently discovered a simple technique to help us innovate consistently without getting overwhelmed. In preparing for each class or course, even those we have taught many times before, we try to ponder this question: "What one change could I make in my lesson plan (or my course design) that would do the most to improve learning?" That question keeps us open to continual improvement without being overwhelmed by a flood of good intentions.

Will taking a more intentional approaching to helping our students with mental health challenges eliminate the need for counseling and medication, or will it magically energize students so overwhelmed by depression that they can't leave their apartments for long stretches of time? Absolutely not. In fact, even when the three of us implement as many of these ideas as we can, we're disappointed to see that some of our students still fail or drop our courses because of their mental health challenges. But we're reminded of the wise counsel a humanitarian leader once gave: "We cannot do everything, but we must do everything we can."[3] With some focused intentionality, we can make life significantly better for many of our students with mental health challenges—and simultaneously help all of our students learn more.

In fact, that's just what happened for Alexis, our research assistant whom we introduced in the first chapter. How has it turned out for her after that rough beginning? As we mention in chapter 2, a turning point in her experience was learning from two professors the art of accepting being good enough. "With the help of this mentality, my shrink, and a good combination of medication/exercise/ diet, I am thriving. I still have my bad days, the days where I want to drop out or disappear, but I am not afraid. I have been given the tools to succeed, and I know that my professors want to help. If I am struggling, I can reach out for help. That is the beauty of this university. Students have professors that are aware of their struggles and are willing to talk about it. I am so grateful for that; it really saved my life."

Doubtless, other students have had similarly transformative experiences at other universities where professors already do many of the things we advocate. And as some of the students in our focus groups made clear, we still have plenty of room for improvement at BYU-Idaho. Our hope is that this book will help more teachers have the kind of impact on students' lives that Alexis's professors have had on hers.

NOTES

....

Introduction

....

1. Lipson and Eisenberg, "Mental Health and Academic Attitudes," 205.
2. Tough, *The Years That Matter Most*, 226.
3. Obama, *Becoming*, 72.
4. Tough, *The Years That Matter Most*, 13.
5. National Center for Education Statistics (NCES), "The NCES Fast Facts Graduation Rates."
6. Lake, "The Cost of Being a College Dropout."
7. Cavanagh, *The Spark of Learning*, 205.
8. American College Health Association, *American College Health Association-National College Health Assessment II*, 13–15.
9. Beers et al., "A Praxis Briefing," 7.
10. Beers et al., "A Praxis Briefing," 13.
11. Brown, *Overwhelmed*, 5.
12. Bristow, Cant, and Chatterjee, *Generational Encounters with Higher Education*, 99.
13. Beers et al., "A Praxis Briefing," 9.
14. Hartocollis. "Feeling Suicidal."
15. Lipson and Eisenberg, "Mental Health and Academic Attitudes," 208–10.
16. Lipson and Eisenberg, "Mental Health and Academic Attitudes," 209.
17. Lipson and Eisenberg, "Mental Health and Academic Attitudes," 206.
18. Beers et al., "A Praxis Briefing," 7.
19. O'Keeffe, "A Sense of Belonging," 606.
20. Baik, Larcombe, and Brooker, "How Universities Can Enhance Student Mental Wellbeing," 2.

21. NCES, "Annual Earnings by Educational Attainment."
22. Georgetown University, "Earning Power Is Increasingly Tied to Education," 1.
23. Lake, "College Dropout."
24. National Institute of Mental Health, "Suicide."
25. National Institute of Mental Health, "Suicide."
26. CDC, "Suicide Rising across the US."
27. Burrell, "The Grim Numbers Suicides and Attempts."
28. Beers et al., "A Praxis Briefing," 8.
29. US Public Health Service, "Protecting Youth Mental Health," 4, 40.
30. Macaskill, "The Mental Health of University Students," 434–35.
31. See Hernandez-Torrano, "Mental Health and Well-Being of University Students," 1–16.
32. See Hernandez-Torrano, "Mental Health and Well-Being of University Students," 1–16.
33. Astin, *Four Critical Years*, 126–36.
34. Gallimore, Braun, and McLaughlin, "A Friend at the Front of the Room."
35. Baik, Larcombe, and Brooker, "How Universities Can Enhance Student Mental Wellbeing," 376, 379, 384.
36. Baik, Larcombe, and Brooker, "How Universities Can Enhance Student Mental Wellbeing," 383.
37. Cavanagh, *The Spark of Learning*, 185.
38. Mukhopadhyay et al., "College Students, Mental Health, and the University's Role."
39. Lang, *Cheating Lessons*, 106.
40. LastingLearning.com, "Using Desirable Difficulties to Enhance Learning, Dr. Robert Bjork."
41. We recognize that calling people either introverts or extroverts is an oversimplification of the ideas of Carl Jung, who originated the terms *introversion* and *extroversion* and believed that we all have elements of both, with one simply being more dominant than the other. Like Cain, however, we find the simplification useful when considering students whose introverted sides are more dominant.
42. Susan Cain, Educators Summit, author's personal notes, July 2019, Philadelphia.

Chapter 1

1. "Protect Your Brain from Stress."

2. Devilbiss, Jenison, and Berridge, "Stress-Induced Impairment."

3. Cavanagh, *The Spark of Learning*, 183

4. Angelidis et al., "I'm Going to Fail!"

5. Medina, *Brain Rules*, 65.

6. Sandi, "Stress and Cognition," 253.

7. Tolkien, *The Hobbit*, 77.

8. Willis, "The Neuroscience Behind Stress and Learning."

9. Vitasari et al., "Student Anxiety and Academic Performance," 496.

10. Cooper, Downing, and Brownell, "Influence of Active Learning Practices on Student Anxiety," 2.

11. Joels et al., "Learning Under Stress," 152–58.

12. Cooper, Downing, and Brownell, "The Influence of Active Learning," 2. For the sake of simplicity, in this and other quotations throughout the book, we have omitted citations within quotes.

13. Joels et al., "Learning under Stress," 153.

14. Medina, *Brain Rules*, 63, 65.

15. Centeno Milton, "Fear Shrinks Your Brain."

16. Medina, *Brain Rules*, 180.

17. Cartreine, "More Than Sad."

18. Deroma, Leach, and Leverett, "Depression and College Academic Performance," 325.

19. Eisenberg, Golberstein, and Hunt, "Mental Health and Academic Success," 1.

20. Baik, Larcombe, and Brooker, "How Universities Can Enhance Student Mental Wellbeing," 2.

21. Cartreine, "More Than Sad."

22. Felitti, "Adverse Childhood Experiences and Adult Health," 44.

23. Felitti, "Adverse Childhood Experiences and Adult Health," 45.

24. Felitti, "Adverse Childhood Experiences and Adult Health," 45.

25. Dube, "Childhood Abuse," 3089.

26. Felitti, "Adverse Childhood Experiences and Adult Health," 45.

27. American College Health Association, *American College Health Association-National College Health Assessment III*, 14.

28. Beck, "How Uncertainty Fuels Anxiety."

29. Hernandez-Torrano, "Well-Being of University Students," 2.

30. Antaramian, "Assessing Psychological Symptoms and Well-Being," 427.

31. Some proponents of positive psychology argue that while the continuum approach has merit, we can obtain an even more accurate image of well-being and mental health pathologies by using two related but distinct continua—one measuring

well-being and another measuring pathology. See Antamarian, "Assessing Psychological Symptoms." And a number of studies support this approach. Still, at the risk of oversimplifying a bit, we will keep things conceptually manageable by referring to a single spectrum for mental health and well-being.

32. Hernandez-Torrano, "Well-Being of University Students," 3.
33. We recognize that college students are vulnerable to a wide variety of mental health conditions beyond depression and anxiety, such as obsessive-compulsive disorder and eating disorders. But because the vast majority of mental health challenges experienced by college students relate to depression and anxiety, for the sake of simplicity, most of our examples and analysis apply to these two conditions.
34. Joels et al., "Learning under Stress," 152.
35. Piray et al., "Emotionally Aversive Cues," 1453.

Chapter 2

1. Felten and Lambert, *Relationship-Rich Education*, 30.
2. Gallup Inc., *Great Jobs Great Lives*, 4.
3. Gallup Inc., *Great Jobs Great Lives*, 6.
4. Gallup Inc., *Great Jobs Great Lives*, 10.
5. Gallup Inc., *Great Jobs Great Lives*, 10.
6. Cuseo, "Student-Faculty Engagement," 87–88.
7. Cuseo, "Student-Faculty Engagement," 89.
8. Clark, "Few Grads Say Alma Mater Prioritizes Mental Health."
9. Felten and Lambert, *Relationship-Rich Education*, 20.
10. O'Keefe, "A Sense of Belonging," 608.
11. O'Keefe, "A Sense of Belonging," 608.
12. Hurd and Zimmerman, "Natural Mentors," 8.
13. Hurd and Zimmerman, "Natural Mentors," 10.
14. Wyman et al., "Peer-Adult Network Structure," 1069.
15. Hurd and Zimmerman, "Natural Mentors," 2.
16. Ferguson et al., "The Influence of Teaching," 82.
17. Ebert et al., "Barriers of Mental Health Treatment," 2.
18. Ebert et al., "Barriers of Mental Health Treatment," 5.
19. Ebert et al., "Barriers of Mental Health Treatment," 9.
20. Ebert et al., "Barriers of Mental Health Treatment," 9.
21. Salaheddin and Mason, "Identifying Barriers," 690.
22. Baik, Larcombe, and Brooker, "How Universities Can Enhance Student Mental Wellbeing," 8.
23. Hsu and Goldsmith, "Instructor Strategies to Alleviate Stress."

24. Active Minds and ACUE, *Creating a Culture of Caring*, 5.
25. Jim Kanan, personal communication with Steve Hunsaker, June 30, 2021.
26. Cuseo, "Student-Faculty Engagement," 91.
27. Cuseo, "Student-Faculty Engagement," 92.
28. Cooper et al., "What's in a Name?" 6.
29. Stephen Courtright, personal communication with Steve Hunsaker, July 18, 2021.
30. Smith et al., " 'Office Hours Are Kind of Weird,' " 17.
31. Smith et al., " 'Office Hours Are Kind of Weird,' " 18–19, 21, 23.
32. Smith et al., " 'Office Hours Are Kind of Weird,' " 15.
33. Smith et al., " 'Office Hours Are Kind of Weird,' " 19.
34. Smith et al., " 'Office Hours Are Kind of Weird,' " 21.
35. University of Washington, "Virtual Office Hours."
36. Johnson, "Moving Office Hours Online"
37. Felten and Lambert, *Relationship-Rich Education*, 118.
38. Cuseo, "Student-Faculty Engagement," 89.
39. Cuseo, "Student-Faculty Engagement," 89.
40. Felten and Lambert, *Relationship-Rich Education*, 87.
41. Felten and Lambert, *Relationship-Rich Education*, 85–86.
42. Felten and Lambert, *Relationship-Rich Education*, 133.
43. Felten and Lambert, *Relationship-Rich Education*, 132.
44. Felten and Lambert, *Relationship-Rich Education*, 157.
45. Nunn, *33 Simple Strategies*, 19.
46. Felten and Lambert, *Relationship-Rich Education*, 150.
47. Felten and Lambert, *Relationship-Rich Education*, 30.
48. Felten and Lambert, *Relationship-Rich Education*, 83.
49. Cuseo, "Student-Faculty Engagement," 92.
50. Lipson and Eisenberg, "Mental Health and Academic Attitudes," 206.
51. Rosenthal and Jacobson, *Pygmalion in the Classroom*, 20.
52. Lipson and Eisenberg, "Mental Health and Academic Attitudes," 205–13.
53. Lipson and Eisenberg, "Mental Health and Academic Attitudes," 210.
54. Cuseo, "Student-Faculty Engagement," 90.
55. Felten and Lambert, *Relationship-Rich Education*, 160.
56. Active Minds and ACUE, *Creating a Culture of Caring*, 5.
57. Active Minds and ACUE, *Creating a Culture of Caring*, 7.
58. Stolzenberg et al., "The American Freshman," 27, 42.
59. Hsu and Goldsmith, "Instructor Strategies to Alleviate Stress," 2.

60. Burnette, Ramchand, and Ayer, "Gatekeeper Training for Suicide Prevention," 16.
61. Brown, *Overwhelmed*, 9.
62. Brown, *Overwhelmed*, 17.
63. Active Minds and ACUE, *Creating a Culture of Caring*, 4.
64. *The Role of Faculty in Student Mental Health*, 11.
65. QPR Institute, "Practical and Proven Suicide Prevention Training."
66. Cross et al., "Suicide Prevention Gatekeeper Training," 149.
67. Felten and Lambert, *Relationship-Rich Education*, 141. The term "warm handoff" comes from Adam Kasarda, director of the Student Disability Resource Center at California State University-Dominguez Hills.
68. Nunn, *33 Simple Strategies*, 33.
69. Felten and Lambert, *Relationship-Rich Education*, 137.
70. Biswas, "How to Mentor Minority Students."

Chapter 3

1. Grupe and Nitschke, "Uncertainty and Anticipation in Anxiety," 497.
2. We are indebted to Salman Khan for this metaphor, which one of the authors heard him give in an oral presentation at Stanford University.
3. Beck, "How Uncertainty Fuels Anxiety."
4. Story et al., "Dread and the Future of Pain," 11.
5. Beck, "How Uncertainty Fuels Anxiety."
6. Boswell et al., "Intolerance of Uncertainty," 630.
7. Beck, "How Uncertainty Fuels Anxiety."
8. Teeselinka et al., "Choking in Darts," 39.
9. Ariely et al., "Large Stakes and Big Mistakes," 463.
10. Angelidis et al., "I'm Going to Fail!" 2.
11. Angelidis et al., "I'm Going to Fail!" 7.
12. Henderson, "Law School Exams and Meritocracy," 975.
13. Gladwell, "The Tortoise and the Hare."
14. Henderson, "Law School Exams and Meritocracy," 975–76.
15. Dastagir, "Why It's So Important to Hope."
16. Comments made to the authors in reviewing this book.
17. Ambrose et al., *How Learning Works*, 106.
18. Ambrose et al., *How Learning Works*, 131.
19. Cavanagh, *The Spark of Learning*, 186.
20. Falk, "Fairness and Motivation."

21. Nunn, *33 Simple Strategies*, 12.
22. Nunn, *33 Simple Strategies*, 16, 61,
23. "If We Have Our Own 'Why.'"
24. Lang, *Distracted*, 42:40.
25. Ambrose et al., *How Learning Works*, 106.
26. Ambrose et al., *How Learning Works*, 105.
27. Ambrose et al., *How Learning Works*, 112.
28. Ambrose et al., *How Learning Works*, 103.
29. As with any other language we suggest or share in this book, readers are welcome to use any portion of this they find helpful in their own syllabi or assignments.
30. Eyler, *How Humans Learn*, 41.
31. Cooper, Downing, and Brownell, "The Influence of Active Learning," 8.
32. Lang, *Cheating Lessons*, 210.
33. Lang, *Small Teaching*, 206.
34. See Khan, *One World Schoolhouse*, 37–44.
35. Lang, *Small Teaching*, 73–75.
36. Lang, *Small Teaching*, 35.
37. Lang, *Cheating Lessons*, 97.
38. Kaufman, "The Will and Ways of Hope."
39. Lemov, *Teach Like a Champion 2.0*, 57.
40. Ferguson et al., "The Influence of Teaching," 89.
41. Khan, "Let's Teach for Mastery."
42. Nunn, *33 Simple Strategies*, 6.
43. Lang, *Cheating Lessons*, 120.
44. Lang, *Cheating Lessons*, 133.
45. Retrieval Practice, "What Is Retrieval Practice?"
46. Brown et al., *Make It Stick*, 36.

Chapter 4

1. Distin, "Kids Ask So Many Questions."
2. Morin, "Developmental Milestones."
3. Khan Academy, "You Can Learn Anything."
4. Elsworthy, "Curious Children."
5. NewsComAu, "Mothers Asked 228 Questions a Day."
6. Adams, "Game of Tongues."
7. Pink, *Drive*, 138–39.
8. Ryan and Deci, "Self-Determination Theory," 70.
9. Dweck, *Mindset*, 29.
10. Lang, *Distracted*, 12:57.

11. Pink, *Drive*, 128.
12. Ambrose et al., *How Learning Works*, 68–69.
13. Ryan and Deci, "Self-Determination Theory," 69.
14. Ryan and Deci, "Self-Determination Theory," 75.
15. Ling et al., "Intrinsic and Extrinsic Goals," 2.
16. Sheehan, Herring, and Campbell, "Associations between Motivation and Mental Health in Sport," 7.
17. Ling et al., "Intrinsic and Extrinsic Goals," 5.
18. Ariani, "Self-Determined Motivation," 1164.
19. See Ambrose et al., *How Learning Works*, 77–87.
20. See Ryan and Deci, "Self-Determination Theory," 71.
21. Ambrose et al., *How Learning Works*, 5.
22. Sheehan, Herring, and Campbell, "Associations between Motivation and Mental Health in Sport," 2.
23. Ambrose et al., *How Learning Works*, 79.
24. Cavanagh, *The Spark of Learning*, 108.
25. Damon, *The Path to Purpose*, 31.
26. Damon, *The Path to Purpose*, 32.
27. LaBier, "A Sense of Awe and Life Purpose."
28. Schaefer et al., "Purpose Predicts Better Emotional Recovery," 1.
29. Duckworth, *Grit*, 64.
30. Duckworth, *Grit*, 91.
31. Duckworth, *Grit*, 145.
32. Duckworth, *Grit*, 147.
33. Damon, *The Path to Purpose*, 40.
34. Yeager et al., "Boring but Important," 566.
35. Twenge, i*Gen*, 167.
36. Twenge, iGen, 168.
37. Twenge, iGen, 169.
38. Parks, *Big Questions, Worthy Dreams*, 211.
39. Damon, *The Path to Purpose*, 22.
40. Damon, *The Path to Purpose*, 113.
41. Felten and Lambert, *Relationship-Rich Education*, 36.
42. Felten and Lambert, *Relationship-Rich Education*, 37–38.
43. Felten and Lambert, *Relationship-Rich Education*, 18.
44. Duckworth, *Grit*, 165–66.
45. Vedantam, "How To Build a Better Job."
46. Duckworth, *Grit*, 166 (italics in original).
47. Duckworth, *Grit*, 166.
48. Weimer, *Learner-Centered Teaching*, 40.
49. Cavanagh, *The Spark of Emotion*, 149.
50. Ryan and Deci, "Self-Determination Theory," 71.
51. Ryan and Deci, "Self-Determination Theory," 71.

52. Weimer, *Learner-Center Teaching*, 97.
53. Cavanagh, *The Spark of Learning*, 179.
54. Cavanagh, *The Spark of Learning*, 150–51.
55. Pink, *Drive*, 155.
56. Kusurkar, Croiset, and Ten Cate, "Twelve Tips to Stimulate Intrinsic Motivation," 979.
57. Pink, *Drive*, 154.
58. Cavanagh, *The Spark of Learning*, 212.
59. Ambrose et al., *How Learning Works*, 83.
60. Kember, Ho, and Hong, "Establishing Relevance," 254.
61. Kember, Ho, and Hong, "Establishing Relevance," 259.
62. Lang, *Cheating Lessons*, 72.
63. Kember, Ho, and Hong, "Establishing Relevance," 256.
64. Ambrose et al., *How Learning Works*, 84.
65. Ambrose et al., *How Learning Works*, 84.
66. Pink, *Drive*, 171.
67. Kusurkar, Croiset, and Ten Cate, "Twelve Tips," 980.
68. Cavanagh, *The Spark of Learning*, 149.
69. Amabile and Kramer, "The Power of Small Wins."
70. Amabile and Kramer, "The Power of Small Wins."
71. Ambrose et al., *How Learning Works*, 86–87.
72. Lang, *Cheating Lessons*, 84.
73. Ferguson et al., "The Influence of Teaching," 85.

Chapter 5

1. Brackett, *Permission to Feel*, 28.
2. Brown, *Overwhelmed*, 45.
3. Dweck, *Mindset*, 14 (italics in original).
4. Dweck, *Mindset*, 74.
5. Dweck, *Mindset*, 16.
6. Dweck, *Mindset*, 58.
7. Dweck, *Mindset*, 58.
8. Dweck, *Mindset*, 58–59 (italics in original).
9. Duckworth, *Grit*, 191.
10. Dweck, *Mindset*, 95.
11. Dweck, *Mindset*, 21.
12. Dweck, *Mindset*, 22.
13. Brackett, *Permission to Feel*, 142.
14. Brackett, *Permission to Feel*, 50–51.
15. Pena-Sarrionandia, Mikolajczak, and Gross, a"Integrating Emotion Regulation," 1.

16. Ackerman, "What Is Self-Regulation?"
17. Brackett, *Permission to Feel*, 158.
18. Ackerman, "What Is Self-Regulation?"
19. Brackett, *Permission to Feel*, 42.
20. Brackett, *Permission to Feel*, 28.
21. Brackett, *Permission to Feel*, 11.
22. Brackett, *Permission to Feel*, 63.
23. Gottman Institute, "Four Parenting Styles."
24. Brackett, *Permission to Feel*, 26.
25. Brackett, *Permission to Feel*, 27.
26. Brackett, *Permission to Feel*, 30.
27. Brackett, *Permission to Feel*, 50.
28. Brackett, *Permission to Feel*, 193.
29. Nunn, *33 Simple Strategies*, 70.
30. Brackett, *Permission to Feel*, 203–4.
31. Dweck, *Mindset*, 101–2.
32. Dweck, *Mindset*, 318.
33. Duckworth, *Grit*, 184.
34. Yeager et al., "A National Experiment," 364.
35. Yeager et al., "A National Experiment," 364, 366.
36. Yeager et al., "A National Experiment," 366.
37. Duckworth, *Grit*, 84.
38. Yeager et al., "A National Experiment," 366.
39. Yeager et al., "A National Experiment," 368.
40. Ackerman, "What Is Self-Regulation?"
41. De la Fuente et al., "Strategies for Coping with Academic Stress," 11, 13.
42. Brackett, *Permission to Feel*, 158.
43. Brackett, *Permission to Feel*, 158.
44. Brackett, *Permission to Feel*, 152.
45. Dweck, *Mindset*, 109.
46. Dweck, *Mindset*, 268–69.
47. Bravata et al., "Impostor Syndrome," 1252.
48. Lang, *Small Teaching*, 200.
49. Brackett, *Permission to Feel*, 146.
50. Brackett, *Permission to Feel*, 154.
51. Brackett, *Permission to Feel*, 155.
52. Brackett, *Permission to Feel*, 17, 23.
53. Duckworth, *Grit*, 189–90.
54. Lemov, *Teach Like a Champion 2.0*, 60.
55. Duckworth, *Grit*, 141 (italics removed).
56. Chowdhury, "What Is Emotion Regulation?" 20.
57. Maxwell, *Failing Forward*, 2.

58. Brown, *Rising Strong*, xxv.
59. Brown, *Rising Strong*, 50.
60. Dweck, *Mindset*, 293.
61. Ferguson et al., "The Influence of Teaching," 8.
62. Ferguson et al., "The Influence of Teaching," 9, 83.
63. Ferguson et al., "The Influence of Teaching," 8.
64. Ferguson et al., "The Influence of Teaching," 44, 46, 48.
65. Ferguson et al., "The Influence of Teaching," 91.
66. Ferguson et al., "The Influence of Teaching," 10.
67. Ferguson et al., "The Influence of Teaching," 7.
68. Ferguson et al., "The Influence of Teaching," 84.
69. Dweck, *Mindset*, 318 (italics in original).
70. Cohen, Steele, and Ross, "The Mentor's Dilemma," 1302.
71. Ferguson et al., "The Influence of Teaching," 8–9.
72. Felten and Lambert, *Relationship-Rich Education*, 90.
73. Gary Wyatt, personal communication with Steve Hunsaker, July 14, 2021.
74. Ferguson et al., "The Influence of Teaching," 12.
75. Felten and Lambert, *Relationship-Rich Education*, 42.
76. Felten and Lambert, *Relationship-Rich Education*, 45.
77. Felten and Lambert, *Relationship-Rich Education*, 43.
78. Nunn, *33 Simple Strategies*, 28.
79. Felten and Lambert, *Relationship-Rich Education*, 89.
80. Ebert et al., "Barriers of Mental Health Treatment Utilization," 2, 3, 5.
81. Redden, "Pandemic Hurts Student Mental Health."

Chapter 6

1. Jeakle, "Learning to Live with Loneliness at a Jesuit College."
2. Stoliker and Lafreniere, "The Influence of Perceived Stress," 147.
3. Tough, *The Years That Matter Most*, 226 (italics in original).
4. Tough, *The Years That Matter Most*, 222.
5. Holt-Lunstad, "Social Isolation and Loneliness," 128.
6. Smith and Applegate, "Mental Health Stigma," 383–84.
7. McPhillips, "Deaths from Police Violence Disproportionately Affect People of Color."
8. Maxwell and Solomon, "The Economic Fallout of the Coronavirus."
9. Strauss, "An Old Story Made New Again."
10. Golden, "Coronavirus in African Americans."
11. Brown, *Overwhelmed*, 8.

12. Anderson, "The Emotional Toll of Racism."
13. Anderson, "The Emotional Toll of Racism."
14. Anderson, "The Emotional Toll of Racism."
15. Cuncic, "What Is Imposter Syndrome?"
16. Romero, "What We Know about Belonging."
17. Weir, "Feel Like a Fraud?"
18. Bravata et al., "Impostor Syndrome," 1260.
19. Bravata et al., "Impostor Syndrome," 1254.
20. Romero, "What We Know about Belonging," 2.
21. Felten and Lambert, *Relationship-Rich Education*, 45–46.
22. Tough, *The Years That Matter Most*, 289.
23. Tinto, "Reflections on Student Persistence," 3.
24. Tinto, "Reflections on Student Persistence," 4.
25. Bowman et al., "Student Adjustment," 276.
26. Bowman et al., "Student Adjustment," 277.
27. Romero, "What We Know about Belonging," 1.
28. Bowman et al., Student Adjustment," 277.
29. Chambliss and Takacs, *How College Works*, 21.
30. Chambliss and Takacs, *How College Works*, 3.
31. Chambliss and Takacs, *How College Works*, 17.
32. Chambliss and Takacs, *How College Works*, 173–74.
33. Felten and Lambert, *Relationship-Rich Education*, 6–7.
34. Posselt and Lipson, "Competition, Anxiety, and Depression," 986.
35. Posselt and Lipson, "Competition, Anxiety, and Depression," 985.
36. Posselt and Lipson, "Competition, Anxiety, and Depression," 984.
37. Posselt and Lipson, "Competition, Anxiety, and Depression," 983.
38. Posselt and Lipson, "Competition, Anxiety, and Depression," 985.
39. Posselt and Lipson, "Competition, Anxiety, and Depression," 974.
40. Scager et al., "Collaborative Learning in Higher Education," 1.
41. Strauss, "The Surprising Thing Google Learned about Its Employees."
42. Posselt and Lipson, "Competition, Anxiety, and Depression," 973.
43. Posselt and Lipson, "Competition, Anxiety, and Depression," 984.
44. Haidet, Kubitz, and McCormack, "Team-Based Learning Literature," 306.

45. Michaelsen, *Team-Based Learning*, 3.
46. Faculty Innovation Center, "Team-Based Learning."
47. Michaelsen, *Team-Based Learning*, 13.
48. Michaelsen, *Team-Based Learning*, 15.
49. Michaelsen, *Team-Based Learning*, 15.
50. Nunn, *33 Simple Strategies*, 52.
51. Kurt Baker, personal communication with Steve Hunsaker, July 16, 2021.
52. Steele, "Race and the Schooling of Black Americans."
53. Tough, *The Years That Matter Most*, 271.

Chapter 7

1. Schell and Butler, "Insights from the Science of Learning," 2.
2. Rocca, "Student Participation in the College Classroom," 194.
3. Cooper, Downing, and Brownell, "The Influence of Active Learning," 15.
4. Cavanagh, *The Spark of Learning*, 37–38.
5. Cooper, Downing, and Brownell, "The Influence of Active Learning," 13.
6. Cooper, Downing, and Brownell, "The Influence of Active Learning," 13.
7. Cooper, Downing, and Brownell, "The Influence of Active Learning," 13.
8. Cooper, Downing, and Brownell, "The Influence of Active Learning," 14.
9. Cooper, Downing, and Brownell, "The Influence of Active Learning," 14.
10. Cooper, Downing, and Brownell, "The Influence of Active Learning," 15.
11. Cooper, Downing, and Brownell, "The Influence of Active Learning," 15.
12. Dallimore, Hertenstein, and Platt, "Impact of Cold Calling," 312, 314, 316.
13. Howard, "How to Hold a Better Class Discussion."
14. Dallimore, Hertenstein, and Platt, "Impact of Cold Calling," 316.
15. Dallimore, Hertenstein, and Platt, "Impact of Cold Calling," 332.
16. Harvard Graduate School of Education, "Expanding Participation through Cold-Calling."
17. Lemov, *Teaching Like a Champion: 2.0*, 240.

18. Northeastern University, "Active Question and Answer Techniques."
19. Dallimore, Hertenstein, and Platt, "Impact of Cold Calling," 307.
20. Cain, *Quiet*, 471–72.
21. Cain, *Quiet*, 64.
22. Cain, *Quiet*, 44–45.
23. Cooper, Downing, and Brownell, "The Influence of Active Learning," 10 (italics added).
24. Cooper, Downing, and Brownell, "The Influence of Active Learning," 10.
25. Cooper, Downing, and Brownell, "The Influence of Active Learning," 8.
26. Cooper, Downing, and Brownell, "The Influence of Active Learning," 12.
27. Rogers, "When Women Don't Speak."
28. Cooper, Downing, and Brownell, "The Influence of Active Learning," 12.
29. Cooper, Downing, and Brownell, "The Influence of Active Learning," 12.
30. Hsu and Goldsmith, "Instructor Strategies to Alleviate Stress," 5.
31. Chang and Brickman, "When Group Work Doesn't Work," 12.
32. Cain, *Quiet*, 48–49, 226.
33. Cain, *Quiet*, 224, 227.
34. Cain, *Quiet*, 51.

Chapter 8

1. Cavanagh, *The Spark of Learning*, 64.
2. Antaramian, "Psychological Symptoms and Well-Being," 427.
3. Hershner, "Sleep and Academic Performance," 51–56.
4. Healthy Sleep Med Harvard, "Sleep and Mood."
5. Okano et al., "Sleep Quality, Duration, and Consistency," 1.
6. Ilardi, *The Depression Cure*, 193–94.
7. Maheshwari and Shaukat, "Impact of Poor Sleep Quality," 1.
8. Huber, "Your Body."
9. Adan et al., "Nutritional Psychiatry," 1322–23.
10. Li et al., "Dietary Patterns and Depression Risk."
11. Tello, "Diet and Depression."
12. Ljungberg, Bondza, and Lethin, "Importance of Dietary Habits," 12.

13. Sharma, Madaan, and Petty, "Exercise for Mental Health," 106.
14. Dunn and Jewell, "The Effect of Exercise on Mental Health," 203.
15. Ilardi, *The Depression Cure*, 14.
16. Ilardi, *The Depression Cure*, 116.
17. See PositivePsychology.com's blog posts on mindfulness at http://positivepsychology.com/category/mindfulness.
18. Ilardi, *The Depression Cure*, 99–101.
19. "Spending Time in Nature Boosts Children's Learning."
20. "Spending Time in Nature Reduces Stress."
21. Keniger et al., "What Are the Benefits of Interacting with Nature?" 914.
22. Keniger et al., "What Are the Benefits of Interacting with Nature?" 917.
23. Ilardi, *The Depression Cure*, 137.
24. Emmanuel-Avina and Delaney, "The Value Assimilation Effect."
25. Wright et al., "Health Behavior Change in the Classroom."
26. Duhigg, *The Power of Habit*, 129–30.
27. Bicknell, "Music and Exercise."

Conclusion

1. Lang, "How to Teach a Good First Day of Class."
2. Lang, "How to Teach a Good First Day of Class."
3. Pace, "A Thousand Times."

BIBLIOGRAPHY

. . . .

Ackerman, Courtney E. "What Is Self-Regulation? (+95 Skills and Strategies)." *PositivePsychology.com*, July 3, 2018. https://positivepsychology.com/self -regulation/.

Active Minds and Association of College and University Educators (ACUE). *Creating a Culture of Caring: Practical Approaches for College and University Faculty to Support Student Wellbeing and Mental Health*. Distributed by Active Minds. 2020. https://www.activeminds.org/wp-content /uploads/2020/04/Faculty-Resource_Creating-a-Culture-of-Caring.pdf.

Adams, Susan. "Game of Tongues: How Duolingo Built a $700 Million Business with Its Addictive Language-Learning App." *Forbes*, July 23, 2019. https:// www.forbes.com/sites/susanadams/2019/07/16/game-of-tongues-how -duolingo-built-a-700-million-business-with-its-addictive-language -learning-app/.

Adan, Roger A. H., Eline M. van der Beek, Jan K. Buitelaar, John F. Cryan, Johannes Hebebrand, Suzanne Higgs, Harriet Schellekens, and Suzanne L. Dickson. "Nutritional Psychiatry: Towards Improving Mental Health by What You Eat." *Science Direct* 29, no. 11 (December 2019): 1321–32. https://doi.org/10.1016/j.euroneuro.2019.10.011.

Ambrose, Susan A., Michael W. Bridges, Michele DiPietro, Marsha C. Lovett, Marie K. Norman. *How Learning Works: 7 Research-Based Principles for Smart Teaching*. San Francisco: Jossey-Bass, 2010.

Amabile, Teresa M., and Steven J. Kramer. "The Power of Small Wins." *Harvard Business Review*, 2011. https://hbr.org/2011/05/the-power-of-small-wins.

American College Health Association. *American College Health Association-National College Health Assessment II: Spring 2017 Reference Group Executive Summary*. Hanover, MD: American College Health Association, 2017.

American College Health Association. *American College Health Association-National College Health Assessment III: Fall 2019 Reference Group Executive Summary*. Silver Spring, MD: American College Health Association, 2019.

America's Health Rankings. "Suicide." 2019. https://www.americashealth rankings.org/explore/annual/measure/Suicide/state/ALL.

Anderson, Greta. "Students in Great Need of Mental Health Support during Pandemic." *Inside Higher Ed*, September 11, 2020. https://www.inside highered.com/news/2020/09/11/students-great-need-mental-health -support-during-pandemic.

Anderson, Greta. "The Emotional Toll of Racism." *Inside Higher Ed*, October 23, 2020. https://www.insidehighered.com/news/2020/10/23/racism-fuels -poor-mental-health-outcomes-black-students.

Angelidis, Angelos, Ericka Solis, Franziska Lautenbach, Willem van der Does, and Peter Putman. "I'm Going to Fail! Acute Cognitive Performance Anxiety Increases Threat-Interference and Impairs WM performance." *PLOS One* (February 7, 2019): 2, 7. https://doi.org/10.1371/journal .pone.0210824.

Antaramian, Susan. "Assessing Psychological Symptoms and Well-Being: Application of a Dual-Factor Mental Health Model to Understand College Student Performance." *Sage Journals, Journal of Psychoeducational Assessment* (November 21, 2014): 419–29. https://doi.org/10.1177 /0734282914557727.

Ariani, Dorothea Wahyu. "Self-Determined Motivation, Achievement Goals and Anxiety of Economic and Business Students in Indonesia." *Educational Research and Reviews* 12, no. 23 (December 2017): 1154–66. https://doi .org/10.5897/ERR2017.3381.

Ariely, Dan, Uri Gneezy, George Lowenstein, and Nina Mazar. "Large Stakes and Big Mistakes." *The Review of Economic Studies* 76, no. 2 (April 2009): 463. https://doi.org/10.1111/j.1467-937X.2009.00534.x.

Astin, Alexander W. *Four Critical Years: Effects of College on Beliefs, Attitudes, and Knowledge*, 126–36. San Francisco: Jossey-Bass, 1977.

Baik, Chi, Wendy Larcombe, and Abi Brooker. "How Universities Can Enhance Student Mental Wellbeing: the Student Perspective." *Higher Education Research & Development* 38, no. 4 (February 11, 2019): 674–87. https://doi .org/10.1080/07294360.2019.1576596.

Bain, Ken. *What the Best College Teachers Do*. Cambridge: Harvard University Press, 2004.

Beck, Julie. "How Uncertainty Fuels Anxiety." *Atlantic*, March 18, 2015. https://www.theatlantic.com/health/archive/2015/03/how-uncertainty -fuels-anxiety/388066/.

Beers, Stephen, Connie Horton, Brad A. Lau, Nathan Greer, C. Skip Trudeau, Kim Stave, and Brenda Roth. "A Praxis Briefing: Mental Health on the Campus: Defining Challenges and Opportunities." *Growth: The Journal of the Association for Christians in Student Development* 18, no. 18 (2019): 7–13. https://pillars.taylor.edu/acsd_growth/vol18/iss18/1/.

Bell, Andrea L. "What Is Self-Regulation and Why Is It So Important?" *Good*

Therapy, September 28, 2016. https://www.goodtherapy.org/blog/what -is-self-regulation-why-is-it-so-important-0928165.

Bicknell, Jeanette. "Music and Exercise: What Current Research Tells Us." *Psychology Today*, January 30, 2013. https://www.psychologytoday.com /us/blog/why-music-moves-us/201301/music-and-exercise-what-current -research-tells-us.

Biswas, Shampa. "Advice on Advising: How to Mentor Minority Students." *Chronicle of Higher Education*, March 13, 2019. https://www.chronicle .com/article/advice-on-advising-how-to-mentor-minority-students /?cid=gen_sign_in.

Bjelland, Ingvar, Steinar Krokstad, Arnstein Mykletun, Alv A. Dahl, Grethe S. Tell, K. Tambs. "Does a Higher Educational Level Protect against Anxiety and Depression? The HUNT study." *Social Science & Medicine* 66, no. 6 (2008): 1344.

Boswell, James F., Johanna Thompson-Hollands, Todd J. Farchione, and David H. Barlow. "Intolerance of Uncertainty: A Common Factor in the Treatment of Emotional Disorders." *Journal of Clinical Psychology* 69, no. 6 (June 2013): 630–45. https://doi.org/10.1002/jclp.21965.

Boucher, Ellen. "It's Time to Ditch Our Deadlines." *Chronicle of Higher Education*, August 22, 2016. https://www.chronicle.com/article/its-time -to-ditch-our-deadlines/.

Bowman, Nicholas A., Lindsay Jarratt, Nayoung Jang, and Timothy J. Bono. "The Unfolding of Student Adjustment during the First Semester of College." *Research in Higher Education* 60: 273–92. https://doi.org/10 .1007/s11162-018-9535-x.

Brackett, Marc. *Permission to Feel: Unlocking the Power of Emotions to Help Our Kids, Ourselves, and Our Society Thrive*. New York: Celadon Books, 2019.

Bravata, Dena M., Sharon A. Watts, Autumn L. Keefer, Divya K. Madhusudhan, Katie T. Taylor, Dani M. Clark, Ross S. Nelson, Kevin O. Cokley, and Heather K. Hagg. "Prevalence, Predictors, and Treatment of Impostor Syndrome: A Systematic Review." *J Gen Intern Medicine* 35, no. 4 (April 2020): 1252–75. https://doi.org/10.1007/s11606-019-05364-1.

Bristow, Jennie, Sarah Cant, and Anwesa Chatterjee. *Generational Encounters with Higher Education: The Academic-Student Relationship and the University Experience*. Bristol: Bristol University Press, 2020.

Brown, Brené. *Rising Strong: How the Ability to Reset Transforms the Way We Live, Love, Parent, and Lead*. New York: Random House, 2015.

Brown, Peter C., Henry L. Roediger III, and Mark A. McDaniel. *Make It Stick: The Science of Successful Learning*. Cambridge, MA: Belknap, 2014.

Brown, Sarah. *Overwhelmed: The Real Campus Mental Health Crisis and New Models for Wellbeing*. Washington, DC: Chronicle of Higher Education, Inc., 2020. https://www.aucccd.org/assets/documents/StatementsPressReleases /MentalHealth_v6_Interactive.pdf.

Burnette, Crystal, Rajeev Ramchand, and Lynsay Ayer. "Gatekeeper Training for Suicide Prevention: A Theoretical Model and Review of the Empirical Literature." *Rand Health Quarterly* 5, no. 1 (July 15, 2015): 16. PMCID: PMC5158249.

Burrell, Jackie. "College Suicide Rates and Statistics." *Verywell Mind*, April 26, 2022, https://www.verywellmind.com/college-and-teen-suicide-statistics-3570768.

Busta, Hallie. "A Look at Trends in College Consolidation Since 2016." *Education Dive*, April 22, 2022. https://www.educationdive.com/news/how-many-colleges-and-universities-have-closed-since-2016/539379/.

Cain, Susan. *Quiet: The Power of Introverts in a World that Can't Stop Talking.* New York: Random House, 2012.

Carter, Christine. "Here's How I Finally Got Myself to Start Exercising." *Ideas. Ted.Com*, November 2, 2020. https://ideas.ted.com/heres-how-i-finally-got-myself-to-start-exercising/.

Cartreine, James. "More than Sad: Depression Affects Your Ability to Think." *Harvard Health Blog*, May 6, 2016. https://www.health.harvard.edu/blog/sad-depression-affects-ability-think-201605069551.

Cavanagh, Sarah Rose. *The Spark of Learning: Energizing the College Classroom with the Science of Emotion.* Morgantown: West Virginia University Press, 2016.

CDC. "Suicide Rising across the US." Accessed January 5, 2022, https://www.cdc.gov/vitalsigns/suicide/infographic.html.

Chambliss, Daniel F., and Christopher G. Takacs. *How College Works.* Cambridge, MA: Harvard University Press, 2014. Kindle.

Chang, Yunjeong, and Peggy Brickman. "When Group Work Doesn't Work: Insights from Students." *CBE—Life Sciences Education* 17, no. 3 (September 5, 2018): 1–17. https://doi.org/10.1187/cbe.17-09-0199.

Chowdhury, Madhuleena Roy. "What Is Emotional Regulation +6 Emotional Skills and Strategies." *PositivePsychology.com*, November 25, 2021, https://positivepsychology.com/emotion-regulation/.

Clark, John. "Few Grads Say Alma Mater Prioritizes Mental Health." *Gallup*, June 9, 2020. https://news.gallup.com/poll/312428/few-grads-say-alma-mater-prioritizes-mental-health.aspx.

Cohen, Geoffrey L., Claude M. Steele, and Lee D. Ross. "The Mentor's Dilemma: Providing Critical Feedback across the Racial Divide." *Personality and Social Psychology Bulletin* 25, no. 10 (1999): 1302–18. https://doi.org/10.1177/0146167299258011.

Cooper, Katelyn M., Virginia R. Downing, and Sara E. Brownell. "The Influence of Active Learning Practices on Student Anxiety in Large-Enrollment College Science Classrooms." *International Journal of STEM Education* 5, no. 23 (June 12, 2018): 2. https://doi.org/10.1186/s40594-018-0123-6.

Cooper, Katelyn M., Brian Haney, Anna Krieg, and Sara E. Brownell. "What's in a Name? The Importance of Students Perceiving That an Instructor Knows Their Names in a High-Enrollment Biology Classroom." *CBE—Life Sciences Education* 16, no. 8 (Spring 2017). https://doi.org/10.1187/cbe.16-08-0265.

Cross, Wendi, Monica M. Matthieu, DeQuincy Lezine, and Kerry L. Knox. "Does a Brief Suicide Prevention Gatekeeper Training Program Enhance Observed Skills?" *Crisis* 31, no. 3 (January 1, 2010): 149–59. https://doi.org/10.1027/0227-5910/a000014.

Cuncic, Arlin. "What Is Imposter Syndrome?" *California Cognitive Behavioral Institute*, March 6, 2021. https://theccbi.com/what-is-imposter-syndrome/.

Cuseo, Joe. "Student Faculty Engagement." *New Directions for Teaching and Learning* 2018, no. 154 (March 7, 2018): 87–97.

Dallimore, Elise J., Julie H. Hertenstein, and Marjorie B. Platt. "Impact of Cold Calling on Student Voluntary Participation." *Journal of Management Education* 37, no. 3 (2012): 305–41. https://doi.org/10.1177/1052562912446067.

Damon, William. *The Path to Purpose: How Young People Find Their Calling in Life.* New York: Free Press, 2008.

Dastagir, Alia E. "Why It's So Important to Hope." *USA Today*, October 10, 2020. https://www.usatoday.com/story/news/nation/2020/10/10/hope-essential-mental-health-and-well-being-psychologists-say/5942107002/.

De la Fuente, Jesus, Jorge Amate, Maria Carmen González-Torres, Raquel Artuch, Juan Manuel García-Torrecillas, and Salvatore Fadda. "Effects of Levels of Self-Regulation and Regulatory Teaching on Strategies for Coping with Academic Stress in Undergraduate Students." *Frontiers in Psychology* 11, no 22 (January 31, 2020): 1–16. https://doi.org/10.3389/fpsyg.2020.00022.

Devilbiss, David M., Rick L. Jenison, and Craig W. Berridge. "Stress-Induced Impairment of a Working Memory Task: Role of Spiking Rate and Spiking History Predicted Discharge." *PLOS Computational Biology.* 8, no. 9 (September 13, 2012): 1–14. https://doi.org/10.1371/journal.pcbi.1002681.

Deroma, Virginia M., John B. Leach, and J. Patrick Leverett. "The Relationship between Depression and College Academic Performance." *College Student Journal* 9, no. 1 (January 2009): 325–34. EBSCOhost.

Dirksen, Debra J. "Hitting the Reset Button: Using Formative Assessments to Guide Instruction." *Phi Delta Kaplan* 92, no. 7 (April 1, 2011): 26–31. https://doi.org/10.1177/003172171109200706.

Distin, Sara. "Why It's a Good Thing Kids Ask So Many Questions." *Tinybop*, February 17, 2016. https://tinybop.com/blog/why-its-a-good-thing-kids-ask-so-many-questions.

Djamasbi, Soussan, Marisa Siegel, Jeanine Skorinko, and Tom Tullis. "Online Viewing and Aesthetic Preferences of Generation Y and the Baby Boom Generation: Testing User Website Experience through Eye Tracking."

Journal of Electronic Commerce 15, no. 4 (2011): 121–57. https://doi.org
/10.2753/JEC1086-4415150404.

Dube, S. R., R. F. Anda, V. J. Felitti, D. P. Chapman, D. F. Williamson, and
W. H. Giles. "Childhood Abuse, Household Dysfunction, and the Risk of
Attempted Suicide throughout the Life Span: Findings from the Adverse
Childhood Experiences Study." *Journal of the American Medical Associaton*
286, no. 24 (December 2001): 3089–96. https://doi.org/10.1001/jama
.286.24.3089.

Duckworth, Angela. *Grit: The Power of Passion and Perseverance.* New York:
Scribner, 2016.

Duhigg, Charles. *The Power of Habit.* New York: Random House, 2012.

Dunn, Andrea L., and Jennifer S. Jewell. "The Effect of Exercise on Mental
Health." *Current Sports Medicine Reports* 9, no. 4 (July–August 2010):
202–7. https://doi.org/10.1249/JSR.0b013e3181e7d9af.

Dweck, Carol. *Mindset: The New Psychology of Success.* New York: Ballantine,
2006.

Ebert, David Daniel, Philippe Mortier, Fanny Kaehlke, Ronny Bruffaerts,
Harald Baumeister, Randy P. Auerbach, Jordi Alonso, et al. "Barriers of
Mental Health Treatment Utilization among First-Year College Students:
First Cross-National Results from the WHO World Mental Health
International College Student Initiative." *International Journal of Methods
in Psychiatric Research* 28, no. 2 (May 9, 2019): 1–14. https://doi.org/10
.1002/mpr.1782.

Eisenberg, Daniel, Ezra Golberstein, and Justin Hunt. "Mental Health and
Academic Success in College." *B. E. Journal of Economic Analysis & Policy*
(May 2009): 1. https://doi.org/10.2202/1935-1682.2191.

Elsworthy, Emma. "Curious Children Ask 73 Questions Each Day—Many of
Which Parents Can't Answer, Says Study." *Independent*, December 3, 2017.
https://www.independent.co.uk/news/uk/home-news/curious-children
-questions-parenting-mum-dad-google-answers-inquisitive-argos-toddlers
-chad-valley-tots-town-a8089821.html.

Emmanuel-Avina, Glory, and Harold D. Delaney. "The Value Assimilation
Effect between University Professors and Their Students in the Classroom."
Journal of Curriculum and Teaching 7, no. 158 (April 2018). https://doi
.org/10.5430/jct.v7n1p158.

Eyler, Joshua R. *How Humans Learn: The Science and Stories behind Effective
College Teaching.* Morgantown: West Virginia University Press, 2018.

Faculty Innovation Center. "Team-Based Learning." Accessed January 15,
2022. https://facultyinnovate.utexas.edu/instructional-strategies/group
-learning.

Falk, Arman. "Fairness and Motivation." *IZA World of Labor* 1, no. 9
(September 2014). https://doi.org/10.15185/izawol.9.

Felitti, Vincent J. "The Relation between Adverse Childhood Experiences and

Adult Health: Turning Gold into Lead." *Permanente Journal* 6, no. 1 (Winter 2002): 44–47. PMCID: PMC6220625.

Felten, Peter, and Leo M. Lambert. *Relationship-Rich Education: How Human Connections Drive Success in College.* Baltimore: Johns Hopkins University Press, 2020.

Ferguson, Ronald F., with Sarah F. Phillips, Jacob F. S. Rowley, and Jocelyn W. Friedlander. "The Influence of Teaching beyond Standardized Test Scores: Engagement, Mindsets, and Agency." The Achievement Gap Initiative at Harvard University, October 2015. https://www.hks.harvard .edu/publications/influence-teaching-beyond-standardized-test-scores -engagement-mindsets-and-agency.

Gallimore, Alec D., Robert D. Braun, and Steven W. McLaughlin. "A Friend at the Front of the Room," *Inside Higher Ed*, Dec. 2, 2019, https://www .insidehighered.com/views/2019/12/02/professors-should-be-more -involved-helping-students-mental-health-challenges.

Gallup Inc. and Purdue University. *Great Jobs Great Lives: The 2014 Gallup-Purdue Index Report.* 2014. Distributed by Gallup Inc. https://www.gallup .com/services/176768/2014-gallup-purdue-index-report.aspx.

Gannon, Kevin. "How to Create a Syllabus: Advice Guide." *Chronicle of Higher Education*, September 12, 2018. https://www.chronicle.com/article/how-to -create-a-syllabus/.

Georgetown University. "New Study Finds That Earning Power Is Increasingly Tied to Education." Georgetown University Center on Education and the Workforce. August 5, 2011. https://cew.georgetown.edu/wp-content /uploads/2014/11/collegepayoff-release.pdf.

Gilbert, Rebecca. "Cognitive Decline in Parkinson's Disease: Is There Anything We Can Do About It?" American Parkinson Disease Association. March 5, 2019. https://www.apdaparkinson.org/article/cognitive-decline-in-parkin sons-disease/.

Gilbert, Rebecca. "Planning for the What-Ifs: Mental Health Concerns in Advanced Parkinson's Disease: Psychosis and Behavioral Problems." American Parkinson Disease Association. December 3, 2019. https://www .apdaparkinson.org/article/psychosis-and-behavioral-problems-in-advanced -parkinsons-disease/.

Gladwell, Malcolm. "The Tortoise and the Hare." *Revisionist History*, June 27, 2019. Season 4, episode 2. Podcast audio. http://revisionisthistory.com /seasons?selected=season-4.

Golden, Sherita Hill. "Coronavirus in African Americans and Other People of Color." *John Hopkins University*, April 20, 2020. https://www.hopkins medicine.org/health/conditions-and-diseases/coronavirus/covid19-racial -disparities.

Gottman, John. *Raising An Emotionally Intelligent Child: The Heart of Parenting.* New York: Simon & Schuster, 1998.

Gottman Institute. "The Four Parenting Styles." Accessed September 10,
    2014. https://www.gottman.com/blog/the-four-parenting-styles/.

Grupe, Dan W., and Jack B. Nitschke. "Uncertainty and Anticipation in
    Anxiety: An Integrated Neurobiological and Psychological Perspective."
    Nature Reviews Neuroscience 14, no. 7 (July 20, 2013): 497. https://doi
    .org/10.1038/nrn3524.

Haidet, Paul, Karla Kubitz, and Wayne T. McCormack. "Analysis of the Team-
    Based Learning Literature: TBL Comes of Age," *Journal on Excellence in
    College Teaching* 25 (2014): 303–33.

Hangen, Tona. "How Can I Write a Course Syllabus That's Worth Reading?"
    Magna 20-Minute Mentors. Accessed May 1, 2020. https://www.magna
    pubs.com/product/program/how-can-i-write-a-course-syllabus-thats
    -worth-reading/.

Harnish, Richard J., Rory O'Brien McElwee, Jeanne M. Slattery, Sue Frantz,
    Michelle R. Haney, Cecilia M. Shore, and Julie Penley. "Creating a
    Foundation for a Warm Classroom Climate." *Observer* 24, January 11,
    2011. https://www.psychologicalscience.org/observer/creating-the
    -foundation-for-a-warm-classroom-climate.

Hartocollis, Anemona. "Feeling Suicidal, Students Turned to Their College.
    They Were Told to Go Home." *New York Times*, August 28, 2018. https://
    www.nytimes.com/2018/08/28/us/college-suicide-stanford-leaves.html
    ?searchResultPosition=1.

Harvard Graduate School of Education: Instructional Moves. "Expanding
    Participation through Cold-Calling." Accessed January 14, 2022. https://
    instructionalmoves.gse.harvard.edu/expanding-participation-through
    -cold-calling.

Harvard Medical School. "Sleep and Mood." Last reviewed December 15, 2008.
    http://healthysleep.med.harvard.edu/need-sleep/whats-in-it-for-you
    /mood.

Henderson, William D. "The LSAT, Law School Exams and Meritocracy: The
    Surprising and Undertheorized Role of Test-Taking Speed." *Texas Law
    Review* 82, no. 975 (2004). https://www.repository.law.indiana.edu/facpub
    /344.

Hernandez-Torrano, Daniel, Laura Ibrayeva, Jason Sparks, Natalya Lim,
    Alessandra Clementi, Ainur Almukhambetova, Yerden Nurtayev, and
    Ainur Muratkyzy. "Mental Health and Well-Being of University Students:
    A Bibliometric Mapping of Literature." *Frontiers in Psychology* (June 9,
    2020): 1–16. https://doi.org/10.3389/fpsyg.2020.01226.

Hershner, Shelley. "Sleep and Academic Performance: Measuring the Impact
    of Sleep." *Science Direct* 33 (June 2020): 51–56. https://doi.org/10.1016/j
    .cobeha.2019.11.009.

Holt-Lunstad, Julianne. "The Potential Public Health Relevance of Social

Isolation and Loneliness: Prevalence, Epidemiology, and Risk Factors." *Public Policy & Aging Report* 27, no. 4 (2018): 127–30.

Howard, Jay. "How to Hold a Better Class Discussion." *Chronicle of Higher Education.* Accessed January 14, 2021. https://www.chronicle.com/article /how-to-hold-a-better-class-discussion/.

Hsu, Jeremy L., and Gregory R. Goldsmith, "Instructor Strategies to Alleviate Stress and Anxiety among College and University STEM Students," *CBE—Life Sciences Education* 20, no. 1 (Spring 2021): 1–13. https://doi .org/10.1187/cbe.20-08-0189.

Huang, Yunhui, Wei Lv, and Jiang Wu. "Relationship between Intrinsic Motivation and Undergraduate Students' Depression and Stress: The Moderating Effect of Interpersonal Conflict." *Psychological Reports* 119, no. 2 (August 3, 2016): 527–38. https://doi.org/10.1177/003329 4116661512.

Huber, Rachel. "Your Body: A Key to Happiness." Speech presented at Brigham Young University–Idaho, Rexburg, ID, November 29, 2019.

Hurd, Noelle, and Marc Zimmerman. "Natural Mentors, Mental Health, and Risk Behaviors: A Longitudinal Analysis of African American Adolescents Transitioning into Adulthood." *American Journal of Community Psychology* 46, no. 1–2 (September 8, 2010): 36–48. https://doi.org/10.1007/s10464 -010-9325-x.

Ilardi, Stephen S. *The Depression Cure: The 6-Step Program to Beat Depression without Drugs.* Boston: Da Capo Press, 2009.

Jeakle, Gabriella. "How I Am Learning to Live with Loneliness at a Jesuit College." *American Magazine*, September 18, 2019. https://www.america magazine.org/faith/2019/09/18/how-i-am-learning-live-loneliness-jesuit -college.

Jeakle, Gabriella. "Not Built to Belong." *America* 222 (2020): 36–37.

Joels, Marian, Zhenwei Pu, Olof Wiegert, Melly S. Oitzl, and Harm J. Krugers. "Learning under Stress: How Does It Work?" *Trends in Cognitive Sciences* 10, no. 4 (April 1, 2006): 152–58. https://doi.org/10.1016/j.tics.2006 .02.002.

Johnson, Sidney. "Will Moving Office Hours Online Get Students to Show Up?" *Ed Surge*, September 27, 2018. https://www.edsurge.com/news/2018 -09-27-will-moving-office-hours-online-get-students-to-show-up.

Kaufman, Scott Barry. "The Will and Way of Hope." *Psychology Today*, December 26, 2011. https://www.psychologytoday.com/us/blog/beautiful -minds/201112/the-will-and-ways-hope.

Kember, David, Amber Ho, and Celina Hong. "The Importance of Establishing Relevance in Motivating Student Learning." *Active Learning in Higher Education* 9, no. 3 (2008): 249–63. https://doi.org/10.1177/146978740 8095849.

Keniger, Lucy E., Kevin J. Gaston, Katherine N. Irvine, and Richard A. Fuller. "What Are the Benefits of Interacting with Nature?" *International Journal of Environmental Research and Public Health* 10, no. 3 (March 6, 2013): 913–35. https://doi.org/10.3390/ijerph10030913.

Key, Kimberly. "The Dark Side of Deadlines." *Psychology Today*, June 15, 2015. https://www.psychologytoday.com/us/blog/counseling-keys/201506 /the-dark-side-deadlines.

Khan Academy. "Sal Khan's Thoughts on Mastery Learning." September 21, 2018. YouTube video, 2:02. https://www.youtube.com/watch?v=lGa QWIV8PZ4.

Khan Academy. "You Can Learn Anything." November 27, 2019. YouTube video, 0:30. https://www.youtube.com/watch?v=beSsSAUf-oc&feature =youtu.be.

Khan, Salman. "Let's Teach for Mastery—Not Test Scores." Filmed November 2015 at TED New York, NY. YouTube video, 10:49. https://www.youtube .com/watch?v=-MTRxRO5SRA.

Khan, Salman. *The One World School House: Education Reimagined.* London: Hodder & Stoughton, 2012.

King, Don Roy, Dave McCary, and Oz Rodriguez, dirs. *Saturday Night Live.* Season 43, episode 1, "Papyrus-SNL." Aired September 30, 2017, in New York, NY. YouTube video, 3:50. https://www.youtube.com/watch?v =jVhlJNJopOQ.

Kusurkar, R. A., G. Croiset, Olle Th. J. Ten Cate. "Twelve Tips to Stimulate Intrinsic Motivation in Students through Autonomy-Supportive Classroom Teaching Derived from Self-Determination Theory." *Medical Teacher* 33, no. 12 (2011): 978–82. https://doi.org/10.3109/0142159X.2011.599896.

LaBier, Douglas. "A Sense of Awe and Life Purpose Increases Your Mental Health." *Psychology Today*, September 15, 2015. https://www.psychology today.com/us/blog/the-new-resilience/201509/sense-awe-and-life-purpose -increases-your-mental-health.

Lake, Rebecca. "The Cost of Being a College Dropout." *Balance*, February 14, 2020, https://www.thebalance.com/the-cost-of-college-dropout-4174303.

Lang, James M. *Cheating Lessons.* Cambridge: Harvard University Press, 2013.

Lang, James M. *Distracted: Why Students Can't Focus and What You Can Do About It.* Read by Caitlin Davies. New York: Hachette, 2020. Audible audio ed., 12:57.

Lang, James M. "How to Teach a Good First Day of Class." *Chronicle of Higher Education*, August 21, 2018. https://www.chronicle.com/article/how-to -teach-a-good-first-day-of-class/.

Lang, James M. *Small Teaching: Everyday Lessons from the Science of Learning.* San Francisco: Jossey-Bass, 2016.

Lang, James M. "The 3 Essential Functions of Your Syllabus, Part 1." *Chronicle*

of Higher Education, February 23, 2015. https://www.chronicle.com
/article/the-3-essential-functions-of-your-syllabus-part-1/.

LastingLearning.com. "Using Desirable Difficulties to Enhance Learning,
Dr. Robert Bjork." October 27, 2015. YouTube video, 4:02. https://www
.youtube.com/watch?v=XPllm-gtrMM.

Lemov, Doug, and Norman Atkins. *Teach Like a Champion 2.0: 62 Techniques
That Put Students on the Path to College*. New York: John Wiley & Sons,
2015.

Li, Ye, Mei-Rong Lv, Yan-Jin Wei, Ling Sun, Ji-Xiang Zhang, Huai-Guo Zhang,
and Bin Li. "Dietary Patterns and Depression Risk: A Meta-analysis."
Psychiatry Research, no. 253 (July 2017): 373–82. https://doi
.org/10.1016/j.psychres.2017.04.020.

Ling, Yu, Yushu He, Yong Wei, Weihong Cen, Qi Zhou, and Mingtian Zhong.
"Intrinsic and Extrinsic Goals as Moderators of Stress and Depressive
Symptoms in Chinese Undergraduate Students: A Multi-wave Longitudinal
Study." *BMC Psychiatry* 16, no. 138 (2016): 1–8. https://doi.org/10.1186
/s12888-016-0842-5.

Lipson, Sarah Ketchen, and Daniel Eisenberg. "Mental Health and Academic
Attitudes and Expectations in University Populations: Results from the
Healthy Minds Study." *Journal of Mental Health* 27, no. 3 (December 21,
2017): 1–205. https://doi.org/10.1080/09638237.2017.1417567.

"Littlewoods Retailer Finds Mothers Asked 228 Questions a Day." *news.com.au*,
March 29, 2013. https://www.news.com.au/lifestyle/parenting/littlewoods
-retailer-survey-finds-mothers-asked-228-questions-a-day/news-story/9cc
a3e25f5981147d1e0bff293f6e3f2.

Ljungberg, Tina, Emma Bondza, and Connie Lethin. "Evidence of the
Importance of Dietary Habits Regarding Depressive Symptoms and
Depression." *International Journal of Environmental Research and Public
Health* 17, no. 5 (March 2020). https://doi.org/10.3390/ijerph17051616.

Lukianoff, Greg, and Jonathan Haidt. *The Coddling of the American Mind:
How Good Intentions and Bad Ideas Are Setting Up a Generation for Failure*.
Westminster: Penguin, 2018.

Macaskill, Ann. "The Mental Health of University Students in the United
Kingdom." *British Journal of Guidance & Counseling* 41, no. 4 (November
2012): 426–41. https://doi.org/10.1080/03069885.2012.743110.

Maheshwari, Ganpat, and Faizan Shaukat. "Impact of Poor Sleep Quality on
the Academic Performance of Medical Students." *Cureus* 11, no. 4 (April 1,
2019). https://doi.org/10.7759/cureus.4357.

Maxwell, Connor, and Danyelle Solomon. "The Economic Fallout of the
Coronavirus for People of Color." *American Progress*, April 14, 2020.
https://www.americanprogress.org/article/economic-fallout-coronavirus
-people-color/.

Maxwell, John C. *Failing Forward: Turning Mistakes into Stepping Stones for Success*. Nashville: Thomas Nelson, 2007.

McCabe, Janice, M. *Connecting in College: How Friendship Networks Matter for Academic and Social Success*. Chicago: University of Chicago Press, 2016.

McPhillips, Deidre. "Death from Police Harm Disproportionately Affect People of Color." *US News*, June 3, 2020. https://www.usnews.com/news/articles /2020-06-03/data-show-deaths-from-police-violence-disproportionately -affect-people-of-color.

Medina, John. *Brain Rules: 12 Principles for Surviving and Thriving at Work, Home, and School*. Seattle: Pear Press, 2008.

Michaelsen, Larry. *Team-Based Learning: A Transformative Use of Small Groups*. Westport, CT: Stylus Publishing, 2002.

Michaelsen, Larry, M. Sweet, and D. Parmalee. *Team-Based Learning: Small Group Learning's Next Big Step. New Directions in Teaching and Learning* (2009): 2–3.

Milton, Carolyn Centeno. "Fear Shrinks Your Brain and Makes You Less Creative." *Forbes*, April 18, 2018. https://www.forbes.com/sites/carolyn centeno/2018/04/18/ar-shrinks-your-brain-and-makes-you-less -creative/.

Mishara, Brian L., Janie Houle, and Brigitte Lavoie. "Comparison of the Effects of Four Suicide Prevention Programs for Family and Friends of High-Risk Suicidal Men Who Do Not Seek Help Themselves." *Suicide and Life-Threatening Behavior* 35, no. 3 (June 2005): 329–42. https://doi.org /10.1521/suli.2005.35.3.329.

Morin, Amanda. "Developmental Milestones for 4-Year-Olds." Accessed April 20, 2020. https://www.understood.org/en/learning-thinking-differences /signs-symptoms/developmental-milestones/developmental-milestones -for-typical-4-year-olds.

Mukhopadhyay, Samhita, Paula Johnson, and Dan Porterfield. "College Students, Mental Health, and the University's Role." *Aspen Ideas To Go*. Podcast audio, August 21, 2018. https://www.aspeninstitute.org/podcasts /college-students-mental-health-and-the-universitys-role/.

Munger, Dave. "The Six-Second Teacher Evaluation." ScienceBlogs. Last modified May 1, 2006. https://scienceblogs.com/cognitivedaily/2006/05 /01/the-sixsecond-teacher-evaluati.

National Institute of Mental Health. "Suicide." US Department of Health and Human Services. Accessed August 24, 2020, https://www.nimh.nih.gov /health/statistics/suicide.shtml.

NCES (National Center for Education Statistics). "Annual Earnings by Educational Attainment." Last modified May 2021. https://nces.ed.gov /programs/coe/indicator/cba.

NCES. "Fast Facts Graduation Rates." Accessed May 1, 2020. https://nces.ed .gov/fastfacts/display.asp?id=40.

Nietzsche, Fredrich Wilhelm. *Twilight of the Idols: Or How to Philosophize with a Hammer.* New York: Penguin Books, 2003.

Northeastern University. "Active Question and Answer Techniques." Accessed January 14, 2022. https://learning.northeastern.edu/active-question-and -answer-approaches/.

Nunn, Lisa M. *33 Simple Strategies for Faculty: A Week-By-Week Resource for Teaching First-Year and First-Generation Students.* New Brunswick, Camden, and Newark: Rutgers University Press. Kindle.

Obama, Michelle. *Becoming.* Read by the author. Toronto: CELA, 2019. Audible audio ed., chapter 6.

Okano, Kana, Jakub R. Kaczmarzyk, Neha Dave, John D. E. Gabrieli, and Jeffrey C. Grossman. "Sleep Quality, Duration, and Consistency Are Associated with Better Academic Performance in College Students." *npj Science of Learning* 4, no. 16 (October 1, 2019): 245–61. https://www .nature.com/articles/s41539-019-0055-z.

O'Keeffe, Patrick. "A Sense of Belonging: Improving Student Retention." *College Student Journal* 47, no. 4 (December 2013): 605–13.

Okon-Singer, Hadas, Talma Hendler, Luiz Pessoa, and Alexander J. Shackman. "The Neurobiology of Emotion-Cognition Interactions: Fundamental Questions and Strategies for Future Research." *Frontiers in Human Neuroscience* 9, no. 58 (February 17, 2015): 1–3. https://doi.org/10.3389 /fnhum.2015.00058.

Pace, Glenn L. "A Thousand Times." Transcript of speech delivered in Salt Lake City, UT, October 1990. https://abn.churchofjesuschrist.org/study/general -conference/1990/10/a-thousand-times.

Parks, Sharon Daloz. *Big Questions, Worthy Dreams: Mentoring Emerging Adults in Their Search for Meaning, Purpose, and Faith.* San Francisco: Jossey-Bass, 2011.

Pena-Sarrionandia, Ainize, Moira Mikolajczak, and James J. Gross. "Integrating Emotion Regulation and Emotional Intelligence Traditions: A Meta-analysis." *Frontiers in Psychology* 6, no. 160 (February 24, 2015): 1–27. https://doi.org/10.3389/fpsyg.2015.00160.

Pink, Daniel H. *Drive: The Surprising Truth About What Motivates Us.* New York: Riverhead Books, 2011.

Piray, Payam, Verena Ly, Karin Roelofs, Roshan Cools, and Ivan Toni. "Emotionally Aversive Cues Suppress Neural Systems Underlying Optimal Learning in Socially Anxious Individual." *Journal of Neuroscience* 39, no. 8 (February 20, 2019): 1446–53. https://doi.org/10.1523/JNEUROSCI .1394-18.2018.

Posselt, Julie R., and Sarah Ketchen Lipson. "Competition, Anxiety, and Depression in the College Classroom: Variations by Student Identity and Field of Study," *Journal of College Student Development* 57, no. 8 (November 2016): 973–89. https://doi.org/10.1353/csd.2016.0094.

"Protect Your Brain from Stress." _Harvard Health Publishing_, August 2018. https://www.health.harvard.edu/mind-and-mood/protect-your-brain-from -stress.

QPR Institute. "QPR Institute: Practical and Proven Suicide Prevention Training." Accessed July 29, 2020. https://qprinstitute.com/.

Redden, Elizabeth. "Pandemic Hurts Student Mental Health." _Inside Higher Ed_, July 13, 2020. https://www.insidehighered.com/news/2020/07/13 /survey-finds-higher-prevalence-depression-among-students-and -difficulties-accessing.

Rello, Luz, and Ricardo Baez-Yates. "Good Fonts for Dyslexia." _ASSETS '13: Proceedings of the 15th International ACM SIGACCESS Conference on Computers and Accessibility_, no. 14 (October 2013): 1–8. https://doi .org/10.1145/2513383.2513447.

Retrieval Practice. "What Is Retrieval Practice?" Accessed January 17, 2022. https://www.retrievalpractice.org/why-it-works.

Rocca, Kelly A. "Student Participation in the College Classroom: An Extended Multidisciplinary Literature Review." _Communication Education_ 59, no. 2 (April 2020): 185–213. https://doi.org/10.1080/03634520903505936.

Rogers, Brittany Karford. "When Women Don't Speak." _Y Magazine_, Spring 2020. https://magazine.byu.edu/article/when-women-dont-speak/.

The Role of Faculty in Student Mental Health. April 2021. Boston University of Public Health, Mary Christie Foundation, The Healthy Minds Network, and Hazelden Betty Ford Foundation. https://marychristieinstitute.org /wp-content/uploads/2021/04/The-Role-of-Faculty-in-Student-Mental -Health.pdf.

Romero, Carissa. "What We Know about Belonging from Scientific Research." _Mindset Scholars Network_, October 2018. https://studentexperience network.org/wp-content/uploads/2018/11/What-We-Know-About -Belonging.pdf.

Rosenthal, Robert, and Lenore Jacobson. _Pygmalion in the Classroom: Teacher Expectation and Pupils' Intellectual Development_. North Stratford: Irvington, 1992.

Ryan, Richard M., and Edward L. Deci. "Self-Determination Theory and the Facilitation of Intrinsic Motivation, Social Development, and Well-Being." _American Psychologist_ 55, no. 1 (2000): 69–73. https://doi.org/10.1037 /0003-066x.55.1.68.

Salaheddin, Keziband, and Barbara Mason. "Identifying Barriers to Mental Health Help-Seeking among Young Adults in the UK: A Cross-Sectional Survey." _The British Journal of General Practice_ 66, no. 651 (2016): 686–92. https://doi.org/10.3399/bjgp16X687313.

Sandi, Carmen. "Stress and Cognition." _Wiley Interdisciplinary Reviews: Cognitive Science_ 4, no. 3 (May 2013). https://doi.org/10.1002/wcs.1222.

Scager, Karin, Johannes Boonstra, Ton Peeters, JonneVulperhorst, and Fred

Wiegant. "Collaborative Learning in Higher Education: Evoking Positive Interdependence," *CBE—Life Sciences Education* 15, no. 4 (Winter 2016): 1–9. https://doi.org/10.1187/cbe.16-07-0219/

Schaefer, Stacey M., Jennifer Morozink Boylan, Carien M. van Reekum, Regina C. Lapate, Catherine J. Norris, Carol D. Ryff, and Richard J. Davidson. "Purpose in Life Predicts Better Emotional Recovery from Negative Stimuli." *PLOS ONE* 8, no. 11 (November 2013): 1–9. https://doi.org/10.1371/journal.pone.0080329.

Schell, Julie A., and Andrew C. Butler. "Insights from the Science of Learning Can Inform Evidence-Based Implementation of Peer Instruction." *Frontiers in Education* 3, no. 33 (May 28, 2018): 1–13. https://doi.org/10.3389/feduc.2018.00033.

Seppala, Emma. "Connectedness & Health: The Science of Social Connection." The Center for Compassion and Altruism Research and Education, Stanford Medicine, May 8, 2014. http://ccare.stanford.edu/uncategorized/connectedness-health-the-science-of-social-connection-infographic/.

Sharma, Ashish, Vishal Madaan, and Frederick D. Petty. "Exercise for Mental Health." *Primary Care Companion to the Journal of Clinical Psychiatry* 8, no. 2 (2006): 106. https://doi.org/10.4088/pcc.v08n0208a.

Sheehan, Rachel B., Matthew P. Herring, and Mark J. Campbell. "Associations between Motivation and Mental Health in Sport: A Test of the Hierarchical Model of Intrinsic and Extrinsic Motivation." *Frontiers in Psychology* 9, no. 707 (May 2018): 1–10. https://doi.org/10.3389/fpsyg.2018.00707.

Smith, Margaret, Yujie Chen, Rachel Berndtson, Kristen M. Burson, and Whitney Griffin. " 'Office Hours are Kind of Weird': Reclaiming a Resource to Foster Student-Faculty Interaction." *InSight: A Journal of Scholarly Teaching* 12 (2017): 14–29. https://doi.org/10.46504/12201701sm.

Smith, Rachel A., and Amanda Applegate. "Mental Health Stigma and Communication and Their Intersections with Education." *Communication Education* 67, no. 3 (May 2018): 382–93. https://doi.org/10.1080/03634523.2018.1465988.

"Spending Time in Nature Boosts Children's Learning." *Technology Networks*, March 14, 2019. https://www.technologynetworks.com/neuroscience/news/spending-time-in-nature-boosts-childrens-learning-316717.

"Spending Time in Nature Reduces Stress." *Science Daily*, February 25, 2020. https://www.sciencedaily.com/releases/2020/02/200225164210.htm.

Steele, Claude M. "Race and the Schooling of Black Americans." *Atlantic*, April 1992. https://www.theatlantic.com/magazine/archive/1992/04/race-and-the-schooling-of-black-americans/306073/.

Stoliker, Bryce E., and Kathryne D. Lafreniere. "The Influence of Perceived Stress, Loneliness, and Learning Burnout on University Students' Educational Experience." *College Student Journal* 49 no. 1 (Spring 2015): 146–60.

Stolzenberg, Ellen Bara, Kevin Eagan, Edgar Romo, Elaine Jessica Tamargo, Melissa C. Aragon, Madeline Luedke, and Nathaniel Kang. "The American Freshman: National Norms Fall 2019." Higher Education Research Institute, 2020. https://www.heri.ucla.edu/monographs/TheAmerican Freshman2019.pdf.

Story, Giles. "Anticipating Pain Is Worse Than Feeling It." *Harvard Business Review*, March 2014. https://hbr.org/2014/03/anticipating-pain-is -worse-than-feeling-it.

Story, Giles, Ivaylo Vlaev, Ben Seymour, Joel S. Winston, Ara Darzi, and Raymond J. Dolan. "Dread and the Disvalue of Future Pain." *PLOS Computational Biology* 9, no. 11 (2013): 1–18. https://doi.org/10.1371 /journal.pcbi.1003335.

Strauss, Valerie. "An Old Story Made New Again: Why Students of Color Are Primed to Be Left behind in the Coronavirus Crisis." *Washington Post*, April 24, 2020. https://www.washingtonpost.com/education/2020/04/24 /an-old-story-made-new-again-why-students-color-are-primed-be-left -behind-covid-19-crisis/.

Strauss, Valerie. "The Surprising Thing Google Learned about Its Employees— And What It Means for Today's Students." *Washington Post*, December 20, 2017. https://www.washingtonpost.com/news/answer-sheet/wp/2017 /12/20/the-surprising-thing-google-learned-about-its-employees-and -what-it-means-for-todays-students/.

Strikwerda, Carl J. "Faculty Members Are the Key to Solving the Retention Challenge," *Inside Higher Ed*, September 4, 2019. https://www.inside highered.com/views/2019/09/04/faculty-must-play-bigger-role-student -retention-and-success-opinion.

Tello, Monique. "Diet and Depression." *Harvard Health Blog*. Last modified January 29, 2020. https://www.health.harvard.edu/blog/diet-and -depression-2018022213309.

Teeselinka, Bouke Klein, Rogier J. D. Potter van Loon, Martijn J. van den Assem, and Dennie van Dolder. "Incentives, Performance and Choking in Darts." *Journal of Economic Behavior & Organization* 169 (January 2020): 39. https://doi.org/10.1016/j.jebo.2019.10.026.

Tice, Dianne M., and Roy F. Baumeister. "Longitudinal Study of Procrastination, Performance, Stress, and Health: The Costs and Benefits of Dawdling." *Psychological Science* 8, no. 6 (November 1, 1997): 454–58. https://doi.org/10.1111/j.1467-9280.1997.tb00460.x.

Tinto, Vincent. "Reflections on Student Persistence." *Student Success* 8, no. 2 (July 2017): 1–8. https://doi.org/10.5204/ssj.v8i2.376.

Tolkien, J.R.R. *The Hobbit: 75th Anniversary Edition*. Boston: Houghton Mifflin Harcourt, 2012.

Tough, Paul. *The Years That Matter Most: How College Makes or Breaks Us*. Boston: Houghton Mifflin Harcourt, 2019.

Twenge, Jean M. *iGen: Why Today's Super-Connected Kids Are Growing Up Less Rebellious, More Tolerant, Less Happy—And Completely Unprepared for Adulthood—And What That Means for the Rest of Us*. New York: Atria Books, 2017.

Udloncampus.cast.org. "UDL On Campus: About UDL." Accessed May 7, 2020. http://udloncampus.cast.org/page/udl_about.

UDL-Universe. "UDL-Universe: A Comprehensive Faculty Development Guide: UDL Syllabus Rubric." UDL-Universe. Accessed May 1, 2020. http://enact .sonoma.edu/c.php?g=789377&p=5650618.

United States Public Health Service. "Protecting Youth Mental Health: The U.S. Surgeon General's Advisory." 2021. https://www.hhs.gov/sites/default /files/surgeon-general-youth-mental-health-advisory.pdf.

University of Washington. "Virtual Office Hours." Accessed July 29, 2020. https://teaching.washington.edu/topics/engaging-students-in-learning /face-to-face-office-hours/virtual-office-hours/.

Urban Dictionary. "Weeder Class." Last Modified April 7, 2014. https://www .urbandictionary.com/define.php?term=Weeder%20Class.

Vaynman, Shoshanna, and Fernando Gomez-Pinilla. "Revenge of the 'Sit': How Lifestyle Impacts Neuronal and Cognitive Health through Molecular Systems That Interface Energy Metabolism with Neuronal Plasticity." *Journal of Neuroscience Research* 84, no. 4 (September 2006): 699–715. https://doi.org/10.1002/jnr.20979.

Vedantam, Shankar. "You 2.0: How to Build A Better Job." *Hidden Brain: A Conversation About Life's Unseen Patterns*. Podcast audio. July 31, 2017. https://www.npr.org/2017/07/31/540648577/you-2-0-how-to-build-a -better-job.

Vitasari, Prima, Muhammad Nubli Abdul Wahab, Ahmad Othman, Tutut Herawan, and Suriya Kumar Sinnadurai. "The Relationship between Student Anxiety and Academic Performance among Engineering Students." *Procedia-Social and Behavioral Sciences* 8, (2010): 496. https://doi.org/10 .1016/j.sbspro.2010.12.067.

Vogel, Susanne, and Lars Schwabe. "Learning and Memory under Stress: Implications for the Classroom." *npj Science of Learning* 1, no. 16011 (June 29, 2016): 6. https://doi.org/https://doi.org/10.1038/npjscilearn.2016.11.

Walter, Ekaterina, and Jessica Gioglio. *The Power of Visual Storytelling: How to Use Visuals, Videos, and Social Media to Market Your Band*. New York: McGraw-Hill Education, 2015.

Weimer, Maryellen. *Learner-Centered Teaching: Five Key Changes to Practice*. Hoboken: John Wiley and Sons, 2013.

Weir, Kirsten. "Feel like a Fraud?" *American Psychological Association*, 2013. https://www.apa.org/gradpsych/2013/11/fraud.

Wikipedia. "Thin-Slicing." Accessed May 18, 2020. https://en.wikipedia.org /wiki/Thin-slicing.

Willis, Judy. "The Neuroscience behind Stress and Learning." *Edutopia*, July 18, 2014. https://www.edutopia.org/blog/neuroscience-behind-stress-and -learning-judy-willis.

Winerman, Lea. "By the Numbers: Stress on Campus." *Monitor on Psychology*, no. 8 (September 2017): 88.

Wright, Robert R., Reese Nelson, Spencer Garcia, and Amanda Butler. "Health Behavior Change in the Classroom: A Means to a Healthy End?" *Journal of Primary Prevention.* 41, no. 5 (October 2020): 445–72. https://doi.org/10 .1007/s10935-020-00605-0.

Wyman, Peter A., Trevor A. Pickering, Anthony R. Pisani, Kelly Rulison, Karen Schmeelk-Cone, Chelsey Hartley, Madelyn Gould, et al. "Peer-Adult Network Structure and Suicide Attempts in 38 High Schools: Implications for Network-Informed Suicide Prevention." *Journal of Child Psychology and Psychiatry* 60, no. 10 (August 8, 2019): 1069. https://doi.org/10.1111 /jcpp.13102.

Yeager, David S., Marlone D. Henderson, Sidney D'Mello, David Paunesku, Gregory M. Walton, Brian J. Spitzer, and Angela Lee Duckworth. "Boring but Important: A Self-Transcendent Purpose for Learning Fosters Academic Self-Regulation." *Journal of Personality and Social Psychology* 107, no. 4 (October 2014): 559–80. https://doi.org/10.1037/a0037637.

Yeager, David S., Paul Hanselman, Gregory M. Walton, Jared S. Murray, Robert Crosnoe, Chandra Muller, Elizabeth Tipton, et al. "A National Experiment Reveals Where a Growth Mindset Improves Achievement." *Nature*, no. 573 (August 7, 2019): 364–69. https://doi.org/10.1038/s41586-019-1466-y.

INDEX

TEACHING AND LEARNING IN HIGHER EDUCATION

Picture a Professor: Interrupting Biases about Faculty and Increasing Student Learning
Edited by Jessamyn Neuhaus

Inclusive Teaching: Strategies for Promoting Equity in the College Classroom
Kelly A. Hogan and Viji Sathy

Teaching Matters: A Guide for Graduate Students
Aeron Haynie and Stephanie Spong

Remembering and Forgetting in the Age of Technology: Teaching, Learning, and the Science of Memory in a Wired World
Michelle D. Miller

Skim, Dive, Surface: Teaching Digital Reading
Jenae Cohn

Minding Bodies: How Physical Space, Sensation, and Movement Affect Learning
Susan Hrach

Ungrading: Why Rating Students Undermines Learning (and What to Do Instead)
Edited by Susan D. Blum

Radical Hope: A Teaching Manifesto
Kevin M. Gannon

Teaching about Race and Racism in the College Classroom: Notes from a White Professor
Cyndi Kernahan

Intentional Tech: Principles to Guide the Use of Educational Technology in College Teaching
Derek Bruff

Geeky Pedagogy: A Guide for Intellectuals, Introverts, and Nerds
Who Want to Be Effective Teachers
Jessamyn Neuhaus

How Humans Learn: The Science and Stories behind Effective
College Teaching
Joshua R. Eyler

Reach Everyone, Teach Everyone: Universal Design for Learning
in Higher Education
Thomas J. Tobin and Kirsten T. Behling

Teaching the Literature Survey Course: New Strategies for
College Faculty
Gwynn Dujardin, James M. Lang, and John A. Staunton

The Spark of Learning: Energizing the College Classroom with
the Science of Emotion
Sarah Rose Cavanagh